SPIRITUAL WARRIOR
The Manual

Dirk Waren

Soaring Eagle Press

SPRITUAL WARRIOR: The Manual

Copyright © 2024 by Dirk Waren

Unless otherwise indicated, all Scripture quotations are taken from the Holy Bible, New International Version®. NIV®. Copyright © 1973, 1978, 1984, 2011 by the International Bible Society. Used by permission of Zondervan Bible Publishers.

Many NIV citations are from the 2011 Revised edition.

Other cited translations are listed in the **Bibliography**.

All underlining, italics and bracketed notes in scriptural citations are added by the author (excluding quotes from the The Amplified Bible).

Pronominal references to Deity in this work are usually not capitalized.

Edited by KEEII with special thanks to Raquel J. for assistance.

ISBN: 979-8-218-48440-8
PUBLISHED BY SOARING EAGLE PRESS
Youngstown

Printed in the United States of America

For though we live in the world, we do not wage war as the world does. The weapons we fight with are not the weapons of the world. On the contrary, they have divine power to demolish strongholds.

- 2 Corinthians 10:3-4

CONTENTS

Introduction

WHAT IS A SPIRITUAL WARRIOR?

A *spiritual* warrior is someone who fulfills their mission in life and resolves challenges through spiritual means. In other words, a Spiritual Warrior achieves goals and tackles problems using wise biblical tactics. If you're a believer, God's calling *you* to be a Spiritual Warrior.

Consider how God is plainly described in the Holy Scriptures as a warrior:

The LORD is a warrior; the LORD is his name.
Exodus 15:3

This is significant because disciples are called to *imitate* the LORD:

Therefore <u>be imitators of God</u> as dear children.
Ephesians 5:1 (NKJV)

Since believers are instructed to imitate God, and the LORD is described as a warrior, then believers are called to be warriors. Simple, right? Yet notice whom we are commissioned to fight:

For <u>our struggle is not against flesh and blood</u>, but against the rulers, against the authorities, against the powers of this dark world and against the spiritual forces of evil in the heavenly realms.
Ephesians 6:12

While there might be times when it's necessary to walk in *tough* love with people, like when Christ cleared the Temple (Mark 11:15-18) or when Peter rebuked Simon the sorceror (Acts 8:20-23), our enemy is spiritual in nature and so our fight is spiritual in nature, first and foremost. Speaking of "fight," Paul instructed the young minister Timothy to "fight the good fight of faith" (1 Timothy 6:12). Anyone who chooses the path of faith—meaning *all* believers—needs to learn to fight the good fight **of faith**.

If there's a fight to faith, there are also enemies to faith. And you'll have to learn how to face these enemies effectively in order to walk in victory and help others. That's what this book—this "manual"—is all about: Learning the knowledge of the Spiritual Warrior and mastering the tactics.

Here's an example from the Bible's book of wisdom:

> **Better a patient person than a warrior,**
> **one with self-control than one who takes a city.**
> **Proverbs 16:32**

The verse is comparing two types of warriors—the spiritual kind and the physical kind. A patient person is *better* than a literal warrior who has material weapons and conquers cities. In other words, patience is a strategic weapon in the arsenal of the wise Spiritual Warrior whereas rashness is foolish and destructive. This is just one example.

The Lord said that "violent people" are the ones who take the kingdom of Heaven by force (Matthew 11:12). He wasn't talking about physically violent people, but rather the *spiritually* violent who further God's kingdom by faith, bearing forth fruit of the spirit in every good work (Colossians 1:10).

Join me now in a journey through the Scriptures to discover myriad wise qualities of God's Spiritual Warrior. Have your Bible handy so you can look up the corresponding passages.

While this manual is designed to be read front-to-back, the chapters are self-contained, so feel free to skip around. Key points are reemphasized throughout because it's an effective method that the apostles themselves used (2 Peter 1:12-13).

<u>1</u>

BE A MODERN DAVID
Against a Modern Goliath

Historical accounts in the Old Testament were chronicled to teach or warn future believers, meaning you and me (Romans 15:4 & 1 Corinthians 10:11). With this in mind, let's take a fresh look at Israel's conflict with the Philistines when David was still a teenager and not yet a soldier. This story is full of foundational lessons for the Spiritual Warrior.

> **Now the Philistines gathered their forces for war and assembled at Sokoh in Judah. They pitched camp at Ephes Dammim, between Sokoh and Azekah. ²Saul and the Israelites assembled and camped in the Valley of Elah and drew up their battle line to meet the Philistines. ³The Philistines occupied one hill and the Israelites another, with the valley between them.**
>
> **1 Samuel 17:1-3**

God's kingdom reigned on Earth in the Old Testament through the *physical* nation of Israel whereas God's kingdom reigns on Earth in the New Testament period via the *spiritual* nation of the Church (1 Peter 2:9). Israel and the Church refer to God's chosen people in two different ages relating to two different covenants. We're currently living in the New Testament era, of course, wherein our New Covenant with the LORD is superior to the Old Covenant that the Israelites had (Hebrews 8:6).

Israel in this historical account is a type of the Church—God's chosen people (1 Peter 2:9)—whereas the Philistines are a type of the enemies of

God's holy nation. In our era, who are the enemies of the Church? The Bible plainly says:

> **For our struggle is not against flesh and blood, but against the <u>rulers</u>, against the <u>authorities</u>, against the <u>powers</u> <u>of this dark world</u> and against the <u>spiritual forces of evil</u> in the heavenly realms.**
>
> **Ephesians 6:12**

Our enemy may operate through physical bodies & the corresponding organization at times, but he is nevertheless a *spiritual* adversary. His filthy minions—demons or evil spirits—are likewise spiritual in nature and function according to ranks of authority. We see this in their description as "rulers," "authorities" and "powers." In every battle you & I face there's a key spiritual adversary on which victory will be won or lost:

> **A champion named Goliath, who was from Gath, came out of the Philistine camp. His height was six cubits and a span** [nine and a half feet tall].
>
> **1 Samuel 17:4**

The camp of the Philistines had a champion who was 9½' tall. Every nation, city and town today have dark *spiritual* forces assigned to them with a 'champion' in each. For instance, in Daniel we observe "the prince of Persia" and "the prince of Greece," both demonic authorities dispatched to these areas (Daniel 10). These particular evil authorities were 'princes' in the kingdom of darkness.

Israel was led by kings, priests, judges and prophets (Jeremiah 2:26) while the Church is led by apostles, prophets, evangelists, pastors and teachers, which means fivefold ministers (Ephesians 4:11-13). 'Minister' means "servant," by the way, so the Church is led by *servant*-leaders (2 Corinthians 4:5). There are of course servant-leaders that function *under* fivefold ministers, like deacons, administrators, contributors, encouragers and so on (1 Corinthians 12:28 & Romans 12:3-8). These positions must be filled and refilled in order for the body of Christ to be effective as a unit in any battle with the enemy.

Now consider the champion warrior of the Philistine camp:

<blockquote>
He had a bronze helmet on his head and wore a coat of scale armor of bronze weighing five thousand shekels; [6]on his legs he wore bronze greaves, and a bronze javelin was slung on his back. [7]His spear shaft was like a weaver's rod, and its iron point weighed six hundred shekels. His shield bearer went ahead of him.

1 Samuel 17:5-7
</blockquote>

The resident spiritual enemy of a location will always present itself in an intimidating manner, making you think it's an impossible-to-win situation. The adversary *wants* you to run away screaming in fear, as was the case with Goliath and the army of Israel:

<blockquote>
Goliath stood and shouted to the ranks of Israel, "Why do you come out and line up for battle? Am I not a Philistine, and are you not the servants of Saul? Choose a man and have him come down to me. [9]If he is able to fight and kill me, we will become your subjects; but if I overcome him and kill him, you will become our subjects and serve us." [10]Then the Philistine said, "This day <u>I defy the armies of Israel!</u> Give me a man and let us fight each other." [11] <u>On hearing the Philistine's words, Saul and all the Israelites were dismayed and terrified</u>.

1 Samuel 17:8-11
</blockquote>

Today, the enemy brazenly defies Christians because the kingdom of darkness is not afraid of believers who are ignorant of their authority and intimidated by their mocking threats. Too many Christ-followers tremble at the thought of satan & evil spirits and their diabolic works. Some liberal Christians even smirk at the thought of the devil & demons, chalking them up to superstition or myth.

Why is this? Why don't most believers know the authority they have over the kingdom of darkness and boldly walk in it? (Colossians 2:15 & Luke 10:19). Why do many walk in fear rather than courageous faith when it comes to fighting the enemy? What's holding potential Spiritual Warriors back from being modern Davids against modern Goliaths?

One reason for the Church's weakness is that many of us aren't following the true God, but rather Christian religion and its teachers. These 'leaders,' like King Saul, are afraid and ineffective. They may have the titles and décor of Christianity, but not the faith and power (2 Timothy 3:5).

Satan & his filthy demons know that if the Church follows the *unbiblical* teachings of Christian religion—as opposed to the *biblical* teachings of Christianity—believers will be powerless against them. Like Saul & his troops, believers will not engage in spiritual warfare with the enemy if they're misled, ignorant and afraid. They'll be ineffective.

Like Saul's army, too many believers are standing away from the warfare, fearful and basically useless. It's safer to hide amidst the ranks and go with the flow than to step out as an individual and take a bold stand against the enemy. Too many of our leaders are just religionists with the corresponding title & garb rather than effective warriors for God's kingdom. The teachers of the Law are a good scriptural example (Luke 20:46).

An Uncompromised Youth

The story in 1 Samuel 17 switches focus to a young male who was tending sheep for his father. This was David when he was about 17-18 years-old and too young for service in the military. His three older brothers were with Saul's troops on the hill and David's father would regularly send the teen to the camp with food supplies (verses 12-20).

Why does Scripture bring up this greenhorn youth? If the LORD cannot depend on the clergy, the elders and their congregants, he will send a willing youth to do what they are unwilling to do. God will raise up someone unsoiled by the ineffective leadership of human religion and develop him to the point where he or she is qualified to fulfill the needs of the hour.

This explains why young people—including those who are young-at-heart—are often the most receptive to revival and active in sparking it. They are willing to fight because they have a fire inside them to carry out the mission, a God-inspired zeal. They're "new wineskins" who can handle the "new wine" as opposed to "old wineskins" (Matthew 9:17).

Young people only become ineffective when they're brainwashed by error and taught the art of comfort & complacency. Woe to Christian 'leaders' who cause pieces of steel to become wilted vegetables!

When David arrived at the camp, dropped off the supplies and met with his older brothers he happened to hear Goliath's daily challenge and was astonished at the terror of the troops (verses 22-24). Notice his response:

> **David asked the men standing near him, "What will be done for the man who kills this Philistine and removes this disgrace from Israel? Who is this uncircumcised Philistine that he should defy the armies of the living God?"**
>
> **1 Samuel 17:26**

He referred to the intimidating Goliath as a "disgrace" and an "uncircumcised Philistine." Since physical circumcision was the sign of being in covenant with the Almighty at the time (Genesis 17:9-11 & Leviticus 12:3), David was emphasizing how this giant wasn't even in covenant with the LORD, like the Israelites, so who was he to defy the armies of the living God?! In other words, David was thinking in terms of covenant and faith. No matter how fearsome Goliath appeared to be, he was not greater than the LORD in whom the Hebrews had an agreement— a contract. They needed not fear because victory was assured according to Scripture (Deuteronomy 20:1-4).

David also inquired what the reward was for slaying the giant because he caught word that King Saul had cited a generous incentive—great wealth, the king's daughter in marriage and exemption from taxes (verse 25). There's nothing wrong with desiring a reward for your faithful service. After all, you didn't give your life to the Lord for nothing: You *expect* forgiveness of sins, reconciliation and eternal life, right?

Weak Christians Will Object to Your Bold Willingness

This can be observed in the response of David's oldest sibling:

> **When Eliab, David's oldest brother, heard him speaking with the men, <u>he burned with anger at him</u> and asked, "Why have you come down here? And with whom did you leave <u>those few sheep</u> in the wilderness? I know <u>how conceited you are</u> and <u>how wicked your heart is</u>; you came down only to watch the battle."**
> **²⁹"Now what have I done?" said David. "Can't I even speak?" ³⁰ <u>He then turned away to someone else</u> and

brought up the same matter, and the men answered him as before.

1 Samuel 17:28-30

Why was David's brother being so hard on him—mocking his job, calling him conceited and wicked? Such mistreatment was unreasonable, to say the least. Obviously, Eliab was challenged by his younger sibling's bold zeal and embarrassed by his own fear and apathy.

No matter what you sincerely do for the LORD you can be sure there will be some "elder" brother or sister who will try to douse your fire with mocking criticisms and putdowns. This "more experienced" Christian will try to discourage you one way or another, including insulting you and sharing a dubious doctrine to defend their position, thus hiding the pain s/he might feel by the threat of having to once again become active.

Notice that David doesn't blow crucial time & energy on fighting with such an "elder." Rather, he simply *turns away*. I call this the Turn-Away Principle.

At some point you too will have to "turn away" from some of your relatives, friends or colleagues if they're treating you the way Eliab treated David. Don't fight with them, as far as it is possible (Romans 12:18). Like David, refuse to enter into life-sapping conflicts of this sort because they'll break your focus and inevitably pull you into the realm of the flesh. If you make a battle out of everything you won't have enough energy left over for what's important. Just turn away.

'Leaders' Who Try to Stifle Your Fire

The leader of the army of Israel was King Saul. Notice how he responds to David's spirit of courageous faith and obedience:

What David said was overheard and reported to Saul, and Saul sent for him.
[32]David said to Saul, "Let no one lose heart on account of this Philistine; your servant will go and fight him."
[33]Saul replied, "You are not able to go out against this Philistine and fight him; you are only a young man, and he has been a warrior from his youth."

1 Samuel 17:31-33

Some leaders in the Church today have the same response. They basically teach apathy to passionate young disciples by insisting that only the clergy can do God's work, which they end up not really doing. "You can't do that," they'll say. "You first have to go off to seminary (for years and years)," assuming you can afford it. Thus revival is stifled.

To defend their decision to not enter into any taxing service for God they naturally try to silence those who would, which ensures no example for comparison and secures their position of employment.

Notice how Saul accentuates Goliath's fearsome power while emphasizing David's inadequacy. He basically praises the darkness and tries to snuff out the only flicker of light at hand. Church leaders like this cripple our forces through misinformation and discouragement, depicting the enemy as unstoppable. They'll say things like, "One person cannot save the whole world." Isn't it great that Jesus Christ didn't heed such advice?

Above all, God is looking for a *willing* heart, regardless of how mature the person is. Maturity can be taught to a degree, but it can't be tested until stepping into the arena! David wasn't mature yet, but he was mature enough for God to use because he was boldly willing to enter the arena, unlike Saul's seasoned soldiers.

Why David Had Faith

David's response to King Saul reveals *how* he had the great faith it took to take on Goliath: When he tended his father's sheep, a lion and a bear attacked the lambs on a couple of occasions and thus David struck the predators and slew them; he reasoned that, just as the LORD gave him victory over the lion and the bear when he boldly acted, so God would give him victory over Goliath (verses 34-37).

We could relate this to us today: If you haven't first been tested with a situation where you needed $100 or $1000 and exercised your faith to receive it (Mark 11:24 & John 16:24), you're not likely going to have the faith to receive $12,000 when it's needed, or more. If you haven't exercised your faith to receive healing for the common cold or back pain, you're not likely going to have the faith to overcome the 'Goliath' of cancer.

Those smaller items would be your 'lion' or 'bear' whereas the bigger challenges would be your 'Goliath.' Are you following? So, I encourage you to praise God when you face those smaller things because God is allowing them in your life so that you can work your faith muscles, which will naturally prepare you for your 'Goliath' down the road.

Since Saul was backed up against a wall with the Philistines & their champion, he wisely gave-in to David's faith & persistence by agreeing to allow him to face the fearsome giant.

Be Led of the Spirit *Not* by What Everyone Else's Doing

The king insisted that David wear full armor and use his personal sword in squaring off with the giant. But David wasn't feeling it and so rejected the armor & sword (verses 38-40). He didn't care "what everyone else was doing" and went with what he had a peace about, what he was gifted at— using a sling weapon. You'll have to do the same if you want to conquer your 'giants.'

Too often in Christendom we are told to do something a certain way or do things we were not designed to do. If we refuse, we are made to feel ashamed, as if we've committed some great sin. Don't allow yourself to be encumbered by someone else's conviction or bondage. The Creator makes every person unique for a reason so disregard "what everyone else is doing" and be led of the Spirit (Romans 8:14). "Let the peace of Christ reign in your heart" (Colossians 3:15); in other words, don't do or say anything you don't have a peace about doing, even if it happens to be the hip thang to do.

That said, one tool *every* believer needs in order to be effective in service of the Kingdom is God's Word since it's the blueprint for genuine Christianity (2 Timothy 3:16-17). Another thing you need, of course, is a tight relationship with the LORD.

March Forward in Faith to Victory

The enemy will naturally despise you, put you down, and mock you when you boldly seek to carry out your God-given mission:

> **Meanwhile, the Philistine, with his shield bearer in front of him, kept coming closer to David. [42]<u>He looked David over</u> and saw that he was little more than a boy, glowing with health and handsome, <u>and he despised him</u>. [43]He said to David, "Am I a dog, that you come at me with sticks?" And the Philistine cursed David by his gods. [44] "Come here," he said, "and I'll give your flesh to the birds and the wild animals!"**
>
> **1 Samuel 17:41-44**

Your adversary will try to distract you from your source of Power by getting you focused on your *own* limitations and flaws, which is why you'll need the breastplate of righteousness, not to mention the full armor & weaponry of God, which we'll examine in chapter <u>19</u>.

Observe David's response to the enemy's hateful intimidation as he confronts him:

> **David said to the Philistine, "You come against me with sword and spear and javelin, but I come against you in the name of the Lord Almighty, the God of the armies of Israel, whom you have defied. [46] <u>This day</u> the Lord will deliver you into my hands, and I'll strike you down and cut off your head. <u>This very day</u> I will give the carcasses of the Philistine army to the birds and the wild animals, and the whole world will know that there is a God in Israel. [47]All those gathered here will know that it is not by sword or spear that the Lord saves; for the battle is the Lord's, and he will give all of you into our hands."**
>
> **1 Samuel 17:45-47**

Forget about tomorrow, march toward victory *today* while the mood strikes (i.e. as the Spirit moves you).

Remember:

> **…"This is the word of the LORD to Zerubbabel: 'Not by might nor by power, but by my Spirit,' says the LORD Almighty.' "**
>
> **Zechariah 4:6**

...the One who is in you is greater than the one who is in the world.

1 John 4:4

The Sovereign God is greater than the "god of this world" (2 Corinthians 4:4). And God lives in you through the Holy Spirit (1 Corinthians 6:19). *You* are a temple of the LORD—*act* like it, *speak* like it!

As far as physicality, skill, experience and weapons technology go, there was no way David could beat Goliath. So, he had to rely on the One who is greater than all of that—the Almighty. He had to act on the leading and power of the Holy Spirit.

Speak the Word of Faith

The Bible teaches that words have the power of life and death (Proverbs 18:21) and Christ emphasized the power of *speaking* in *faith* (Mark 11:23). In the literal rendition of that passage the mighty Messiah stressed speaking **three times** as opposed to believing, which he noted **once**. So, if you're having trouble believing something biblical or something the Spirit wants you to get a hold of, start speaking it in faith, even if you're struggling with believing it. Paul taught on believing & speaking too (2 Corinthians 4:13).

Both Goliath and David understood this powerful principle because they *both* utilized it in their pursuit of victory, as shown in verses 41-47. Since Goliath was the champion of the Philistines for many years, he obviously had much success with this principle of believing & speaking. The difference between the two, however, is that David was in covenant with God while Goliath was not. This tipped the scales in the former-shepherd boy's favor and thus he beat Goliath even though—physically speaking—his chances for victory were minuscule. Do you want victory over the giants that surface in your life and threaten you & your loved ones? Of course you do. Then learn to speak God's blessings & truths into the situation by faith; and then take action led of the Spirit (Romans 8:14).

Take Out the Lead Bully and the Others Will Flee

We see this principle at play after David used his sling to plant a stone in Goliath's forehead, the giant's "Achilles' heal," which dropped him facedown to the ground. David wasted no time in cutting off his head as a grisly trophy (this is definitely an R-rated story), which sent the Philistine troops fleeing like curs with their tails between their legs (verses 48-54). This "woke the dead" as it inspired the Israelite soldiers to break free from their fog of fear & comfort to route the enemy!

The same can be observed in the New Testament in a spiritual sense:

> **Submit yourselves, then, to God. <u>Resist the devil</u>, <u>and he will flee from you</u>.**
>
> **James 4:7**

Get ahold of this fact: The powers of darkness don't have spiritual authority over you; *you* have authority over them:

> **And having <u>disarmed the powers and authorities</u>** [of darkness], **he** [Christ] **made a public spectacle of them, triumphing over them by the cross.**
>
> **Colossians 2:15**

> **"I have given you authority to trample on snakes and scorpions and to overcome all the power of the enemy, nothing will harm you."**
>
> **Luke 10:19**

There are myriad ways that the principles covered in this chapter will apply to your specific situation depending upon what particular 'Goliath' you are facing. Use your God-given imagination and be led of the Spirit.

When you set the example by taking a risky stand, only then will the religious dead in your midst be inspired to wake up from their apathy and take on the enemy with renewed zeal. Those who refuse should retire from service.

This is how the wicked giants of this fallen world are slain by modern Davids.

Do it.

<u>2</u>

THE SEVEN FREEDOMS:
Your Rewards

David needed to know what he'd get if he beat Goliath (1 Samuel 17:25-27). I bring this up because, let's face it, few people will be motivated to be a Spiritual Warrior unless they have good reason to be one. In other words, what's the payoff? That's the purpose of this chapter—to show you the *rewards* of being a Spiritual Warrior beyond the obvious forgiveness of sins and acquiring eternal life.

Life-Transforming Truth

The truths of God's Word are literally **life-transforming** and will set believers free in every area of life, just as the Lord declared:

> **"<u>If</u> you <u>continue in my word</u>, you are truly my disciples; and you will know the truth, and <u>the truth will make you free</u>."**
>
> **John 8:31-32** (NRSV)

The truth will indeed set you free, but notice the two conditions: **1.** You must **"continue in"** God's Word and **2.** you must **"know the truth."** Simply put, if you give up at some point or choose to stay in the darkness of ignorance the truth *can't* set you free, and understandably so.

To "know the truth" means more than just mental assent. "Know" conveys the idea of *union*, as in the connection between a husband and wife. It's necessary, as Jesus said, to "continue" in his Word for the truth to become a part of you in this sense.

How can you know the truth like this? Practice what you know and understand. If you miss it, immediately get back up (Proverbs 24:16). You don't drown by falling in the water, you drown by staying there.

Also, if you're a "believer," it's naturally necessary to **believe**, meaning you don't disagree with the truth of God's Word. Don't get me wrong here, it's wise to question dubious teachings, including traditional doctrines that simply aren't biblical—and there are many of these—but it's of the utmost importance that believers *believe* the clear truths and promises of the Scriptures. Your words have the power of life and death (Proverbs 18:21), so be careful not to cancel out the awesome promises and blessings of God's Word with words of unbelief. Doing so is double-mindedness and the Bible warns that the double-minded person should not think s/he will receive anything from the Lord (James 1:6-7).

For instance, the Bible emphasizes that you are "**more than a conqueror**" who will "**reign in life**" (Romans 8:37 & 5:17), but you go around saying, "I can't do anything right; I'm a failure: I *can't, I can't, I can't.*" If you do this, guess what? You *won't* be more than a conqueror and you *won't* reign in life. More likely you'll be a depressed failure. What's the cure for double-mindedness? Simple, just do what Christ said: *Continue* in his Word with a spirit of faith, don't give up, and when you inevitably miss it, be quick to repent (1 John 1:8-9). As you do this, you will come to know the truth more and more fully, "and the truth will set you **free**."

Speaking of which, there are seven vital freedoms available to you:

1. FREEDOM to Know and Walk With God

There's a big difference between knowing *about* the LORD and actually knowing him. Too many Christians know a lot about God but don't actually walk *with* him. The gospel is referred to as the "message of reconciliation" in the Scriptures (2 Corinthians 5:17-21). 'Reconciliation' means "to turn from enmity to friendship." In other words, **you** can be God's friend just as Moses was (Exodus 33:11), **you** can be a "man [or woman] after God's own heart" just like David (1 Samuel 13:14, Acts

13:22 & Jeremiah 3:15), and **you** can be a "disciple whom Jesus loves" just as John (John 13:23, 19:26 & 21:7,20).

There are levels of glory in spiritual growth (1 Corinthians 3:17-18), so rise up O man of God, rise up O woman of God, to new levels of closeness and strength with the Mighty One! In the LORD's presence is fullness of joy (Psalm 16:11)!

Christianity is not a religion in the sense of Islam, Hinduism or Sciencefictionology,[1] but rather a *relationship* with the Creator of the Universe. Pursue a closer walk with the LORD. Developing a good relationship with God takes time and effort, just like any good relationship. Make sure part of your prayer time consists of simple communion—you hanging out with your heavenly Father and friend. Resist religious-tinged lingo when fellowshipping; shoot for a conversational tone and **be real**. Any step you genuinely take toward God will bring the LORD closer to you (James 4:8). You'll be blessed.

2. FREEDOM to Soar in the Spirit

The Bible promises that those who hope in the LORD "will soar on wings like eagles" (Isaiah 40:31), but too many believers are grounded from the spiritual heights due to one or more of the five encumbrances listed below. Part of the awesome news of the gospel of Christ is that we can escape these impediments and walk in **newness of life** by "participating in the divine nature" (2 Peter 1:4). This is called living in the spirit or clothing yourself with Christ (Galatians 5:16 & Romans 13:14). When you do this, you activate "the law of the spirit of life in Christ" and neutralize "the law of sin and death" (Romans 8:1-2).

These are spiritual laws. The higher law naturally *deactivates* the lower law, as long as it's in motion. For example, the law of lift and propulsion in the natural enables aircrafts of all sizes to defy the law of gravity and fly. As long as the former law is activated, the law of gravity is rendered powerless.

Are you getting this? YOU can soar in the spirit above the limitations of the mental realm and the darkness of the flesh. People who see life only

---

[1] That's not a typo since L. Ron Hubbard was a science fiction author. I was trying to be amusing.

from the mental sphere and five physical senses will be limited by **the human perspective**. However, believers can activate the "law of the spirit of life in Christ" and "participate in the divine nature," which enables them to experience life from **the divine viewpoint**, which is the eminent perspective.

You were born to *soar in the spirit!*

3. FREEDOM From the Flesh or Sinful Nature

The flesh or sinful nature is the ugly beast within us all that naturally produces sin as we embrace its lusts (James 1:14-15). Sin is more than just murder, stealing, adultery and being a drunkard or druggie, it's also things like arrogance, envy, jealousy, malice, gossip, slander, sloth, gluttony, deceit, fits of rage, faction-ism (i.e. rigid sectarianism), greed and the corresponding pompous airs of wealth (Galatians 5:19-21 & Proverbs 6:16-19). Some in the Church may be freed up from the overt transgressions but, because they show consistent evidence of the "smaller" ones, it's clear that their flesh is doing quite well and, in some cases, going full blast. The great news of the message of Christ is that we can walk free of the flesh, as described in the previous section, by "**participating in the divine nature**" (2 Peter 1:4).

This potent passage offers details on how to do this:

> **You were taught, with regard to your former way of life, to <u>put off the old self</u>** [the flesh], **which is being corrupted by its deceitful desires;** [23]**to <u>be made new in the attitude of your minds</u>;** [24]**and to <u>put on the new self</u>** [the spirit], **created to be like God in true righteousness and holiness.**
>
> **Ephesians 4:22-24**

The key here is two-pronged: **A.** You must **put off the flesh**, which means you don't flirt with it and embrace its lusts, but rather "count yourself dead to sin but alive to God in Christ Jesus," as taught in Romans 6:11. You must "count yourself dead to sin" by faith because sometimes you won't *feel* dead to sin—particularly when you're tempted by its lusts—but, spiritually speaking, you *already are* dead to sin. For instance, I used to have a problem with fits of rage; to walk free of these carnal fits it was necessary for me to start counting myself dead to such antics by faith. So

I made it my regular confession: "I Dirk Waren am dead to fits of rage." You can do this with any area of the flesh with which you struggle.

B. You must **put on the new self**, which means living according to who you are spiritually with the help and guidance of the Holy Spirit. This is "clothing yourself with Christ" (Romans 13:14) or "participating in the divine nature." Remember, the gospel is "Christ IN YOU, the hope of glory" (Colossians 1:26-27). The only way you can live according to **who you are** in your spirit is by first *knowing* who you are in the spirit and, of course, accepting it. This explains why the passage above instructs believers to "be made new in the attitude of your minds," which could be viewed as a third prong to walking free of the flesh. Your mental attitude is made new simply by accepting and believing who you are in your spirit!

Who are you in the spirit? How does God see you *in* Christ? Ten things:

- You are a **child of God** (John 1:12-13).
- You are a **new creation** (2 Corinthians 5:17).
- You are **holy** (Colossians 1:21-22).
- You are the **righteousness of God** (2 Corinthians 5:21).
- You are **dead to sin** (Romans 6:11,14,18).
- You are **more than a conqueror** (Romans 8:37).
- You are **a temple of the Holy Spirit** (1 Corinthians 6:19-20).
- You are **rich** (2 Corinthians 8:9).
- You are **healed** (1 Peter 2:24).
- You are **a royal priest of the Most High God** (1 Peter 2:9)!

These are positional truths because they reveal your *position* in covenant with God through Christ. The more these spiritual realities become a part of you, the more you'll be set free of the flesh and fulfill your God-given mission. A good example from the Old Testament is Gideon, who viewed himself as the weakest and least, but God saw him as a "mighty warrior" (Judges 6:12-16). He had to change his thinking in order to fulfill his call.[2]

Yet please don't try putting on the new self (the spirit) without first putting *off* the old self (the flesh). To do so would be like changing a baby's soiled

---

[2] See the Fountain of Life (FOL) videos *How God Sees YOU* and *How to Walk FREE of the Flesh*.

diaper by putting the new diaper over the old one. It doesn't work, not to mention it's absurd.

To repent, by the way, simply means to change your mind for the positive. This doesn't mean a meaningless mental exercise, but a change of mind with **the corresponding actions**, like the resolve to fulfill God's will (Acts 26:20) and turn from that which is opposed to God's will, i.e. sin (Acts 8:22 & 2 Corinthians 12:21). Repentance and faith are two sides of the same coin (Acts 20:21) and so for repentance to be effective **it must be combined with faith**, otherwise repentance is just a dead exercise. Is it any wonder that repentance and faith are the first two of the six basic doctrines of Christianity, as observed in Hebrews 6:1-2. We'll examine these chief doctrines in chapter **4**.

If you're having difficulty wrapping your head around the concepts of "who you are in the spirit" and "putting off the flesh or old self," we'll look at human nature in chapter **17**.

4. FREEDOM From Curses of the Law

The "curses of the Law" are relayed in excruciating detail in Deuteronomy 28:15-68. They can be condensed into five basic curses: **physical illness, mental illness, defeat to human enemies, premature death** and **financial lack**. The great news of the gospel includes this fact:

> **Christ <u>redeemed us from the curse of the law</u> by becoming a curse for us, for it is written: "Cursed is everyone who is hung on a tree."**
>
> **Galatians 3:13**

"Redeemed" literally means to purchase a slave with intent of liberating. You see, the Messiah set us free from all such curses by becoming a curse for us when he was crucified!

Am I saying that Christians can walk in victory over all five of these general maladies? Yes. What I'm *not* saying is that you won't be attacked in these areas. The Bible repeatedly says you will be attacked (1 Peter 5:8 & James 4:7). Take, for instance, the satanic attack on Job's life, which took place over the course of **several months** (see the book of Job). We also need to realize that believers may have one or more of these curses evident in their lives when they turn to God due to a generational curse and any associating impure spirit(s), but the truth can set them free!

When you are attacked—and *you will* be attacked—you must recognize it and **take a stand**. utilizing the armor & arms of God at your disposal. **Resist in faith**. In fact, put up your "shield of faith" even before you're attacked, which will shield you from many of the enemy's flaming arrows (Ephesians 6:16); in other words, the enemy's fiery darts will be extinguished *before* they can harm you. Pull out your "sword" as necessary. Your sword is the Word of God spoken in bold, persistent faith (Ephesians 6:17). Slice down all lies and curses.

Take a stand in faith and persevere. Continue walking according to the Word in general and learn to follow the leading of the Holy Spirit. **Don't back back**. If you make a stand in faith and persevere, the devil will flee from you like a yelping cur with his tail between his legs (1 Peter 5:8-10). This means that the curse in question will flee from you (I'm not talking about some comic booky red figure with a pitchfork). The Bible guarantees it. It's your covenant agreement with the Most High.

Just make sure there's no sin in the camp, so to speak (Joshua 7). Keep your spiritual arteries clear of the build-up of *unconfessed* sin. Always be quick to 'fess up when you miss it and God will faithfully "purify you from all unrighteousness" (1 John 1:8-9).

These things are addressed in detail in chapters **19-20**.

5. FREEDOM From the Dead Religiosity, i.e. Legalism

"Legalism" is a condition where people are obsessed with rules, which is why it's called *legal*-ism. It could just as well be called law-ism or rule-ism. This spiritual disease focuses on the outward veneer of godliness at the expense of inward genuineness. It's the idea that faith is an outward job. Real Christianity, by contrast, changes from the inside out, starting with spiritual rebirth and reconciliation with the Creator.

Legalism in its broadest sense is a spirit of dead religiosity that can manifest in six ways: general legalism or pharisaical-ism; rigid sectarianism; a spirit of religious-formal death, which is spiritual sterility wherein people just go through the motions; a spirit of bondage; a spirit of condemnation & authoritarianism; and bondage to Old Testament laws that were *fulfilled* in Christ (Colossians 2:13-17). By the way, when I use the term 'spirit' in this way—like "the spirit of authoritarianism"—I mean it in the sense of "established character" or a person's overall vibe. For instance, Joshua and Caleb had a "different spirit" compared to the 10 unbelieving Israelite spies because they had a spirit of faith (see Numbers 13-14, particularly 14:24).

As you can see, legalism is at odds with genuine Christianity because true Christianity offers grace, life, freedom and joy, not condemnation, death, bondage and religious drudgery. Too many Christians fall into the pitfall of legalism in one or more of these six ways, yet—thankfully—the Bible declares: "It is for freedom that Christ has set us free. Stand firm, then, and do not let yourselves be burdened again by a yoke of slavery" (Galatians 5:1). The "yoke of slavery" here is referring to being *under* the yoke of religious law. Believers have been released from the Law and serve in the new way of the Spirit, not in the old way of the written code for "the letter kills, but the Spirit gives life" (Galatians 5:18, Romans 6:14, Romans 7:6 & 2 Corinthians 3:6).[3]

6. FREEDOM From False Doctrine

God's Word is truth (John 17:17). A false doctrine is any belief or teaching that simply isn't true, meaning it's not genuinely biblical. Christ said, "the truth will set you free" but the truth *can't* set us free if we embrace teachings that are false. Let's be honest here: Every sect, camp and individual believer adheres to false doctrine to some degree. The only antidote is being open to the truth and willing to change, like the Bereans to whom Paul ministered (Acts 17:10-12).

Truth is discerned simply by "rightly-dividing" the Scriptures, which means "correctly handling" them (2 Timothy 2:15). Error is perpetuated by *incorrectly* handling the Scriptures. This explains why those who teach God's Word will be judged more strictly because of the power and influence they wield (James 3:1).

How does one rightly divide or correctly handle the Scriptures? Simply by adherence to **the four rules of hermeneutics**, which is the science of Bible interpretation:

---

[3] Check out *Legalism Unmasked* and *LAW and the Believer* for more details; or see the corresponding free articles at the FOL site.

- **"Context is king"** means your interpretation of a passage must gel with the meaning given it by the surrounding texts, which is the context.
- **Scripture interprets Scripture** means your interpretation of a passage must coincide with what the rest of Scripture teaches; the more detailed and overt passages obviously trump the more sketchy or ambiguous ones.
- **Take the Bible literally unless it's obvious that the language is figurative**, in which case you simply look for the literal truth the symbolism intends to convey.
- **If the plain sense makes sense—and is in harmony with the rest of Scripture—don't look for any other sense lest you end up with nonsense**. This means that every passage has an obvious meaning within its context, as well the context of the entire Bible. Deeper meanings are possible, like Paul's figurative exposition on Hagar and Sarah in Galatians 4, but these will conform with obvious scriptural truth. The plain meaning of a passage will dawn on the believer with greater insight as s/he grows in the Lord. The purpose of this fourth rule is to prevent bizarre and unbiblical interpretations of passages.

The Spiritual Warrior will master these four common-sense guidelines because they help keep you from being misled by false doctrine and religious cons, including those who are simply **ignorant of their error** and don't know any better. (Usually they're ignorant due to *sectarianism,* which is when people are rigidly loyal to the official doctrines of their sect rather than to what the Bible actually teaches. We'll look at this further in chapter **4**). As you master these principles, you'll be increasingly empowered and start to discern false doctrine—which includes *partially* true teachings—even from your own assembly/camp, which comprises the ministers thereof.

Strive to be like the Bereans in Acts 17:10-12 by maintaining a **humble spirit that's *open* to the truth, willing to search for the truth** through regular reading of the Scriptures, and **willing to change in light of the truth** when you see it. The regular influx of accurate knowledge will naturally cleanse you of error and sin (Ephesians 5:26). I would estimate that 99% of people's problems are due to *not* being regularly washed through the Word (Hosea 4:6). So, *keep yourself washed in the Word!*

Unfortunately, people infected by a legalistic religious spirit don't want the rightly-divided Word of God and the freedom that goes with it. They want human religion and the questionable doctrines thereof, not to mention the rules, which are often eye-rolling. It goes without saying, flee life-stifling, growth-stultifying sectarianism and false religiosity like the plague (Luke 9:49-50 & Matthew 15:14)!

7. FREEDOM From Doubt and Unbelief

The Bible points out that "without faith it is impossible to please God" (Hebrews 11:6). What is faith? Some people think faith means believing in fairy tales. No, faith is knowing and believing something to be true even if you can't prove it via your five physical senses. It's something you just *know*. You know it because you discern it by your sixth sense, your spirit. Take love (not lust), for example: Love is an ethereal quality that can't be proven through science or the five physical senses and, yet, we all know it exists.

The first twenty years of my life I was an unbeliever. I grew up in a non-Christian environment but, somehow, I just knew there was a God. I would go out at night by the lake where I lived and try to commune with the Creator under the stars. Although my five physical senses didn't discern God—that is, beyond the evidence *of* God in nature (Romans 1:20 & Psalm 19:1-4)—and practically all the people around me didn't advocate belief in God (quite the opposite), somehow I just knew there was a Supreme Creator. This mustard seed of faith led to my salvation—reconciliation with the LORD and attainment of eternal life once I accepted the gospel of Christ at the age of 20.

Here's another example: When I was around 8 years-old, my family and I were walking the trails of Theodore Wirth Park in Minneapolis when we came to the edge of a baseball field where a softball game was being played. As soon as we entered the outskirts of the field, I just knew that the current batter was going to hit the ball and it was going to hit me right on the face. I knew it, but didn't know how I knew it. I just knew. I knew it by faith, even though I was only 8 years old (!). Next thing you know the batter hits the ball high into the air—it was like slow motion—and it came and hit me right on the cheek! Good thing it was a softball, huh? How did I *know* this was going to happen? Obviously by my sixth sense, my spirit.

Every believer has "a *measure* of faith" (Romans 12:3), otherwise he or she wouldn't be a 'believer.' The awesome news is that **your faith can**

grow. One important way to grow in faith is by simply getting closer to your heavenly Father, as encouraged in the first area of freedom above; after all, it's nigh-impossible for someone to tell you God doesn't exist when you actually *know* the LORD rather than merely know about God. It would be like someone trying to convince you that your mother doesn't exist (or never existed, if she's already passed on).

Faith also grows by feeding on the rightly-divided Word of God (Romans 10:17). God's Word is spiritual bread that feeds your inner being; Yeshua said, "Man does not live upon bread alone but on every word that comes from the mouth of God" (Matthew 4:4). God's Word doesn't just increase faith, it also gives wisdom (2 Timothy 3:15). Wisdom is the ability to discern difference, including the ability to distinguish good and evil, truth and error, what's proper and what's improper in any given environment, etc. Needless to say, seek out God's Word—hear it, read it, study it, memorize it, and meditate on it (Psalm 119:9-16). Just as important, live it, speak it, and believe it in the same spirit of Joshua and Caleb who entered their "promised land" (Numbers 14:6-9,24). You will consequently enter *your* "promised land," and I'm not talking about Heaven, but here on Earth.[4]

Lastly, your faith can be energized and grow by regularly **praying in the spirit** (Ephesians 6:18, Jude 1:20 & 1 Corinthians 14:14-15). We'll look at this in the section *Knowing the Six Basic Doctrines* in chapter **4**.

Too Good to Be True?

Are these seven freedoms too good to be true? No! **They're actually part of the gospel of Christ.** Why do you think it's called the **"good news"**? It's sad and tragic that too many sects and leaders of the body of Christ today don't proclaim these truths, whether due to ignorance, truth-stifling sectarianism, religious traditionalism or what have you.

Know this: If the enemy can't keep you from salvation in Christ, the next thing he'll attempt to do is to keep you from walking in these seven freedoms, which are your birthright. The reason the enemy will try to keep you from walking in them is because believers who are totally free are **a serious threat to the kingdom of darkness** and will **automatically advance the kingdom of God**.

---

[4] This is elaborated on in chapter **20**.

Make it your ambition to grow in all seven of these freedoms as you continue in your walk with the LORD. Cultivate the learning spirit of a disciple and regularly expose yourself to the fivefold ministry gifts (apostles, prophets, evangelists, pastors and teachers), but learn to identify life-draining legalists amongst them and "leave them; they are blind guides" (Matthew 15:14). Cultivate a relationship with the LORD via your prayer life and feed regularly from God's Word with the teaching help of the Holy Spirit (1 John 2:27).

Freedom is a *process*, so don't allow temporary struggles in any of these areas to disillusion you. **Life's a fight, fight it!** The Bible says we are to "fight the good **fight** of faith" (1 Timothy 6:12). Of course there will be temptations, trials and tests—"higher levels, bigger devils," as they say— but **believers *overcome* by faith** (1 John 5:4)!

Let's close this chapter on freedom with this powerful relevant insight…

God Exists in a State of TOTAL FREEDOM

People in the world sometimes perceive God as some old fuddy duddy in the sky who can't stand folks having a "good time" and therefore is obsessed with removing anything "fun" from our lives. While human religion and forms of legalism might be like this, the LORD is quite different and actually operates from a state of absolute freedom. See for yourself:

> **Now the Lord is the Spirit, and where the Spirit of the Lord is, there is freedom.**
>
> **2 Corinthians 3:17**

Thus in the Scriptures you'll find several statements like this:

> **Our God is in heaven;**
> **he does whatever pleases him.**
>
> **Psalm 115:3**

> **The LORD does whatever pleases him,**
> **in the heavens and on the earth,**
> **in the seas and all their depths.**
>
> **Psalm 135:6**

> **"But he stands alone, and who can oppose him?**
> **He does whatever he pleases."**
>
> **Job 23:13**

In other words, **God functions in a state of total freedom and therefore does whatever he wants**.

What's interesting is that people—male and female—are created in God's image and likeness and so **we have this same desire** (Genesis 1:26-27). We intrinsically *hate* captivity and the restraints thereof. **We want freedom!** This explains why we have an instinctive revulsion of slavery. No wonder efforts to end the slave trade in the West were spearheaded by *godly* people, like William Wilberforce in Britain and William Lloyd Garrison in America.

Satanic people & their godless ideologies, by contrast, *love* tyranny and bondage in one form or another. Communism is a good example. And this explains why citizens in Socialist states East of the Iron Curtain always tried to escape to the freedom-oriented republics of the West and not vice versa.

Remember during the plandemic of 2020-2022, how **LIE**beral politicians told us to "trust the science" while they absurdly taped off benches at parks or filled skateparks with sand, outlawing fresh air & sunshine because they cared so much about our health? They closed down our small businesses en masse, churches too, coerced citizens to wear masks that impeded fresh air and tried to lock us in our homes. It was okay to crowd into Walmart, though, not to mention strip joints and bars were kept open (rolling my eyes).

Christians and wise people with common sense had a revulsion to these despotic tactics. Unfortunately, the deceived masses complied for the most part. This is the *opposite* to the spirit of freedom that God wants us to walk in!

<u>3</u>

THE LORDSHIP
of Jesus Christ

You've of course heard the appeal to "accept Jesus Christ as your Lord and Savior." Is this just a religious expression or is there a biblical basis to it? It *is* scriptural. Look no further than this popular evangelistic verse:

> **If you declare with your mouth, "Jesus <u>is Lord</u>," and believe in your heart that God raised him from the dead, <u>you will be saved</u>.**
>
> **Romans 10:9**

As you can see, Jesus Christ is both Lord and Savior. For a person to apprehend eternal salvation—that is, reconcile with God and receive eternal life (2 Corinthians 5:19 & John 3:16,36)—they have to first acknowledge that Yeshua is Lord, combined with belief in the gospel.

While not everyone in the three realms—Heaven, Earth and the Underworld—presently acknowledges Christ's Lordship, they eventually will, even the unredeemed on Judgment Day (Philippians 2:5-11 & Revelation 20:11-15).

Thus every genuine believer acknowledges that Jesus Christ is Lord and is therefore saved from the wages of sin, eternal death (Romans 6:23). But what about…

The LORDSHIP of Jesus Christ in the Believer's Life

If Christ is Lord to a believer, what exactly does that mean? The Greek word for 'Lord' is *kurios (KOO-ree-os)*, which means "lord, master—a person exercising absolute *ownership* rights." This indicates a profound truth of Christianity: We are not our own since God purchased us through the precious blood of Christ (1 Corinthians 6:19-20 & 1 Peter 1:18-19). We are therefore to offer our bodies as **living sacrifices** to our LORD on a continuing basis (Romans 12:1) and, more than that, our thoughts as well since the passage goes on to instruct us to be "transformed by the renewing of **our minds**" (Romans 12:2).

Since we've been purchased by God, each believer is to offer every part of himself/herself to the LORD as "instruments of righteousness" (Romans 6:13). How do you do this? Simple: Find out what God's Word says and simply put it into practice (James 1:22-25). Just as important, find out who you are in Christ and make that your mindset and confession since it reveals **how God sees you**, which we looked at last chapter.

This is how the believer increasingly acquiesces to the **Lordship** of Christ and this relates to spiritual growth. The very word 'growth' suggests a *process*, something that naturally happens over time. It's the day-to-day progression of sanctification. John the Baptist put it like this:

> **"He must become greater; I must become less."**
> **John 3:30**

This doesn't mean that the individual loses his/her identity, but rather that **the will of the Lord becomes increasingly paramount** (1 Peter 4:2). Things and activities that used to seem so important gradually lose their appeal and you find yourself content and at peace simply serving your Lord in the unique way that God has called you, which corresponds to your talents and distinct situation.

This process involves years, even decades, wherein you may experience relapses with certain issues of the old self, but keep getting back up and moving forward. The Bible stresses that the LORD has compassion on the plight of his children in this fallen creation (Psalm 145:9). Compassion means "sympathetic understanding." Christ is our High Priest who fully emphasizes with our weaknesses and struggles because he dwelt in a flesh-and-blood body on this fallen world, just like us (Hebrews 4:15).

It's crucial to understand that **God is *for you*** and not against you (Romans 8:31).

Focus on relationship with God because this will anchor your faith when you face the inevitable hard times of life. Also keep in mind that your relationship with the LORD isn't one-dimensional in the sole sense of servant and Lord. Christ is also your friend (John 15:15), you are a precious son or daughter to the Father (Matthew 6:9 & 23:9), a rightful co-heir with Christ (Romans 8:17 & Ephesians 3:6), and the Holy Spirit is your teacher, guide, comforter and helper (John 14:26, 16:13 & 16:17).

Since the LORD is the Fountain of Life (Psalm 36:9) it's imperative that you develop closeness with your Creator and stay close. Why? Because, as *the* Fountain of Life, the LORD will constantly gush forth life into your being and give you the grace to overcome the great challenges of this fallen world, not to mention fulfill your unique call and purpose.

Why am I stressing all of this and encouraging growing believers? Two reasons:

1. I've heard sermons on Christ's Lordship that tend to dish out the condemnation, which is an unbalanced approach, not to mention legalistic. As such, I want to emphasize the positive side of this vital topic.
2. It's necessary in the name of balance to also look at the unfortunate reality of…

Believers Who Don't Acquiesce to Christ's Lordship

If Jesus Christ is truly your Lord and Savior, would you not seek to know him and find out what he wants you to do and not do with your life—a life that he literally purchased with his life's blood? Of course you would, as explained above. **Acquiescing to Christ's Lordship is a natural part of spiritual development and increases with growth.** As John the Baptist put it above, "He must become greater; I must become less." It's a *process*. It doesn't happen overnight, but it does happen and naturally so.

But what about those who foolishly choose not to do so? Here's what the Lord said:

> "Why do you call me, 'Lord, Lord,' and do not do what I say? [47]As for everyone who comes to me and hears my words and puts them into practice, I will show you what they are like. [48]They are like a man building a house, who dug down deep and laid the foundation on rock. When a flood came, the torrent struck that house but could not shake it, because it was well built. [49]But the one who hears my words and does not put them into practice is like a man who built a house on the ground without a foundation. The moment the torrent struck that house, it collapsed and its destruction was complete."
>
> **Luke 6:46-49**

The Messiah is talking about those who call him 'Lord,' but aren't interested in putting his teachings into practice. As Titus put it, "They claim to know God, but by their actions they deny him" (Titus 1:16). Jesus then links this to the issue of spiritual development, which can be observed in his parable of building a foundation along with the phrasing "well built." This succinct parable speaks of two separate people building foundations for their houses:

1. **The wise one** digs deep and builds his house on a rock foundation; when the storms eventually come, his house stands strong.
2. **The foolish one**, however, builds his house without a foundation and thus it *collapses* when the storms manifest.

Interestingly, the LORD is repeatedly described in the Bible as **a rock** to those who trust in him (Psalm 18:2, 18:46, 19:14 & 95:1). Why? Because, like a rock foundation, God is unmovable and impregnable. Christ is saying that **believers need to build their spiritual houses on the solid rock of the LORD**. If we don't, our spiritual house will collapse when facing the inevitable hardships and temptations of life.

For instance, I was reading up on some believers who were in Christian bands in the 80s-90s and held up as Christian leaders, often interviewed in magazines & newspapers wherein they gave their wise advice to other believers. I was surprised to discover that several key ones are no longer walking with the Lord and some are even evangelistic atheists. What happened? I thought these were Christian leaders? The sad truth is that they didn't build their house on the Rock of the LORD. Thus when the torrents of life's difficulties and the challenge of secular ideologies threatened their faith, their spiritual houses collapsed.

I'm sharing this with zero condescension, but as a scriptural warning. The lesson is that **the LORD must be the believer's rock foundation in spiritual development**. This can be seen in Christ's coinciding statement in Matthew:

> **"Not everyone who says to me, 'Lord, Lord,' will enter the kingdom of heaven, but <u>only the one who does the will of my Father who is in heaven</u>. [22]Many will say to me on that day, 'Lord, Lord, did we not prophesy in your name and in your name drive out demons and in your name perform many miracles?' [23]Then I will tell them plainly, '<u>I never knew you</u>. Away from me, <u>you evildoers!</u>' "**
>
> **Matthew 7:21-23**

As with his similar statement in the above passage (Luke 6:46-49), Christ emphasizes those who readily call him 'Lord,' but *don't* practice God's Word. However, this passage adds that the Lord didn't *know* these people and even calls them evildoers or "workers of lawlessness," as some translations put it (verse 23). In short, these people:

- **Didn't know the LORD**, that is, they didn't have a relationship with him, even though they confessed him as 'Lord.'
- **They walked in the flesh** on a regular basis without penitence.

They also trusted in their religious works, rather than the Lord (Ephesians 2:8-9), as observed in verse 22. Hence, the Messiah plainly tells them when they stand before him for evaluation, "I never knew you. Away from me you evildoers!"

So merely calling Jesus 'Lord' and performing religious works doesn't necessarily mean a believer is acquiescing to the Lordship of Christ, but rather:

1. Practicing the Word of God you currently understand,
2. Having a relationship with the Lord and…
3. Walking in the spirit as opposed to the flesh.

Any believer who wisely attends to these three things will build a solid rock foundation to spiritual growth and fruit-bearing service in God's kingdom. All three signify that the believer is acquiescing to the Lordship of Christ. Those who fail to do these things are apparently only interested in Jesus as Savior, but not Lord. They want what Christ can *give* them—forgiveness of sin and salvation from eternal death—but they don't want *who* he ultimately is, Lord.

The Spiritual Warrior, of course, belongs in the former group.

A Church That Made Something Other-Than-Christ Lord

Here's what the resurrected Lord had to say to the historical assembly in Laodicea (which was located in what is today southwestern Turkey):

> **"So, because you are lukewarm—neither hot nor cold—<u>I am about to spit you out of my mouth.</u> [17] <u>You say, 'I am rich; I have acquired wealth and do not need a thing.'</u> But you do not realize that <u>you are wretched, pitiful, poor, blind and naked.</u> [18]I counsel you to buy from me gold refined in the fire, so you can become rich; and white clothes to wear, so you can cover your shameful nakedness; and salve to put on your eyes, so you can see."**
> **[19]"Those whom I love I rebuke and discipline. So be earnest and <u>repent.</u> [20]Here I am! <u>I stand at the door and knock. If anyone hears my voice and opens the door, I will come in and eat with that person, and they with me.</u>"**
>
> **Revelation 3:16-20**

Christ rebuked these believers for being "lukewarm" and threatened to spit the whole fellowship out of his mouth if they didn't repent, meaning he would "pull the plug" on them and they'd be a church in name only.

The Lord desired that they were cold or hot rather than lukewarm. This was an allusion to nearby cold and hot springs. The cold springs were useful for refreshing and the hot springs for bathing, but lukewarm water was useless. Thus this assembly was useless.

What was the root problem? They made something *other than* Christ Lord of their lives; and verse 17 reveals that this 'thing' was material wealth. I want to stress that it's okay to have physical wealth, but it's not okay for physical wealth to have the person wherein it basically becomes their 'god' (Luke 12:15). As the Messiah put it, "You cannot serve God and money" (Matthew 6:24).

Sadly, riches replaced Christ's Lordship in the lives of the Laodicean believers, which can be observed in their boasting of their great wealth and the claim that they had need of nothing. But the Lord gave them a rude awakening by informing them that they were, in reality, "wretched, pitiful, poor, blind and naked" and needed to repent (verses 17 & 19).

Further support for the fact that material wealth was their 'lord' and not Christ can be seen in the fact that Jesus was *outside* the fellowship knocking on the door wanting to come in and commune with them. In short, **the very Lord they claimed to serve wasn't even in their fellowship!** He was outside politely asking them to let him in while threatening to spit them out of his mouth if they foolishly refused.

The obvious moral is: Be careful *not* to make anything other than Jesus Christ Lord in your life.

What Does It Mean to "Take Up Your Cross Daily"?

This question applies to what the Lord said here:

> **And he said, "The Son of Man must suffer many things and be rejected by the elders, the chief priests and the teachers of the law, and he must be killed and on the third day be raised to life."**
> **[23]Then he said to them all: "Whoever wants to be my disciple <u>must deny themselves</u> and <u>take up their cross daily and follow me</u>. [24]For whoever wants to save their life will lose it, but whoever loses their life for me will save it. [25]What good is it for someone to gain the whole world, and yet lose or forfeit their very self?"**
>
> **Luke 9:22-25**

The Lord first informs his disciples concerning the grim reality of his ultimate mission on Earth—to die for humanity as a substitutionary sacrifice, which of course opened the door to reconciliation with God and eternal life (Romans 5:10 & John 3:16). He then switches to what is expected of his disciples, aka his Spiritual Warriors: To deny themselves, take up their cross daily, and follow him. To "deny yourself" means to deny the flesh or sinful nature. It also includes throwing off any "weights" that hinder your service in the Lord (Hebrews 12:1).

Christ's instruction to "take up their cross daily" was no doubt startling since "taking up a cross" literally meant facing the humiliation and horrible pain of Roman crucifixion wherein the condemned were usually required to carry their cross to the place of execution (and the corresponding hole in the ground where the pole fit).

The difference between the Messiah and condemned criminals of the Roman Empire was that Yeshua laid down his life voluntarily (John 10:15). He asks us to do likewise in a figurative sense: To commit our lives wholeheartedly to the LORD, accepting any humiliation, ridicule and hardship that this eventually brings.

Since starting this ministry in late 2011, for instance, I've had to face humiliation and ridicule from arrogant people & slanderers and even lose relationships. The Spiritual Warrior might sometimes feel as Hosea felt: "the prophet is considered a fool, the inspired person a maniac" (Hosea 9:7). These types of challenges are plainly chronicled in the Scriptures:

> **[3]Have mercy on us, Lord, have mercy on us,**
> **for <u>we have endured no end of contempt</u>.**
> **[4]We have endured no end**
> **of <u>ridicule from the arrogant</u>,**
> **of <u>contempt from the proud</u>.**
>
> **Psalm 123:3-4**

> **"Truly I tell you," Jesus replied, "no one who has left home or brothers or sisters or mother or father or children or fields <u>for me and the gospel</u> [30]will fail to receive a hundred times as much in this present age: homes, brothers, sisters, mothers, children and fields—<u>along with persecutions</u>—and in the age to come eternal life. [31]But many who are first will be last, and the last first."**
>
> **Mark 10:29-31**

Carol & I have also had to sacrifice certain luxuries, which I won't go into, but nothing we've experienced compares even slightly to the myriad challenges that Paul had to face in service of God's kingdom, as detailed in 2 Corinthians 11:16-33. Please read it and marinate on it.

This is what it means to take up your cross daily and follow the Lord. Keep in mind, however, that God deals with people according to the light they have and this naturally corresponds to the individual's stage of spiritual growth and calling (John 9:39-41, John 15:22 & John 15:24). If you're a half-pint, live up to being a half-pint; if you're a gallon, live up to being a gallon; if you're a two-ton tank, live up to being a two-ton tank. The ex-thief on the cross, for instance, was a brand new believer (Luke 23:39-43).

What Makes a Person a "Legitimate Believer"?

A believer's legitimacy in Christianity doesn't depend on being doctrinally correct on every peripheral issue. While it's certainly good to be as accurate as possible on any given topic, it's one's **faith** in the message of Christ that marks a true believer (John 3:16 & 3:36). As the Lord said:

> **"The work of God is this: to believe in the one he has sent."**
>
> **John 6:29**

As far as practice or lifestyle goes, legitimate believers are those who walk in the spirit and produce the fruit thereof in every good work (Colossians 1:10), the primary fruit being **love** (Colossians 3:14), which includes walking in tough love when appropriate. Genuine Christians naturally live by the 'golden rule' (or should I say *super*naturally live by it, with the help of the Holy Spirit?). Walking in the spirit of course includes **keeping with repentance** (1 John 1:9, Matthew 3:8 & Luke 3:8). Any confessing believer who refuses to keep with repentance and stubbornly lives a *lifestyle* of sin is deceiving himself or herself. As it is written:

> **Do not be deceived: God cannot be mocked. A man reaps what he sows. [8]Whoever sows to please their flesh, from the flesh will reap <u>destruction</u>; whoever sows to please the spirit, from the spirit will reap <u>eternal life</u>.**
>
> **Galatians 6:7-8**

<u>4</u>

SPIRITUAL GROWTH BASICS

This chapter is devoted to the basics that every Spiritual Warrior must master if you want to grow spiritually in a healthy manner and fulfill the LORD's will in your unique life. A lot of this material has been covered at length in my other works, so we'll just brush up on these things here. If you're already up on a particular topic, just jump to the next section.

The Foundation of the Fear of the LORD and Humility

The "fear of the LORD" isn't talked about much in Christian circles these days, including sermons. Why? Possibly because the Mighty LORD has been essentially reduced to a cuddly teddy bear in the sky or perhaps a genial genie. The idea that the Almighty Sovereign God—the Creator of all things in Heaven, Earth & the Universe—is to be feared, respected and awed seems to be unhip. But what does the Bible say about the fear of the LORD, both Old and New Testaments?

The fear of the LORD is **foundational** to the Spiritual Warrior. Foundational to what? See for yourself:

> **The fear of the LORD is the _beginning_ of knowledge,**
> **but fools despise wisdom and discipline.**
>
> **Proverbs 1:7**

> **The fear of the LORD is the *beginning* of wisdom;**
> **all who follow his precepts have good <u>understanding</u>.**
> **Psalm 111:10**

> **The fear of the LORD is the *beginning* of wisdom,**
> **and knowledge of the Holy One is <u>understanding.</u>**
> **Proverbs 9:10**

These verses show the connection between **knowledge, understanding** and **wisdom**. Knowledge, of course, is factual information, whether mundane or spiritual, while understanding has to do with comprehension. It's possible to know something, including trivia, but not really understand the subject. Meanwhile wisdom is the application of what you know and understand. Many people know & understand certain important things, but they fail to live it or live in light of it, which means they lack wisdom.

Observe what these passages say is the *beginning* of all three—**the fear of the LORD**. If the fear of the LORD is the *beginning* of knowledge, understanding and wisdom then a person who seeks to attain these *without* the fear of the LORD is off track from the start! Consequently, the conclusions they'll come to in their journey of enlightenment will be off. We see this today with all these highly intelligent and "educated" people who are trying to reinvent morality: What is bad is now good and what is good is bad (Isaiah 5:20). Their journey has brought them to a place of twisted understanding because they failed to start with the fear of the LORD, which is **acknowledging the Creator and respecting God**.

Someone might argue that the "fear of the LORD" is an outmoded Old Testament principle, but Christ himself said we are to fear God:

> **"Do not be afraid of those who kill the body but cannot**
> **kill the soul. Rather, <u>be afraid of the One</u> who can**
> **destroy both soul and body in hell."**
> **Matthew 10:28**

For more proof, Revelation 19:5 depicts a scene in Heaven in which a voice coming from God's throne says: "Praise our God, all you his servants, **you who fear him**, both great and small!" Furthermore, after Ananias and Sapphira were slain by the LORD for their unrepentant lying **"great fear seized the whole church** and all who heard about these events" (Acts 5:5,11). Great fear of whom? God!

Furthermore, when Paul noted that all *believers* will have to stand before Jesus Christ and give an account of our lives at the Judgment Seat, he followed it up with "since, then, we know what it is to fear the Lord" (2 Corinthians 5:10-11). Why do we fear the Lord? Because we're going to stand before Christ and give an account of our lives for what we did in the body, whether good or bad. Of course, any deeds repented of beforehand will *not* be evaluated because God forgave you when you 'fessed up and "purified you from all unrighteousness" (1 John 1:8-9). Those sins were cast into the sea of forgetfulness (Micah 7:19). Isn't that awesome?

The type of fear Paul was talking about—led of the Holy Spirit—was obviously fear of being held accountable to something negative. In other words, fear of punishment (Proverbs 16:6, 3:7 & 8:13). This is the most elemental kind of fear, which compels people to stay on the straight and narrow. For instance, a guy might not believe in God, but he won't commit murder because he fears going to prison for decades or the death penalty. A married woman might find a man attractive, but she refuses to entertain adultery because she doesn't want to ruin her family and life. Of course, the Lord wants us to grow past fear of punishment on our spiritual journey and be motivated by love of God led of the Holy Spirit (1 John 4:16-18 & Romans 8:14). This naturally comes with spiritual growth.

So, the fear of the LORD is the beginning of knowledge, understanding and wisdom, and it's not just an Old Testament principle, but what exactly *is* the fear of the LORD? Since fear is another word for reverence and worship, this suggests that knowledge and wisdom begin when we properly acknowledge God and offer our Creator the reverence and adoration due. The writer of Hebrews put it like this:

> **Therefore, since we are receiving a kingdom that cannot be shaken, let us be thankful, and so worship God acceptably <u>with reverence and awe</u>, for our "God is a consuming fire."**
>
> **Hebrews 12:28-29**

There's also the respectful fear that a son or daughter has toward the just correction and discipline of his/her loving father. It's a healthy respect for authority; in God's case, the *ultimate* authority.

A key trait of the fear of the LORD is, of course, humility, the attitude that we're not all that and a bag of chips, which brings to mind a simple yet potent passage:

God <u>opposes</u> the proud but <u>gives grace</u> [favor] to the humble.
James 4:6; 1 Peter 5:5; Proverbs 3:34

This is quoted **three times** in the Bible, once in the Old Testament and twice in the New. God's trying to get something across to us! He "opposes" the proud, which means he *resists* them. Proverbs 16:5 even says "The LORD *detests* all the proud of heart." Those who are arrogant resist God and the Lord resists them in return. They resist, God resists. It's a doomed cycle.

The good news, of course, is that the LORD gives grace to the humble, the meek, not the weak. This means his **favor**! God says:

"These are the ones I look on with favor:
those who are humble and contrite in spirit,
and who tremble at my word."
Isaiah 66:2

God's favor, blessing and enlightenment only flow to the humble who genuinely acknowledge their Creator, not the arrogant who are stubborn, hard-hearted and think they know it all. The latter includes religious leaders, like the Pharisees and teachers of the law, who put on airs that they knew and honored God when nothing could've been further from the truth. The Pharisees, for instance, claimed to be God's children but the Messiah told them point blank that they were children of the devil (John 8:41-47)! Don't think that such religious leaders only existed in Christ's day. They're all over today, just open your eyes; they even go by the tag 'Christian' and say "Lord, Lord" (Matthew 7:15-23).

What can we conclude from all of this? If we want freedom we have to want truth, which means *the way it really is*. Why? Because truth is the very thing we need to set us free, as Jesus taught (John 8:31-32). Truth consists of knowledge, understanding and wisdom from God's Word and the *foundation* of these is **the fear of the LORD.**

Needless to say, let's be wise sons & daughters of God and cultivate a healthy reverence and awe of the Holy One. Always strive for humility, which is the opposite of stubbornness and arrogance. Cultivate the attitude of an unworthy servant who's only doing his/her duty (Luke 17:10). If you do this, God's favor will surely flow to you. But please understand that persecutions will increase (2 Timothy 3:12). Higher levels, bigger devils.

Cultivating the Heart of a *Learner,* aka a Disciple

Anyone who aspires to be a Spiritual Warrior must be a disciple of Christ as opposed to someone who merely says they're a believer while their actions tell a different story (Titus 1:16). The word 'disciple' is *mathétes (math-ay-TAYS)* in the Greek, which means "learner." So, a true disciple of the Lord—a Spiritual Warrior—is a *learner* of the Lord. In this world, does a person ever get to a place of knowing it all and not needing to learn anymore? Of course not. How much more so in a spiritual sense for those who are disciples of the Lord?

Even those who are called to the fivefold ministry—whether apostle, prophet, evangelist, pastor or teacher (Ephesians 4:11-13)—continue to learn as they mature and fulfill their calling. In Christ, you never stop learning; you never stop being a disciple, a learner, no matter how far you go or highfalutin your position.

This of course ties into the humility from the previous section because arrogant people tend to think they know it all and therefore resist learning. They hate it when someone tries to teach them something or, God forbid, corrects them (Proverbs 9:7-9).

Arrogance and the corresponding stubborn ignorance are the kiss of death, spiritually. Take heed; truer words have rarely been spoken.

Utilizing the Seven Keys to Spiritual Maturity

The Bible speaks of seven virtues that believers need to regularly apply to their faith if they want to keep growing spiritually and fulfill their God-given mission while bearing fruit of the spirit (2 Peter 1:3-11). These qualities *go together* and are to be added *one to the other*. They are:

1. Goodness, which refers to virtue or moral excellence. In the Greek it's *arête (ar-ET-ay)*. The reason *arête* is a vital ingredient to your spiritual growth is because the human heart is likened to **soil** in the Bible (Luke 8:15) and it takes *good* soil to produce a *good* crop. So be careful to guard your heart from contaminants that would hinder the productiveness of God's Word that's sown in your heart. Guard your heart as the wellspring of life—the source that determines the very boundaries of your life; that is, how far you go or don't go (Proverbs 4:23). Throw off every *thing* that hinders your walk and every sin that so easily entangles you (Hebrews

12:1). The "thing" isn't a sin in-and-of-itself, but rather something that hampers your output in Christ because you spend too much time with it. Since things get planted in your heart through **A.** what you see, **B.** what you hear and **C.** the company you keep or the atmosphere you permit, it's important to discipline what you allow your eyes to see, your ears to hear and the people with whom you spend time. We'll look at this in more detail next chapter.

Adding goodness can be viewed as removing the "dross" from your life so that the LORD can forge a worthy vessel for his purposes. This coincides with Proverbs 25:4: "Remove the dross from the silver and out comes material for the silversmith." Dross is waste material that a metallurgist removes in order to forge the quality instrument of choice. It's the same thing with God and you (2 Timothy 2:20-21).

2. Knowledge is *gnosis (NOH-sis)* in the Greek and refers to textual knowledge or sound teaching. You add to the soil of your heart the seed of knowledge, which includes the Word of Truth on any given topic, such as how to walk free from sin or receive a healing by faith (2 Timothy 2:15 & 3:16). Like David, cultivate a passion for knowledge (Psalm 119:20). As you search for it as if it were a hidden treasure, you'll "find the knowledge of God" (Proverbs 2:3-6). Learn to distinguish fact from opinion (which we'll address at in the last section of this chapter).

3. Self-control refers to controlling yourself *according to* the knowledge you received because the text says to add self-control *to* knowledge (2 Peter 1:6). This simply means to put into practice the Word of God that you've learned, whether it's a practical truth, historical truth or revelational truth. Practical truths are of course practiced by *doing* them whereas historical and revelational truths involve changing your thinking accordingly.

For instance, if you receive a truth that describes your *position* in Christ, such as how you're "holy **in God's sight**, without blemish and free from accusation" (Colossians 1:22), then make this your mindset and confession. Say: *"I am holy in God's sight, without blemish and free from accusation!"* Remember, the words you speak have power; in fact, the Bible says they have the power of life and death (Proverbs 18:21). How much more so the words you speak over yourself!

4. Perseverance is *hupomoné (hoop-om-on-AY)* in the Greek, which means endurance, steadfastness, or to wait patiently. After preparing the soil of your heart to ensure that it's good soil and then adding the Word of God coupled with putting it into practice, it's then necessary to persevere in order for the Word to produce fruit in your life. You see, it's through faith *and* patience that we inherit what is promised, not just faith (Hebrews 6:12). What good is faith that believes for a while but ultimately gives up?

This is relevant to the rocky soil in the Parable of the Sower: People who fail to add perseverance "last only a short time. When trouble or persecution come **because of the word**, they quickly fall away" (Mark 4:17). You see, whenever someone receives the Word on any given topic, the enemy will try to steal it via some kind of attack. The wise person who puts into practice God's Word and perseveres will withstand the attack whereas the foolish person who fails to put it into practice or fails to endure challenges will not. The latter person naturally concludes that "God's Word doesn't work" when it has nothing to do with the truthfulness of the Word or the faithfulness of the Lord (Matthew 7:24-27).

Applying these first four "keys" to your faith—goodness, knowledge, self-control and perseverance—*will* result in fruit in your life. In short, these four virtues guarantee the fruitfulness of God's Word. They concern the planting, cultivation and productiveness of the Word of Truth.

The following three keys, by contrast, involve **walking in love** in your **relationships**, starting with the LORD ("godliness"), then fellow believers ("mutual affection") and, lastly, people in the world ("love").

The reason this is important is revealed in this passage:

> **For in Christ Jesus neither circumcision nor uncircumcision means anything, but <u>faith working through love</u>.**
>
> **Galatians 5:6** (NASB)

Our covenant with God is a covenant of faith and therefore it works through faith; and faith *works through* **love**. If you cancel out love, you cancel out faith and your covenant won't "work" as it should. You see, the foundation of the New Covenant is the law of Christ, which is the law of love (1 Corinthians 9:19-21 & Galatians 6:2). With this understanding, consider these last three "keys" that need to be added to your faith:

5. Godliness is not the same as "religion" in the Greek. The former word is *eusebeia (yoo-SEB-ee-ah)* whereas the latter is *thréskeia (thrays-KIH-ah)*. This is how scholar E.W. Bullinger distinguished the two:

> *Eusebeia* [godliness] relates to a real, true, vital, and spiritual relation with God while *thréskeia* [religion] relates to the outward acts of religious observances or ceremonies, which can be done in the flesh. Our English word "religion" was never used in the sense of true godliness. It always meant the outward forms of worship (Bullinger 335).

So **godliness refers to genuine spiritual relationship with the LORD** as opposed to religion, which refers to outward religious acts. Godliness *cannot* be performed by the flesh whereas religion can.

Godliness could simply be translated as "like-God-ness." In other words, it's behaving and speaking as the Lord would behave and speak. You could say it's *imitating* God, which we are plainly instructed to do in the Bible (Ephesians 5:1 & 1 Peter 4:11). There are two ways to do this. One is to find out what Holy Scripture instructs and simply put it into practice. Since this is *already covered* in verses 5-6 of our main text (2 Peter 1)—i.e. adding knowledge and self-control—this is not what verse 6 is talking about when it says we're to add godliness. Godliness in this context refers to loving God in a different way than obeying his Word (1 John 5:3); it's referring to loving the LORD in a relational sense.

How would this make a person godly, i.e. *like*-God? Simple: The more time you spend with a person, particularly someone you love and respect, the closer you'll become and the more *like* him or her you'll naturally be. It's the same thing with your relationship with God. The more time you spend together, the closer you'll become and the more *like* God you'll be. The LORD will "rub off" on you and you'll thus be increasingly godly.

Hence, we are encouraged to *pursue* godliness in the Bible (1 Timothy 6:10-11) and to *train* ourselves to be godly (1 Timothy 4:7-8). This shows that godliness—an active and increasingly intimate relationship with the LORD—won't automatically happen. It must be pursued and you have to "train yourself" to habitually walk in it. This is understandable when you consider that all good relationships take time, energy, attention and discipline. It's no different with your relationship with God.

6. Mutual affection is *philadelphian* in the Greek (one word) and refers specifically to loving your Christian brethren and sistren. As Paul instructed, "Be devoted to one another in <u>love</u> *(philadelphia)*. Honor one another above yourselves" (Romans 12:10). Notice how Peter phrased it:

> **Now that you have purified yourselves by obeying the truth so that you have sincere <u>love</u> *(philadelphia)* for each other, <u>love</u> *(agapaó)* one another deeply, from the heart.**
>
> **1 Peter 1:22**

Two kinds of love are stressed here. The first kind refers to the affection/respect of brotherly and sisterly love in Christ. The second refers to *agape* love, which is love **in practice**, as defined in 1 Corinthians 13:4-7. With this understanding, let's apply this verse to us: Now that we are spiritually regenerated Christians and therefore have genuine affection—*phileo* love—for our fellow believers let's be sure to *agape* love one another—that is, walk in practical love toward each other—and let it stem from the heart, that is, the warm affection of *phileo* love.

Hebrews 10:24 instructs us to "spur one another on toward love and good deeds." Do this in accordance with your particular grace gifts:

> **We have different gifts, according to the grace given to each of us. If your gift is <u>prophesying</u>, then prophesy in accordance with your faith; [7] if it is <u>serving</u>, then serve; if it is <u>teaching</u>, then teach; [8] if it is to <u>encourage</u>, then give encouragement; if it is <u>giving</u>, then give generously; if it is to <u>lead</u>, do it diligently; if it is to <u>show mercy</u>, do it cheerfully.**
>
> **Romans 12:6-8**

Utilize whatever gift you have to bless your brothers & sisters in the Lord. My gifts are teaching, encouraging and showing mercy. What are yours?

7. Love in the context of 2 Peter 1:7 refers to walking in love toward those who are lost and dying in the world (since loving God and loving fellow believers have already been addressed). The Greek word for 'love' here is *agape*, which refers to practical love as shown in this popular passage:

> **Love is patient, love is kind. It does not envy, it does not boast, it is not proud. ⁵ It does not dishonor others, it is not self-seeking, it is not easily angered, it keeps no record of wrongs. ⁶ Love does not delight in evil but rejoices with the truth. ⁷ It always protects, always trusts, always hopes, always perseveres.**
> **1 Corinthians 13:4-7**

Since *agape* love is practical love, it doesn't require *phileo* love in order to walk in it, not to mention *storge* love (familial love) or *eros* love (romantic love). In other words, you don't have to have any affection or respect whatsoever toward an individual to *agape* love him or her, which explains Jesus and Paul's instructions to love our enemies (Matthew 5:44 & Romans 12:14-21). You don't have to have warm feelings or respect for your enemies to *agape* love them because the **biblical definition of *agape* love** shows that it's practical in nature.

Nor does *agape* loving someone mean always being sugary-sweet nice. Yes, *agape* love is kind, but sometimes the kindest thing you can do for a person is boldly tell them the truth. After all, only the truth will set him/her free. Christians aren't mandated to be nice; we're mandated to be good. And sometimes doing the good thing for a person or situation isn't the nice thing; but it is the right thing, as long as you're led of the Holy Spirit. I'm talking about *tough* love. Christ walked in it on occasion (Mark 11:15-18 & Luke 11:37-54), not to mention Peter (Acts 8:20-23) and Paul (Acts 13:8-12). These people are *your* examples as a Spiritual Warrior.

Of course, you should only take the tough love route if it's absolutely necessary and more gentle measures have proven ineffective.

The Bible encourages us to add *agape* love for unbelievers to our faith because it's easy to get saved, hook up with a fellowship and not have much to do with unsaved people. There are Christians who pretty much refuse to have anything to do with unbelievers, not unlike the Israelites during Jesus' era who shunned Samaritans. Let's not be like that. Yeshua wasn't. He went out of his way to talk with the outcast Samaritan woman and ministered to her. He *agape* loved her (John 4:4-26). Even though Christ was called specifically to "the lost sheep of Israel," he ministered to a Canaanite woman and, indirectly, her daughter (Matthew 15:21-28).

What are some ways that you can *agape* love unbelievers? Pray for them regularly, consider ways to bless them, do a good deed, share the message of Christ, "turn the cheek" when necessary and, by all means, don't be a Pharisaical hypocrite. Here's a good passage:

> **But in your hearts revere Christ as Lord. Always be prepared to give an answer to everyone who asks you to give the reason for the hope that you have. But do this with gentleness and respect,**
>
> **1 Peter 3:15**

The important thing is that you don't forget the lost on your Christian pilgrimage and act like they don't exist. *Agape* love them!

As a Spiritual Warrior, "make every effort" to add these seven qualities to your faith because they guarantee spiritual productivity and growth (2 Peter 1:5). Paul said "he who began a good work in you will carry it on to completion" (Philippians 1:6), but this will only happen *if* you're attentive to adding these seven "keys" to your faith. It's no accident that there are seven because the number 7 signifies completeness or completion.

Our text promises that if you do this "in increasing measure" you will never stumble and it guarantees a "rich welcome" into the eternal kingdom when you come face to face with the LORD (2 Peter 1:10-11). A *rich* welcome is opposite of a *poor* or *lousy* welcome.

Believers Are *Under* the Law of Christ, Not the OT Law

The Spiritual Warrior understands the foundational truth that New Covenant believers are *not* under the Mosaic law:

> **But if you are led by the Spirit, <u>you are not under the law</u>.**
>
> **Galatians 5:18**

> **For sin shall not be your master, because <u>you are not under law, but under grace</u>.**
>
> **Romans 6:14**

> **...<u>we have been released from the law</u> so that we serve in the new way of the Spirit, and <u>not in the old way of the written code</u>.**
>
> **Romans 7:6**

In the New Testament era, **we've been released from the Law**—the Torah—to "serve in the new way of the Spirit, and *not* in the old way of the written code." We're "not under law, but under grace," meaning we're under God's *graciousness*—favor—through the work of Christ wherein we obtain spiritual regeneration and are reconciled with the LORD, not to mention indwelt by the Counselor, the Holy Spirit.

While New Testament believers are not under the Mosaic law, we are under **Christ's law**, aka **the law of Christ** (1 Corinthians 9:19-21 & Galatians 6:2). The rest of the New Testament reveals what the law of Christ is. For instance, notice Jesus' answer to an expert in the Law who sought to test him:

> **"Teacher, which is the greatest commandment in the Law?"**
> **[37]Jesus replied: "'<u>Love the Lord your God</u> with all your heart and with all your soul and with all your mind.' [38] <u>This is the first and greatest commandment.</u> [39]And the second is like it: '<u>Love your neighbor as yourself.</u>' [40] <u>All the Law and the Prophets hang on these two commandments.</u>"**
>
> **Matthew 22:36-40**

The phrase "the law and the prophets" is a reference to the Old Testament Scriptures; and, specifically, to the moral law since the dietary and ceremonial laws of the Old Testament were foreshadows of Christ and were **fulfilled** in him:

> **Therefore do not let anyone judge you by <u>what you eat or drink</u>, or <u>with regard to a religious festival, a <u>New Moon celebration</u> or a <u>Sabbath day</u>. [17] These are <u>a shadow</u> of the things that were to come; the reality, however, is found <u>in Christ</u>.**
>
> **Colossians 2:16-17**

The passage is addressing the dietary and ceremonial laws of the Old Testament: "what you eat or drink" refers to dietary laws and the others refer to ritualistic laws. We are **not** to allow legalists to judge us negatively by these things. In fact, all of them—dietary laws, the Jewish festivals, the New Moon celebration and the Sabbath day—were mere **shadows** of what was to come, meaning Jesus Christ, the Anointed One. "A shadow" means a *foreshadow*, which is something that testifies to the reality to come. The real thing, however, is not the shadow. "The reality is found in Christ" and if you're a believer **YOU** are "in Christ."

As for the moral law, believers are not under it, yet we uphold it:

> **Do we, then, nullify the law by this faith? Not at all! Rather, <u>we uphold the law</u>.**
>
> **Romans 3:31**

How exactly do we uphold the moral law; that is, establish it and fulfill it?

> **so that <u>the righteous standard of the Law</u> might be <u>fulfilled in us</u>, who do not live according to the flesh but according to the spirit.**
>
> **Romans 8:4** (BSB)

The "righteous standard of the Law" refers to the moral law, which is fulfilled in believers "who do not live according to the flesh, but according to the spirit." This means living out of your new spiritual nature as led of the Holy Spirit:

> **So I say, walk by the spirit, and <u>you will not gratify the desires of the flesh</u>.**
>
> **Galatians 5:16**

You see? **Walking in the spirit** is the key to fulfilling the moral law for the New Testament believer. This is one-in-the-same as "**participating in the divine nature**" (2 Peter 1:4). It means being spirit-controlled rather than flesh-ruled and is the automatic result of loving God, which is the primary part of the law of Christ and includes "coming near to God" (James 4:8). If you are "near to God" that obviously means that you have a close *relationship*. So relationship with the LORD is key.

Getting back to Matthew 22:37-40, all of the Old Testament moral laws can be condensed into two basic rules with three applications: LOVE GOD and LOVE PEOPLE as you LOVE YOURSELF. When you do this, you automatically fulfill the whole moral law of the Old Testament.

Walking According to the Golden Rule

What we call "**the golden rule**" applies to the general guideline on how we should treat other people:

> **"In everything, then, do to others as you would have them do to you. For this is the essence of the Law and the prophets."** Matthew 7:12

> **"Do to others as you would have them do to you."** Luke 6:31

This social guideline is referred to as "the royal law" in the Bible:

> **If you really fulfill the royal law stated in Scripture, "Love your neighbor as yourself," you are doing well.** James 2:8

True believers live a lifestyle that reflects the "golden rule" or "royal law." This rule is the simplest of guidelines to live by: **Do to others as you would have them do to you.** For instance, if you don't want people to be rude and insulting to you for no justifiable reason, don't be rude and insulting to others. If you want people to be respectful and courteous towards you, be so toward them. If you don't want people to gossip about you, like a pathetic two-face, don't badmouth others behind their backs.

Imagine the global revolution if *everyone* lived this way—there'd be no theft, no adultery, no malicious lying, no backbiting, no racism, no wars.

I'm stunned when I come across intelligent confessing believers who've gone to quality assembles for decades and yet don't follow this simple rule, with zero qualms about it. They might as well get out a megaphone and say, *"I'm not a true believer! I'm a fake Christian!"*

Of course, the golden rule doesn't mean you have to be nicey wicey in situations where tough love is in order:

> **5Better is open rebuke**
> **than hidden love.**
> **6Wounds from a friend can be trusted,**
> **but an enemy multiplies kisses.**
> **Proverbs 27:5-6**

How is this relevant to the golden rule—doing to others as you would have them do to you? Simple: truly godly people *want* others to correct them if they are in the wrong because it will improve the quality of their lives and their service to God. Only an arrogant fool—a mocker—hates legitimate correction:

> **7Whoever corrects a mocker invites insults;**
>   **whoever rebukes the wicked incurs abuse.**
> **8Do not rebuke mockers or they will hate you;**
>   **rebuke the wise and they will love you.**
> **9Instruct the wise and they will be wiser still;**
>   **teach the righteous and they will add to their learning.**
>   **Proverbs 9:7-9**

Kindness is a fruit of the spirit (Galatians 5:22-23) and the kindest thing you can do for someone who's walking in harmful error is correct him/her with the truth. As such, there's example after example of believers boldly confronting & reprimanding others in the New Testament, such as Matthew 16:23, 18:15-17, 23:13-33, Acts 8:9-24, 13:8-12 and Galatians 2:11-14. These are examples of tough love.

Grasping the Four Stages of Spiritual Growth

The Four Stages of spiritual growth are revealed in **1 John 2:9-14**:

STAGE ONE is "in the darkness," which refers to spiritual darkness and is the state of every human being separate from covenant with God. Not everyone in this stage is frothing at the mouth with evil, of course. There are *levels* within each stage. For instance, the Lord spoke of those "not far from the kingdom of God" (Mark 12:34), which refers to those on the verge of...

STAGE TWO is the "childhood" stage of spirituality, which takes place after reconciling with the LORD through spiritual rebirth, thus becoming "children of God" (Titus 3:5 & John 1:12-13). As children in a spiritual sense, these believers are *dependent* upon their pastors and the sect thereof, just as children in the natural are dependent on their parents or caretakers. These Christians tend to believe whatever their spiritual parents say and naturally develop an allegiance to them, as well as the sect thereof. Hence, believers in this stage tend to be overly sectarian.

STAGE THREE is the "young man" stage and of course refers to young females as well (Galatians 3:28). Believers in this stage experience spiritual growth pangs similar to teenagers and young adults in the natural. They're *becoming* more independent and so naturally question what they were taught as spiritual children. It can be a challenging stage and some people unfortunately use it as an excuse to backtrack to STAGE ONE. Those who continue to apply the aforenoted seven keys to spiritual maturity, however, will eventually enter into…

STAGE FOUR is where believers *know* the LORD rather than just know *about* God (verse 13 & Galatians 4:9). They have developed a living relationship on a day-to-day basis and have become spiritual parents, whether "fathers" or "mothers." This is a limitless stage and those in it are the furthest thing from arrogant. Remember, God actively opposes and resists the carnally proud, but gives favor to the *humble* (James 4:6). As spiritual parents, they naturally propagate in a spiritual sense.

Ideally, believers in STAGE TWO should start to grow in STAGE THREE and STAGE FOUR before fully entering them, as illustrated here:

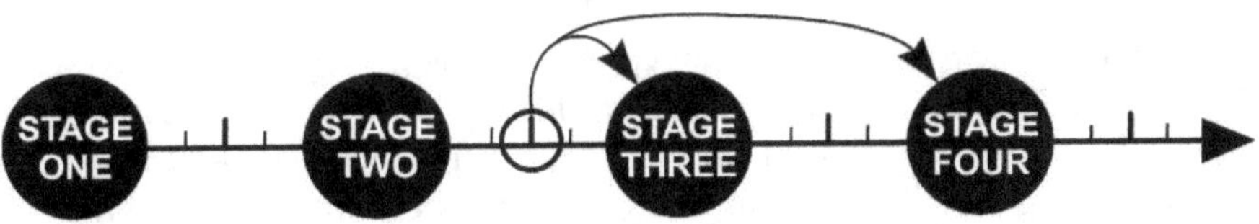

Unfortunately, this isn't always the case. Some believers—too many—choose to stay in STAGE TWO and never truly grow beyond it. These are dear brothers & sisters in the Lord, of course. They're just stuck in the fundamentalist, sectarian mode of spiritual growth and the typical dependence thereof.

People in the lower levels of STAGE ONE usually wind up in a penal institution where they find the structure and discipline necessary to keep the inner beast, the flesh, at bay. This is STAGE TWO in a substitutionary sense. When they're eventually released, they can't handle the freedom and so inevitably commit some heinous crime, which lands them back in the needed structure of the institution, their proxy STAGE TWO.

Why should the Spiritual Warrior know about these stages of spiritual growth? Because it helps you locate where *you* are spiritually and where you need to go, as well as where other people are, which will help you minister to them accordingly.

Knowing the Six Basic Doctrines of Christianity

While most believers seem to be unaware of them, the Bible itself cites the six chief teachings of Christianity in Hebrews 6:1-2. They are:

1. Repentance from Dead Works. It's necessary that believers turn from both dead religious works and sin, which are "acts that lead to death," as the NIV puts it (Romans 6:23). 'Repent' means to change your thinking and therefore your actions in response to the truth received, whatever that might be. It was the first word of the first sermons of John the Baptist and Jesus Christ (Matthew 3:2 & 4:17). The former stressed that "keeping in repentance" on a regular basis was fundamental to bearing fruit for God (Matthew & Luke 3:8).

Curiously, such repentance seems to be unpopular in Evangelical circles these days. Yet the apostle John cited it as a requirement to receiving the LORD's grace and forgiveness when we miss it (1 John 1:8-9). Meanwhile the Lord exhorted the Ephesian believers to repent for abandoning their first love (Revelation 2:4-5). Obviously, he didn't get this dubious memo.

2. Faith in God. Everything received in the New Covenant is received by faith, which is belief. Faith goes hand-in-hand with repentance because the individual *believes* based on the particular truth received; and responds with changing their mind along with the corresponding actions, which is repentance. This explains why repentance and faith are coupled together in Scripture (Mark 1:15 & Acts 20:21). They're two sides of the same coin.

Our covenant is a covenant of faith and so everything in our covenant is by faith (Hebrews 11:1,6). Do you want eternal salvation? It's by faith. Healing? It's by faith. Intimacy with God? Faith. Answers to prayer? Faith. Power to overcome? Faith. I find it puzzling when I come across Christians who are "anti-faith" because it's an oxymoron. They defend their position on the grounds that there have been some extremists in the faith movement, but every movement in the body of Christ inspired by the Holy Spirit has its lunatic fringe. You don't throw the baby out with the bathwater!

Notice that this second fundamental doctrine is called faith **in God**, which shows that our faith is the result of knowing the LORD—the product of relationship—as well as knowing God's Word and the promises thereof. So, it's faith *in God*, not faith in faith. The LORD is the *object* of our faith.

Remember that faith must be *combined with* perseverance in order to be effective (Hebrews 6:12). Faith that gives up is not true faith. So, be sure to continue feeding your faith and avoid people or things that would rob you of it. While every believer starts out with a "measure of faith" (Romans 12:3), faith will grow as you feed it (2 Thessalonians 1:3 & Romans 10:17).

3. Instructions on Baptisms. This core doctrine reveals the importance of the three baptisms of Christianity. They are: **A.** the baptism into Christ, which is one-and-the-same as receiving spiritual regeneration (Galatians 3:26-27 & Romans 6:3); **B.** water baptism, which is the *public testimony* of receiving the prior baptism (Acts 10:47-48); and **C.** the baptism of the Holy Spirit (Acts 10:44-48 & 19:4-7).

The baptism into Christ reveals that a person can't even be in the New Covenant *without* spiritual rebirth (John 3:3,6 & Titus 3:5). So, if you come across a group that deemphasizes being "born-again" in Christ, head for the hills.

Meanwhile there are whole sects that deny the baptism of the holy Spirit, which enables the believer to speak in tongues and is synonymous with praying in the spirit as a supplement to praying in one's own language, as evidenced by 1 Corinthians 14:14-15,18-19 and Ephesians 6:18. This is a source of power, love, self-discipline and faith for the believer (2 Timothy 1:6-7 & Jude 1:20).While you can certainly be a believer without it, loved of the Lord, I strongly encourage getting it and taking advantage of it.

All three of these baptisms can be observed in this passage:

> **Paul said, "John's baptism was a baptism of repentance. He told the people <u>to believe in the one coming after him, that is, in Jesus."</u> [5]On hearing this, they were [water] <u>baptized in the name of the Lord Jesus.</u> [6]When <u>Paul placed his hands on them, the Holy Spirit came on them, and they spoke in tongues and prophesied.</u> [7]There were about twelve men in all.**
>
> **Acts 19:4-7**

4. The Laying on of Hands. This refers to the transference of four things through physical contact:

- Blessing (Mark 10:13,16 & Matthew 19:13,15).

- Anointing and consecration for service, that is, ministry (Acts 6:1-6 & 13:2-3).
- The baptism of the Holy Spirit, as detailed in the previous section.
- Healing or deliverance (Luke 4:40-41).

Elaborating on the last one, a woman who was subject to bleeding for twelve years heard about Jesus' anointing to heal and therefore **had faith** to receive healing from him (Mark 5:25-34). When the woman touched his cloak Christ sensed "power had gone out from him" (verse 30).

The Messiah had an anointing to heal, but his ministry was very limited in his hometown because of the people's lack of faith due to a "spirit of familiarity"—meaning they were so familiar with Yeshua during his first three decades that they were hindered from acknowledging his divine anointing and receiving from it (Mark 6:1-6). This example reveals that getting a healing is a matter of faith in regards to **A.** the person praying (i.e. the human conduit of God's power), as well as **B.** the recipient of the healing. So receiving a healing via a human conduit involves a combination of faith. Needless to say, there's power in agreement (Matthew 18:20 & Leviticus 26:8). However…

People with the greatest faith do not require hands to be laid on them for healing or deliverance. This type of faith accepts the LORD at his Word, like the centurion from Matthew 8:5-10,13. In other words, they don't require a human conduit to receive healing or deliverance from God. The baptism of the Holy Spirit can be received this way as well (Luke 11:13).

5. The Resurrection of the Dead. This doctrine establishes that everyone will be bodily resurrected—both the righteous and the unrighteous—as Jesus and Paul plainly declared (John 5:28-29 & Acts 24:15). This doesn't mean, however, that there will only be two resurrections in number, just that there are two *types* of resurrections: **A.** The resurrection of the righteous and **B.** the resurrection of the unrighteous. The former is called "the first resurrection" in Scripture (Revelation 20:5-6), which makes the latter the second resurrection.

The second resurrection takes place at the time of the Great White Throne Judgment (Revelation 20:11-13). This massive resurrection concerns every dead soul contained in Hades (Sheol) after the millennial reign of Christ on this Earth, which means it involves every unredeemed person throughout history. It does not include Old Testament holy people because they had a covenant with the LORD and will be resurrected after the 7-

year Tribulation and before the Millennium (Matthew 19:28-30, Luke 22:30 & Daniel 12:1-2).

The first resurrection is the resurrection of the righteous, meaning those in right-standing with God. While there's only one resurrection of the unrighteous, the resurrection of the righteous takes place in stages, which correspond to the analogy of a biblical harvest. This harvest began with **the firstfruits**, which concerned the first fruits or grains to ripen in the season and were offered to the LORD as a sacrifice of thanksgiving (Exodus 23:16,19). Later came **the general harvest** (Exodus 23:16) and, lastly, **the gleanings**, which were leftovers for the poor and needy (Leviticus 19:9-10). Here's how each of these apply to the resurrection of the righteous:

- **The Firstfruits.** Paul described Christ as the firstfruits in 1 Corinthians 15:21-23.
- **The General Harvest.** Verse 23 shows that the main harvest takes place when Jesus returns for the Church—his "bride"—which is the Rapture, detailed in 1 Thessalonians 4:13-17. This harvest includes physically-alive believers translated to Heaven.
- **The Gleanings** refer to the righteous who were not included in the main harvest and are, as such, "leftovers." This resurrection happens at the time of the Lord's return at the end of the Tribulation. This return to Earth to establish his millennial reign is separate from the Rapture, which is when the general harvest occurs. Remember, when Christ comes for his Church, he doesn't return to Earth, but rather meets believers in the sky (1 Thessalonians 4:13-17). The gleanings include the resurrection of Old Testament saints as well as the bodily resurrection of believers who died during the Tribulation (and the Millennium).

Here's a helpful diagram to visualize these resurrections:

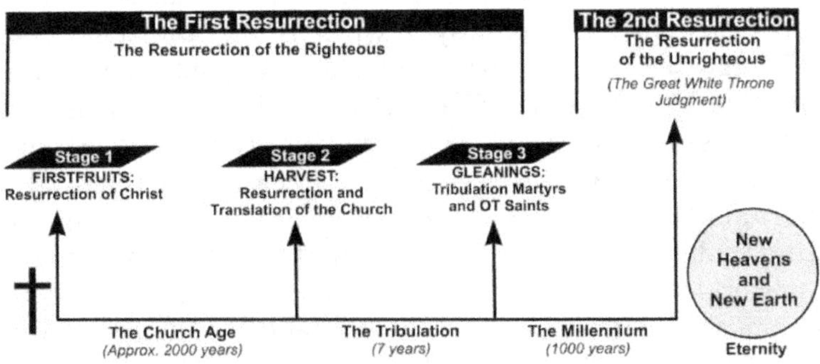

6. Eternal Judgment is the basic doctrine of Christianity that all persons will stand before the LORD for assessment and this will have eternal ramifications. The book of James plainly says "There is only one Lawgiver and Judge, the one who is able to <u>save</u> and <u>destroy</u>" (James 4:12). This is a New Testament passage and it describes the LORD in terms of being a Judge, a Judge who's going to do one of two things with people depending on what they choose to do or not do on this Earth: He's either going to **save** or **destroy**. Whether salvation or destruction, the judgment is eternal, meaning it applies to the never-ending age to come, which is the age of the new Heavens and new Earth (2 Peter 3:7,13).

There are four judgments involving people and they apply to:

- New Covenant believers at the Judgment Seat of Christ, aka the Bema Judgment (2 Corinthians 5:10-11, Hebrews 4:13 & James 3:1). Some Evangelical ministers preach that believers won't have to stand before the LORD and have their lives evaluated, but this is a false doctrine in light of the plain teaching of Scripture.
- The unsaved still alive when Christ returns to the Earth at the end of the Tribulation. This is the Sheep and Goat Judgment (Matthew 25:31-46). Those designated as "goats" will be denied eternal life and cast into the lake of fire to suffer the "eternal punishment" of the second death, which is defined in Scripture as "everlasting destruction," that is, destruction that lasts forever (2 Thessalonians 1:9). The "sheep" will be granted eternal life through spiritual regeneration and allowed to enter the Millennium as mortals (just as you and I are during this current Church Age).
- Old Testament saints (Matthew 19:28-30).
- The unredeemed who have died throughout history, i.e. the lost (Revelation 20:13-15). The text says "The lake of fire is the second death. Anyone whose name was not found written in the book of life was thrown into the lake of fire." What happens to those cast into the lake of fire who suffer this "second death"? James 4:12 (quoted above) says they'll be destroyed, which is what Christ plainly taught (Matthew 10:28). The writer of Hebrews said "raging fire will **consume** the enemies of God" (Hebrews 10:26-27). This coincides with Jesus' unmistakable illustrations (Luke 19:27) and the scriptural fact that "the wages of sin is **death**, but the gift of God is **eternal life** in Christ Jesus" (Romans 6:23); not to mention what the Lord said in the most popular verse of the Bible: "For God so loved the world that he gave his one and only Son, that whoever believes in him shall not **perish** but have **eternal life**." Notice what the two

polar opposites offered to humanity are: destruction/death or eternal life. Get ahold of this fact: Immortality and eternal life are only available to people *through* the message of Christ (2 Timothy 1:10).

For important details on the six basic doctrines see my book of the same name or *The Four Stages of Spiritual Growth*.

Understanding the Fivefold Ministry Gifts

When most people think of occupational ministry they automatically think of a pastor, someone who heads a local assembly. Actually, there are *five* ministry positions and being a pastor is only one of them, as observed in Ephesians 4:11-13. Each of these can be briefly described as follows:

- **Apostles** have an anointing to go out and start assemblies, as well as oversee them (at least more than one). In order to start or oversee fellowships, an apostle obviously has to have the gift of pastoring, i.e. managing a group of believers. This can be observed by the examples of apostles in the Bible, like Paul and John. Furthermore, a true apostle is marked by "signs, wonders and miracles" (2 Corinthians 12:12), but this might be hard to come by in these days of gross unbelief; they should at least have an anointing with the laying on of hands. Lastly, beware of "false apostles" (2 Corinthians 11:13-14). I once met a joyless, stern believer who insisted on being addressed as "Apostle Harrad" at all times even though he wasn't remotely an apostle in any biblical sense.
- **Prophets** in the New Testament sense are not the same as Old Testament prophets. The gift of prophecy was not given to the body of Christ for the purpose of leading and guiding God's people, as was the case in the Old Covenant, because believers are spiritually regenerated and have the Holy Ghost within them for this very purpose (John16:13). Since it is the Holy Spirit's job to guide believers in the New Testament era, we don't need the gift of prophecy for this function. The prophetic word is encouraging and is able to **touch believers in that specific area where they need ministered**. For example, Acts 15:32 says that the prophets Judas and Silas "said much to encourage and strengthen the believers." This is the purpose of the prophetic gift in the Church and reveals why it is so necessary—**it encourages and strengthens believers**. The original Greek word for 'encourage' means **"to cause to move forward."** In other words, a prophetic word will **inspire believers**

and **provoke them to go forward and fulfill God's call on their lives**. This shows that prophets are more preachers than teachers. They see things in the spirit realm and proclaim God's will that's applicable to the situation or person, but they don't go into scriptural details on doctrine, like a teacher would.

- **Evangelists** are preachers and not teachers. They proclaim by unction the truths of the gospel and the Word of God in general, but they're not effective at detail-oriented teaching. This can be observed in the definition of 'evangelist' in the Greek, which is *euaggelistés (yoo-ang-ghel-is-TAYS)*, meaning "a bringer of good news." Evangelists can certainly minister to *believers* at revivals and what have you, but their drive & focus is reaching the lost with the life-changing Good News of the message of Christ (2 Corinthians 5:17-21). I knew a pastor who simultaneously had the gift of an evangelist, which was also the case with Timothy (2 Timothy 4:5). This particular pastor wasn't good at teaching, although he could preach and—as a pastor—he was gifted at overseeing an assembly. I saw him at several services where he was exceptional at preaching the gospel and inspiring people to turn to the Lord in repentance and faith (Acts 20:21). In fact, my aged father got saved at one of his services. This shows that ministers can have more than one of the fivefold gifts, although only Jesus Christ functioned in all five.
- **Pastors** have the gift of oversight and are called to shepherd local assemblies, as is commonly known. They have a social gift and are skilled at teaching or preaching God's Word.
- **Teachers** don't have the gift of oversight, but are anointed to logically explain the Scriptures in detail. While they might be called to focus on a few particular topics in their service, they can actually teach on hundreds of subjects effectively. This happens to be my gift in the fivefold ministry.

The reason this info is important to the Spiritual Warrior is because you may be called to one (or more) of these ministries. If not, you're at least called to walk according to one or more of the "body gifts" detailed in Romans 12:6-8—prophesying, teaching, encouraging, generous giving and administrative work. The difference between the fivefold ministry gifts and the body gifts is the degree of anointing and scope of service.

How to Discern OPINION and FACT in Theology

'Theology' means the study of God. In Christian theology, how do we distinguish what's true and what's not true concerning anything related to the LORD and the things of God, including Church doctrine and practice? Is it "all just opinion," as I heard someone recently argue? Absolutely not. Notice what the Bible says:

> **All Scripture is God-breathed and is useful for teaching, rebuking, correcting and training in righteousness, [17]so that the servant of God may be thoroughly equipped for every good work.**
>
> **2 Timothy 3:16-17**

This shows that the basis for teaching and correction in Christianity is **the God-breathed Scriptures**. If what a denominational handbook or minister teaches cannot be substantiated by rightly-dividing the Holy Scriptures, then it's not a valid doctrine or practice. I said "rightly dividing" because the Scriptures need to be correctly interpreted in line with the common sense hermeneutical guidelines (2 Timothy 2:15), which are detailed in chapter **2** in the section *FREEDOM From False Doctrine*. After all, if the Scriptures can be *rightly* divided, they can also be *wrongly* divided. This explains Paul's rule "Do not go beyond what is written" (1 Corinthians 4:6).

It also explains the wise response of the Bereans to Paul's gospel message when he shared it with them:

> **As soon as it was night, the believers sent Paul and Silas away to Berea. On arriving there, they went to the Jewish synagogue. [11]Now the Berean Jews were of more noble character than those in Thessalonica, for they received the message with great eagerness and examined the Scriptures every day to see if what Paul said was true. [12]As a result, many of them believed, as did also a number of prominent Greek women and many Greek men.**
>
> **Acts 17:10-12**

The Bereans **went to the Scriptures** to determine if what Paul taught was true. They viewed the Word of God as the basis for truth, not the word of a religious organization or the word of man—even an apostle as great as

Paul. Understanding this is especially important today when there are *hundreds* of sects of Christianity with each group usually insisting that they're the most correct version of Christianity and, in some cases, "the one true church."

Notice what the Lord said to believers:

> **As Jesus spoke these things, many believed in Him. ³¹So He said to the Jews who had believed Him, "<u>If you continue in My word</u>, you are truly My disciples. ³²<u>Then you will know the truth</u>, and <u>the truth will set you free</u>."**
>
> **John 8:31-32** (BSB)

This tells us three things:

1. There most certainly is truth to discover in God's Word, which proves that theology *isn't* "all just opinion."
2. You have to *continue* in God's Word, if you want to know **the truth** fully on any given issue. 'Truth' is *alétheia (ah-LAY-thee-ah)* in the Greek, meaning **"the way it really is."**
3. This is a prerequisite to being set **free**, including being set free of false doctrines that may be religious and popular, but they're not actually correct, at least not wholly correct (in other words, they may be *partially* accurate, which also means they're partially *inaccurate)*.

Now observe what some disciples of the Pharisees and Herodians—two Judaic sects—said about Jesus Christ:

> **"Teacher," they said, "we know that you are a man of integrity and that <u>you teach the way of God in accordance with the truth</u>. You aren't swayed by others, because you pay no attention to who they are."**
>
> **Matthew 22:16**

This reveals what set Christ above his religious luminaries in the 1st century—He taught the way of God **in accordance with the truth** as opposed to in accordance with this or that sect and their biased sectarianism. Shortly later, Jesus responded to another sect of Judaism, the Sadducees:

> **"You are in error because <u>you do not know the Scriptures</u> or the power of God."**
>
> **Matthew 22:29**

The Sadducees didn't believe in the resurrection, which is error. (This, by the way, reveals the power of sectarianism, which can convince masses of people into believing something *isn't* scriptural even though it's blatantly scriptural; and vice versa). Christ said the Sadducees didn't believe in the resurrection because **they did not know the Scriptures**. In other words, the answer to doctrinal error is **to *know* the Scriptures**. The more you get to know the Word of Truth and rightly divide it (2 Timothy 2:15), the more easily you'll be able to screen-out error, whether totally false doctrine or partially false doctrine.

Speaking of partially false teachings, two believers may be right on a certain doctrine in a broad sense, but one will be false in the details whereas the other will be accurate because s/he is more faithful to the *specifics* of Scripture. Here's an example:

Two Christians rightly believe that eternal life is one of the main benefits of Christianity (e.g. John 3:16 & Romans 6:23). While they are both correct on this, one is off on the details and the other more fact-based and therefore correct. For instance, the former may think that eternal life revolves around living on a cloud playing a harp forever while the latter understands the truth about the new Jerusalem (Revelation 21-20) and the new Heavens and new Earth (2 Peter 3:13).

Each of them is a sincere believer, loved of the LORD, and both rightly believe the truth about eternal life, but one is mistaken on the particulars while the other is more scriptural and therefore more accurate. One is tripped-up by false religious ideas whereas the other *knows* the truth and is therefore set free by it, at least on this specific topic. It all comes down to who is more detailed in their studies and "rightly divides" the God-breathed Scriptures free of sectarian bias. This is the person who knows the truth and is therefore set free on the issue.

The average believer will, of course, side with the official doctrines of their sect, whatever group that might be. It's just the way it is because they're in the childhood stage—STAGE TWO—and this explains why God holds those who teach the Scriptures to stricter accountability:

> Not many of you should become teachers, my fellow believers, because you know that <u>we who teach will be judged more strictly</u>.
>
> **James 3:1**

Since the average believer in STAGE TWO tends to just go along with whatever their favored minister teaches, like their pastor, I generally don't debate the Scriptures with them because it's unprofitable. You could say it's a waste of time.

Here are a few relevant passages about the uselessness and potential damage of such debates:

> But <u>avoid foolish controversies, genealogies, arguments, and quarrels about the law</u>, because these things are pointless and worthless. [10]<u>Reject a divisive man</u> after a first and second admonition, [11]knowing that such a man is corrupt and sinful; he is self-condemned.
>
> **Titus 3:9-11**

> <u>Don't have anything to do with foolish and stupid arguments</u>, because you know <u>they produce quarrels</u>. [24]And <u>the Lord's servant must not be quarrelsome</u> but must be kind to everyone, able to teach, not resentful. [25]<u>Opponents must be gently instructed</u>, in the hope that God will grant them repentance leading them to a knowledge of the truth, [26]and that they will come to their senses and escape from the trap of the devil, who has taken them captive to do his will.
>
> **2 Timothy 2:23-26**

> It is to one's honor to avoid strife,
>   but every fool is quick to quarrel.
>
> **Proverbs 20:3**

> Starting a quarrel is like breaching a dam;
>   so drop the matter before a dispute breaks out.
>
> **Proverbs 17:14**

Unless a certain topic comes up, by the Spirit, and the other person is interested in discussing it with an open mind regarding what the Word of

Truth actually teaches (2 Timothy 2:15), I don't try to convince believers of this or that doctrine. Their pastors will be held accountable for what these people believe or don't believe (1 Corinthians 3:8-17). In light of this, the truths conveyed in this section apply more to those who have grown past the confines of pastoral-dependency and sectarianism (or are in the process of doing so). How do believers "grow past" these? See *Grasping the Four Stages of Spiritual Growth* earlier in this chapter.

Wrapping this up, how do you separate opinion from fact on any Judeo-Christian doctrine? By being as biblically-accurate as possible along with discarding the bias of a particular camp/sect, as well as popularity. Then you will know the truth and the truth will set you **free** (John 8:31-32).

<u>5</u>

GOD-GIVEN GOALS
And Evading Time-Wasters

The Spiritual Warrior will seek to discover God's calling for their lives and the regular assignments within that calling. Without this, you'll struggle with the meaningless of life and the melancholy thereof, as witnessed in Solomon's life chronicled in the book Ecclesiastes. Christ is our greatest example. He said, "My food is to do the will of him who sent me and to finish his work" (John 4:34). In other words, Jesus' sustenance and drive were rooted in fulfilling his God-given mission and the many works thereof.

The Biblical 3-Point Strategy to Fulfill Goals

We've got to get away from this idea that, unless you're called to be a pastor, God is uninterested in your life. This is a lie straight from the enemy. The LORD is very interested in your life and has a calling for you and the corresponding assignments or works within that mission. How do you discern God's calling? Proverbs 3:6 says "In all your ways acknowledge Him, And He shall direct your paths" (NKJV). But how does the LORD direct your paths? The answer can be found in Proverbs 16:3. The original Amplified Bible puts it like this: "Roll your works upon the LORD [commit and trust them wholly to Him; <u>He will cause your thoughts to become agreeable to His will</u>, and] so shall your plans be established and succeed."

As you acknowledge the LORD in prayer, seeking his will, God will cause your thoughts to become agreeable with his will. In other words, you'll *desire* to do what God's calling you to do. Religion has taught us that all human desire is bad, but that's not what the Bible says. Sure, flesh-based desires are bad, like the desire to fornicate or engage in gluttony, but God-given desires are good. Proverbs 11:23 says this point blank: "The desire of the righteous is only good" (NASB/KJV). It's talking about the desires of the righteous, not the wicked. The word 'desire' here is a form of the Hebrew *ta'avah (tah-âv-AW)*, which means "that which you earnestly **long** for." It's a desire that **stays with you** and you can't get rid of it.

You can't obtain your (righteous) desires until you know what they are. So, get close to the LORD, look deep within (remember, the Holy Spirit indwells you), and draw them out. This is in line with godly wisdom as shown in Proverbs 20:5: "The **purposes of a person's heart** are deep waters, but one who has insight **draws them out**."

I turned to the LORD at the age of 20 with my whole heart. In the ensuing years I grew as a believer while writing songs and recording them on a 4-track recorder with drum machines. I was eventually in a Christian band. However, as I kept seeking God, my desire to do this changed and I developed a longstanding desire for the Word of God and teaching ministry. So, here I am at the age of 60 doing this full-time and loving it. Whatever God calls you to do, you'll have a passion for it, whether that's to be a minister, a writer, a nurse or to create a family. Maybe the LORD will give you the desire to get a home in a certain area. Whatever the case, God will make your desires agreeable with his will as you acknowledge him. This is the first phase of the 3-point strategy to fulfill God's will.

Once you have a longstanding desire, a *ta'avah,* what do you do with it? This is the second phase of fulfilling God's will. Proverbs 16:9 says "**The mind of a person plans their way**, but the LORD directs their steps" (NASB). God gave you a mind, so use it: Plan your way based on the available resources to fulfill your God-given goal. No one plans to fail, but failures fail to plan. A goal without a plan is just a wish.

So come up with a basic plan. Keep it simple. Let's say you have the desire to be an electrician or a nurse. What schools are available for you to acquire the necessary skills and credentials? How will you pay for it? Where will you live? Will you work part-time? Say you want to be a recording musician. You'll need an environment where you can practice your instrument daily. Where can you record? Can you do it at home?

Remember, you develop your plan based on *existing* resources, not dubious ones that *might* manifest at some ambiguous point in the future. The plan you come up with must be a plan **of action**, not a plan of procrastination, which is the pathway to frustration and failure.

Now that you have a plan, it's time to get up and follow it. As you do, the LORD will "direct your steps" by the Holy Spirit (Proverbs 16:9). Think of the guided missile: It cannot be guided *until* it blasts off. This is the third and final phase of the 3-point strategy. You'll be on your way to fulfilling your God-given assignment, whatever that may be.

Consider the example of this book you're reading. Months ago, I was seeking the LORD about whether or not to publish a book this year. The idea to do a manual on being a Spiritual Warrior came to mind. As I kept praying about it, **the desire** got stronger. So, I came up with a basic outline of the contents, which was **my plan**, and then started putting it together and writing, which is **taking action** wherein the Spirit is guiding my steps on a day-to-day basis. I'm currently several weeks into it and I'm excited about the project. It's invigorating! As Christ said, "My *food* is to do the will of him who sent me and to complete his work."

Keep in mind the difference between **course**, **path** and **steps**:

- Your **course** is your objective, goal, assignment or mission, which is based on the longstanding desire—the *ta'avah*—the LORD gave you as you sought him.
- Your **path** is the way you planned with your mind to fulfill your course or obtain your goal, based upon the available resources (as opposed to unavailable resources).
- Your **steps** are you walking down that path day-by-day utilizing God's direction via the Holy Spirit.

How exactly are you "led of the Holy Spirit" as you're walking the **path** to your **objective** according to your **plan**? A few things come to mind:

- Be alert for "**golden opportunities**," which are **open doors** of opportunity that manifest, such as Paul's "open door" for ministry noted in 2 Corinthians 2:12.
- Be alert for "**golden connections**," which are people who can link you to your goal one way or another.
- "Let the **peace** of Christ rule in your heart" (Colossians 3:15) concerning every potential opportunity or connection since not every

opportunity or person is from the LORD. For instance, Potiphar's wife was a connection for Joseph, but it was an *ungodly* connection that would've kept him from reaching the palace (Genesis 39:6-7).

Also be conscious of proper timing: **The time for research is not the time for production or marketing.** A good example is Moses, who had a strong desire—a *ta'avah*—from God to deliver the Israelites from Egyptian bondage, but he acted prematurely, not to mention foolishly, which caused him to be exiled to the desert for 40 years (Exodus 2-3).

I use this simple 3-point plan for every goal I accomplish. I encourage you to master it and do the same. Use it for small goals too, not just big ones.

For instance, you can apply it to mundane projects. Say you want to paint your deck. That's your *ta'avah* or righteous desire. Now come up with a plan of action, which will obviously involve acquiring the necessary tools & materials, cleaning the deck, putting wood filler where necessary, sanding it, and then applying a couple of coats of paint. Once you have a plan, take action on the scheduled days (assuming weather permits). When it's done, you have an empowering sense of fulfillment and satisfaction.

Keeping Balanced in Every Area of Life

As alluded to, there are different areas of your life, such as family, marital, work, devotional, ministerial, educational, social, homestead, recreational, fitness, and so on. You can discern God's will in each of these areas using the above method. But how do you achieve and maintain **balance**? How do you keep from being sidetracked—hindered—by things that drain your time & energy and aren't conducive to your God-given goals? This has to do with walking in moderation, which means to have a spirit of self-control that avoids excess or extremes.

The problem with excess is that the person loses sight of self-control and becomes obsessed with the thing in question, which wastes his/her time & energy that could be spent on more productive pursuits. I'm not talking about things that apply to one's occupation since your work pays the bills, but even that can become a problem if you make earning money an idol and become a workaholic.

First, keep in mind that the Bible doesn't teach us to seek the LORD only, but rather to seek God first (Matthew 6:33). In short, we're to make the

Creator **first priority**—that is, "sell out" to God—but don't get out of balance by seeking God **only**. That's a ticket to looney religiosity and burnout.

Once you know your purpose in one or more of the areas of life, you then have a goal. Hebrews 12:1 instructs us to "throw off **1. every *thing* that hinders** and **2. the sin that so easily entangles**." The passage then encourages us to **run with perseverance the race (goal, mission)** marked out for us.

The "thing that hinders" is something that holds you down and prevents you from fulfilling your God-given objective. The thing itself is neutral and not a sin, but it saps your time and energy so much that it hinders you from completing your assignment. It therefore becomes a **weight** in your life (as the KJV and NKJV put it)—something that weighs you down and impedes more productive output. People can become somewhat obsessed with such a thing and it thus creates **imbalance**, hampering the person from fulfilling their current assignment (God-given goal).

This "weight" could be any number of things depending on the individual—computer games, movies, sports-watching, golf, boating or fishing, a certain relationship, etc. These things are not evil in-and-of themselves, but because they distract you from your calling and drain your time & energy, they become a negative thing **for you**. As such, you must either carefully guard the time you spend with such things—guarding your heart as the wellspring of life (Proverbs 4:23 & Matthew 12:34) or, if necessary, remove them from your life altogether in order to fulfill your mission, at least for a season.

This is part of maintaining moderation in all you do, which means cultivating a spirit of self-control that avoids excess or extremes.

Consider this example from Scripture: Christ didn't completely abstain from alcohol (Matthew 11:19) and Paul instructed Timothy to drink a little wine apparently for health reasons (1 Timothy 5:23). Moreover, the LORD permitted the Israelites to drink fermented beverages at certain celebrations (Deuteronomy 14:26). Yet the Bible also instructs "Do not **get drunk** on wine, which leads to debauchery" (Ephesians 5:18), not to mention candidly points out the negatives of drunkard-ness (Proverbs 20:1). So the problem isn't the alcoholic beverage itself, but rather the individual who loses a proper sense of **moderation**.

Proverbs 25:28 stresses the importance of self-control: "Like a city whose walls are broken through is a person who lacks self-control." Back when this verse was written cities required walls for defense against enemy invasion. The comparison is obvious: The individual who loses sight of moderation is like a defenseless city. The enemy can come in and misdirect his/her life anytime.

If something has a "hold" on you and you've become obsessed with it to a degree, consider fasting from it. This will swiftly break the "spell." By "fasting" I mean **abstaining from it**—putting it on the sideline for a period of time. Seek the LORD and the Holy Spirit will guide you on how long to refrain from the thing in question. Consider 40 days. If you find that excessive, how about 21 days, 10 days, 7 days or 3 days—whatever it takes to break the thing's hold over you and bring back **balance** in that particular area of your life. Be led of the Holy Spirit.

If I ever sense myself becoming obsessed with something and it's hindering me spiritually, I make a clean break from it for a determined season. Recently, I fasted from something for 40 days and it broke the 'spell' that I discerned was cooling my fire for the Lord and my ministry assignment. My enthusiasm almost immediately returned and I finished my project in 21 days!

Take sports-viewing, I like to watch a game now and then for R&R,[5] but one game is about 3 hours. If you watch 2 games that's 6 hours of your time! Needless to say, guard how much time you spend on sports each week. Decide *beforehand* how many games a week you're going to watch and stick to your plan. The same goes for movies, TV shows, computer activities, boating/fishing and so forth. This frees-up your time so you can spend it on your Spirit-led goal/assignment, whatever that may be.

As for the "sin that so easily entangles," this is any flesh proclivity that you've developed a taste for and it therefore seriously tempts you from time to time. You must make it a top priority to remove this transgression from your life, whatever the cost (Genesis 4:7). If you don't, it will prevent you from obtaining your God-given desire/goal.

---

[5] Sloth is of the flesh, of course, but **R&R is necessary and healthy**, as long as it doesn't become an idol, figuratively speaking. The Bible teaches that there's "a time to weep and **a time to laugh**, a time to mourn and **a time to dance**" (Ecclesiastes 3:4).

Put these things into practice and you will keep **balanced** in every area of life. I practice them daily and could give examples from my life and the lives of others. They're tried & true.

To close this chapter, I'd like to share something indispensable to the topic, originally featured in my book *Legalism Unmasked*…

New Testament Advice on Moderation

Paul brought up the topic of personal moderation *twice* in his first letter to the believers at Corinth. Here's the first time:

> **"Everything is permissible for me"—but <u>not</u> <u>everything is beneficial</u>. "Everything is permissible for me"—but <u>I will not be mastered by anything</u>.**
>
> **1 Corinthians 6:12**

The apostle was quoting a popular phrase of some believers at the assembly in Corinth: "Everything is permissible for me." This is the attitude of libertines in a nutshell. *"I can do anything I want"* is what they believe. Now Paul wasn't against freedom since he preached liberty to these very same believers when he said, "the Lord is the Spirit and where the Spirit of the Lord is there is freedom" (2 Corinthians 3:17). Yet **Paul adds some wise framework for freedom here**: Whilst people have the power of volition and can essentially do whatever they want if they *decide* to do it, Paul points out that **"not everything is beneficial."** This is an obvious fact, of course, but he had to stress it because not every believer in Corinth realized it. Since following the deceitful desires of the sin nature is never beneficial, anything sinful is off-limits to the believer. Why? Obviously because it's not beneficial; it's destructive.

Say, for example, if a married man meets an alluring woman at work and entertains the idea of committing adultery with her, would this be beneficial to his life or destructive? Even if he's not a believer, it's a destructive course of action because it would hurt his wife and could harm his marriage, possibly even destroy it, not to mention the domino effect of hurting his hypothetical children and losing the respect of the community. No sane person respects unfaithfulness, not even unbelievers.

Paul quotes the popular phase again in the second half of the verse and this time adds "but **I will *not* be mastered by *anything***." Here Paul isn't just talking about the corrupt desires of the flesh but rather **anything neutral that has the capacity to master him and put him in bondage**. Today, we see people mastered by many destructive addictions, like alcohol, drugs and various forms of sexual immorality. But millions are just as mastered by things that aren't considered bad, such as food, computer games, watching or playing sports, TV, surfing the internet, "meds," forms of recreation and even church activities.

Again, none of these things are bad in-and-of themselves, but they can become bad if a person is *mastered* by them—becomes *obsessed* with them—in which case they become idols. (I should emphasize that something like playing sports—e.g. tennis, golf, pool, chess, basketball or football—can't become an idol if one *uses it* to make a living; in other words, the sport is the person's occupation).

We don't see many people in modern Western Civilization worshiping literal idols, but people can become so addicted to certain things that it becomes a form of idolatry because idolatry is the worship—the *adoration, glorification*—of something over God. Christians are free, but we have to be careful to guard our hearts as the wellspring of life so that nothing takes us away from our devotion to the Lord (Proverbs 4:23).

Paul brings up the popular phrase a second time in his letter:

> **"Everything is permissible"—but not everything is beneficial. "Everything is permissible"—<u>but not everything is constructive</u>. [24] Nobody should seek his own good, but the good of others.**
>
> **1 Corinthians 10:23-24**

The apostle again points out the obvious: Everything is permissible because we have been blessed with freewill and therefore have the power of decision. We have the power to *choose* to act or not act on any impulse, whether good or bad; but Paul stresses, once again, that not everything is beneficial. This is a repeat denouncement of engaging in the deceitful desires of the flesh, which are never beneficial. Christians are free in the Lord but the appetites of the sinful nature are off-limits because they are destructive. If there's any doubt, Paul cleared it up with his statement to the Roman believers: "What then? Shall we sin because we are not under law but under grace? By no means!" (Romans 6:15).

He repeats the phrase again, "everything is permissible" and this time adds **"but not everything is constructive."** This obviously refers to neutral things. The believer is free to do the neutral activity, but we have to ask ourselves if it is constructive. He then adds that "Nobody should seek his own good, but the good of others." For instance, if you're blowing so much time & energy on some*thing* that it significantly subtracts from your relationship with your spouse or kids, it becomes a negative thing.

Teachers and preachers can share these principles until they're blue in the face but some believers don't seem to "get it," evidently because they lack wisdom in this particular area. Wisdom is the ability to distinguish difference. Anyone who wants wisdom must seek it as if it were a treasure; and God will give it to him/her (James 1:5). This is an encouragement to acquire wisdom for moderation concerning any *thing* that can become a weight in your life and prevent you from fulfilling your call or responsibilities.

The bottom line is this: Believers have freedom in Christ but it's not freedom to embrace the flesh, but rather freedom *from* the bondages of the flesh. **We have true freedom in Christ, but we must be careful to not allow anything to master us. And we must use wisdom—common sense—in what we choose to do, and how much time we spend with it, since not everything is constructive, for ourselves or others.**

<u>6</u>

THE SEVEN WAYS TO HEAR FROM GOD

Obviously, the Spiritual Warrior will need to discern the will of God on a regular basis. We looked at how to discern God's will in regards to one's calling and assignments last chapter. What are some other ways that you can hear from the LORD and discern divine will on a matter? Here are seven ways:

1. Through the Holy Scriptures

The Judeo-Christian Scriptures are said to be "God-breathed" and therefore they're "useful for teaching, rebuking, correcting and training in righteousness" (2 Timothy 3:16). Every believer has an anointing to receive insights from God's Word with the help of the Holy Spirit, who is our Counselor and Teacher that guides us into all truth (1 John 2:27, John 14:26 & 16:13).

Notice what David said about the revealed Scriptures of his day:

> **[7]The law of the LORD is perfect,**
> **refreshing the soul.**
> **The statutes of the LORD are trustworthy,**
> **making wise the simple.**
> **[8]The precepts of the LORD are right,**
> **giving joy to the heart.**
> **The commands of the LORD are radiant,**

giving light to the eyes.
⁹The fear of the LORD is pure,
    enduring forever.
The decrees of the LORD are firm,
    and all of them are righteous.
¹⁰They are more precious than gold,
    than much pure gold;
they are sweeter than honey,
    than honey from the honeycomb.
¹¹By them your servant is warned;
    in keeping them there is great reward.

                              Psalm 19:7-11

¹⁴I rejoice in following your statutes
    as one rejoices in great riches.
¹⁵I meditate on your precepts
    and consider your ways.
¹⁶I delight in your decrees;
    I will not neglect your word.

                              Psalm 119:14-16

If you're a person who doesn't like to read, then get an audio version of the Scriptures. You can listen to them while you're doing this or that around the house or driving in your vehicle, etc.

2. Through Responses in Prayer

Such answers from the LORD can manifest in several ways:

- **The peace of God** (Philippians 4:6-7).
- **An "inner witness"** or **impression/revelation** (Amos 4:13).
- **A gentle whisper**, aka **"still small voice"** (1 Kings 19:12), or **a clear audible voice** (1 Samuel 3:1-14, Acts 8:29 & Acts 13:2).

Concerning that last one, for anyone who argues that Samuel wasn't praying when the LORD spoke to him in 1 Samuel 3:1-14, 'prayer' simply means "communion with God" and so, if the LORD speaks to you, *that's* communion with the Creator, aka prayer. We'll look at the different kinds of prayer in chapter **18**.

3. Through the Peace of Christ in Your Heart

We are instructed to let the peace of Christ rule us from within; that is, *govern* us (Colossians 3:15). In light of this, don't do anything you don't have a peace about doing (assuming you have a choice in the matter). For instance, if someone is trying to sell or convince you of something using manipulation or pressure and you don't have a peace about it, don't buy it or accept it.

You might have noticed that this is relevant to the first point of the previous section.

4. Through the Wise Council of Others

The truths of Holy Scripture are able to make us wise (2 Timothy 3:15) and so you can receive God's leading on a crucial matter through the wise council of worthy souls (Acts 27:31, Proverbs 13:20, Proverbs 11:14, Proverbs 20:18 & Proverbs 24:6).

By contrast, don't listen to the council of fools—such as those who embrace and advocate **LIE**beral idiotology—for that is the path to destruction (Proverbs 14:7 & Proverbs 13:20).

5. Through Dreams and Visions

Peter quoted Joel 2:28, saying:

> **" 'In the last days, God says,**
> **I will pour out my Spirit on all people.**
> **Your sons and daughters will prophesy,**
> **your young men will see visions,**
> **your old men will dream dreams."**
>
> **Acts 2:17**

While this prophecy is referring to the New Covenant era, the LORD spoke to people through dreams and visions even in earliest times (Job 33:14-17).

6. Through a Prophetic Word

God spoke to people through genuine prophets in the past (Hebrews 1:1 & Amos 3:7), yet still uses prophets in the New Covenant era. For instance, the prophet Agabus came to the assembly at Antioch and prophesied that a famine would hit Judea, which moved the believers to provide for their brothers & sisters down there; this was God's will (Acts 11:27-30).

Please keep in mind, however, that it is the Holy Spirit's job to guide believers in the New Testament era (John16:13 & Romans 8:14) so you don't need the gift of prophecy for this function. If a prophet prophesies over you and says you're to do this or that and go here or there, don't receive it unless the Spirit has already been leading you in this direction and you have a peace about it. In other words, prophecies in the New Testament are to confirm what the Holy Spirit has already been leading you to do. You could say it's an external source to confirm or compliment the believer's internal source of direction from God.

This explains why Paul instructed believers to test prophecies and "hold on to the good," which means to eat the meat and spit out the bones (1 Thessalonians 5:19-21). Nowhere are we instructed to blindly accept a prophecy spoken over us, especially from a supposed prophet who's arrogant and likes to throw his/her weight around in an obnoxious manner. Christ said "By their fruit you will know them" (Matthew 7:15-23). If a prophet or any minister is pompous and unnecessarily rude, head for the hills (Matthew 15:14).

7. Through Circumstances and Events

This can be observed when Jonah tried to flee from the LORD's instructions and so God had to get his attention through a life-threatening storm at sea to turn him around so he would fulfill his commission (Jonah 1:4-16).

Let's close this chapter with the relevant topic of…

God's Perfect Will vs. God's Permissive Will

God's general will is revealed in the Holy Scriptures. For instance, does the LORD want you to live a life of fornication or adultery? Obviously not. Theologians call this God's preceptive will, based on the word 'precept,' which means rule, mandate, guideline or principle.

God's more *specific* will is revealed to the individual believer by the Holy Spirit (John 14:26 & John 16:13), which would also technically be the LORD's preceptive will.

Both of these would fall under the category of "God's perfect will" for the individual.

Since our Creator reigns supreme, God is sovereign, but within that sovereignty he allows humans freewill, which opens the door to the LORD's permissive will. In other words, God permits humans to make decisions or conduct themselves in a way that isn't in accord with God's perfect will.

In addition, the LORD *permits* humans to make decisions about things that are of little concern to the Almighty. For instance, the color of the socks/shoes you are wearing today are up to you, depending on your resources.

To complicate matters, Yahweh's permissive will can involve:

- Decisions/behaviors that are *not* sinful.
- Decisions/behaviors that *are* sinful.

An example of the former would be the Israelite's wanting a king in order to be "like all the other nations," which was against God's perfect will, yet the LORD permitted it (1 Samuel 8:4-22). An example of the latter would be God permitting David to commit adultery with Bathsheba and indirectly murder her husband, which of course had negative repercussions (2 Samuel 11-12).

An attack by the enemy or human enemies would fall under God's permissive will. For instance, it was satan's idea to attack Job, God just allowed it (Job 1-2). Also, it was Joseph's wicked siblings who captured & sold their young brother into slavery, the LORD merely permitted it and ultimately brought about good from it (Genesis 37 & 50:20).

Consider some examples from the New Testament. Mark 3:35 and 1 John 2:17 would (presumably) refer to God's preceptive will whereas 1 Peter 4:19 refers to God's permissive will.

A small book could be written on this topic, but these are the basics. Chew on the ideas and you'll gain further insight in your studies.

7

ALTARS AND ALTAR CALLS

The Spiritual Warrior needs to be up on "altar experiences," as recorded in the Scriptures, for reasons which will be revealed. An altar in the Old Testament was typically a raised platform used for offering sacrifices. It's not surprising therefore that the Hebrew word for 'altar' stems from the root *zabach (zaw-BAKH)*, which means "to slaughter for sacrifice." The LORD instructed that these structures be made from either soil or rock, albeit uncut, likely to avoid the temptation of pride over craftsmanship or viewing the altar itself as an idol (Exodus 20:24-25, Deuteronomy 27:5-6, Joshua 8:31, Judges 6:20-21 & 13:19).

There was, of course, an altar at the Temple and tent Tabernacle that was used for regular sacrifices, such as the annual Day of Atonement (Leviticus 16:34 & Hebrews 10:3), as well as individual offerings (Leviticus 4 & Luke 2:24). But we're going to focus on "altar experiences," which involved:

- Significant moments for worship (Genesis 8:20),
- Receiving a divine commission (Judges 6:12-24),
- Commemoration (Exodus 17:14–15 & Joshua 22:26–27) and
- Establishing a covenant (Exodus 24:4–8).

These somewhat overlap and mark a notable sequence in one's life (Genesis 12:7). Taken together, they point to **a potent encounter with the**

LORD and the revelation or new directive thereof coupled with the appropriate sacrifice and of course the decision/resolve to comply.

God is omnipresent, of course, but an "altar experience" is when the LORD *manifests* his presence to the individual and it naturally results in reverent awe, some kind of profound change, a sacrifice, and a fresh directive (2 Chronicles 7:1-3).

With this understanding, there are arguable "altar experiences" in the Old Testament that don't mention an actual altar, like when Jacob wrestled with God and was renamed Israel (Genesis 32:27-32), Moses' divine meeting at the burning bush (Exodus 3) and Joshua's awesome encounter with the Commander of the LORD's Army (Joshua 5:13-15).

Altars in the New Testament

Since the need to sacrifice animals ceased with the spilling of Christ's blood (Hebrews 9:23-10:12) we have no need for physical altars in the New Covenant era in the sense of sacrificing animals, which is why you won't find believers doing this in the New Testament.

Rather, believers are *themselves* to be "**living sacrifices**" (Romans 12:1) because we "are not [our] own" since we were "bought at a price" via the blood of Christ (1 Corinthians 6:19-20). In other words, *our whole lives* are God's possession, not just 10% of our financial earnings. Our bodies, our thoughts, our material possessions, our incomes—they're *all* God's already.

Of course, people have to grow into this mind-blowing truth and this is where altars have their place in the New Covenant. The altar is invisible, but a personal "altar call" is when we encounter God by the Spirit where we receive new revelation and make the decision to comply. Usually, a sacrifice is involved whereby we cut something out of our lives and consecrate—set apart—ourselves to serve the Lord in a new capacity. This becomes an important moment in our lives, which we'll naturally commemorate, sort of like how we commemorate our birthdays and anniversaries.

Every believer's first "altar experience" is when we received the Lord and partook of spiritual regeneration (Titus 3:5). Once saved, the LORD works with us through the leading of the Spirit (John 16:13), the feeding of the

Word (Matthew 4:4) and the service of the fivefold ministry (Ephesians 4:11-13).

We'll continue to have "altar experiences" throughout our spiritual journeys, just as Old Testament saints did, except that believers have the benefit of a vastly superior covenant (Hebrews 8:6). Again, these altar experiences are encounters with God where we receive a potent revelation and make the necessary sacrifices. Such encounters are separate from—and should not be confused with—one's daily fellowship with the LORD in which the believer has (or, at least, can have) a 24/7 rapport with God by the Spirit (1 Thessalonians 5:17).

They are also distinguished from entering into the Lord's presence during praise & worship. How so? Simply that "altar experiences" naturally involve **a sacrifice**, whether physical or mental (which we'll address momentarily). That said, one can certainly have an "altar experience" *during* praise & worship when encountering God's "manifest presence."

To illustrate, consider the salvation experience: An individual hears the gospel and is moved by the Spirit to believe and repent. The sacrifice is the old self—the sinful nature—and the person resolves to walk in newness of life, reconciled with the Lord, while "keeping with repentance" (Matthew & Luke 3:8; 1 John 1:8-9). This is an altar experience, a critical turning point in one's life. Paul's powerful conversion on the road to Damascus is a great example (Acts 9:1-22).

Or take a genuine believer who backslides. The Spirit will inevitably move that person to rededicate his/her life to the Lord. This is likewise an altar experience.

Yet *all* growing believers—that means each one of us—will have altar experiences from time to time during our spiritual growth; this goes with the lifelong process of sanctification.

Altar experiences can involve some type of pruning, like the removal of a piece of flesh that's hanging on (John 15:1-4), a new directive or a release to serve in greater capacity. These encounters with God are between you and your Creator. They *can* take place at an assembly gathering, but they can actually occur anywhere, as was the case in the Old Testament examples noted earlier. For instance, when I was 20, I had an altar experience in a woman's shower room while working at a fitness center, which I'll share momentarily.

Speaking of altar experiences at church services, let's look at…

Altar Calls

An "altar call," as it is known today, is an invitation to come forward and pray the sinner's prayer or rededicate one's life. The altar is the area in front of the assembly. Methodist preachers began practicing this circa 1800 as a method to help determine who had been converted at their gatherings. Charles Finney made altar calls more popular in the 1830s.

Because of this, I've heard ministers say that altar calls have only been around for a couple hundred years, which suggests that altar calls didn't exist in the Church prior to about 1800. Really? Like there was never a call to repentance/consecration at *any* assembly in the previous 1800 years *anywhere* on Earth? *Why Sure!*

Biblical support for altar calls includes Christ's exhortations to follow him (Mark 1:17 & Luke 5:29) and the importance of boldly confessing Christ before others if we expect the Lord to do the same (Luke 12:8), as well as Paul's emphasis that "today is the day of salvation" (2 Corinthians 6:2). The first "altar call" is chronicled in the Scriptures, fittingly taking place the very day the Church was birthed on the Day of Pentecost after Peter preached to those gathered:

> **When the people heard this, they were cut to the heart and said to Peter and the other apostles, "Brothers, what shall we do?"**
> **[38]Peter replied, "Repent and be baptized, every one of you, in the name of Jesus Christ for the forgiveness of your sins. And you will receive the gift of the Holy Spirit. [39]The promise is for you and your children and for all who are far off—for all whom the Lord our God will call."**
> **[40]With many other words he warned them; and he pleaded with them, "Save yourselves from this corrupt generation." [41]Those who accepted his message were baptized, and about three thousand were added to their number that day.**
>
> **Acts 2:37-41**

The apostle passionately preached, urged repentance, and the listeners were "cut to the heart"—obviously convicted by the Holy Spirit (John 16:3-11)—and so 3000 people got saved.

Peter was led of the Spirit and the results were natural (and supernatural). It doesn't mean ministers have to try to *manufacture* an "altar call" every time they preach. But it does make sense to invite listeners to reconcile to their Creator now and again (Romans 10:9-15) as this is part of the "ministry of reconciliation" and the responsibility of "ambassadors" of Christ (2 Corinthians 5:17-21).

Yet some ministers choose not to implement a conventional altar call for one reason or another when they teach/preach and that's perfectly fine. This is especially so at more unconventional meetings. We all have to be led of the Spirit in our particular services.

However, there's something called a "mini-altar call" wherein one or more believers seek the LORD in prayer for this or that—salvation, rededication, healing, etc.—and they encounter the Lord (Matthew 18:20). Mini-altar calls can take place before, during or after a Christian service; they can take place in the parking lot or in a car. I ran into a couple of believers at the local mall and could see that they needed prayer urgently, so we huddled right there and had a mini-altar call in the central concourse. (We were careful, of course, not to draw undue attention to ourselves since the occasion had nothing to do with showing off to passersby and everything to do with meeting with the Lord on the spot).

One criticism of conventional altar calls is that unbelievers might pray the sinner's prayer or rededicate their lives simply because they're caught up in the emotion of the moment or they're socially pressured to do so. They haven't really "counted the cost" of being a believer (Luke 14:25-35). In other words, such converts quickly fall away, yet Christ plainly said that a certain percentage of people would respond this way, so it's not really an issue (Luke 8:13). It's just the way it is.

There are some interesting linking topics to altar calls that I'd like to address. Let me breach them by sharing my first "altar experience"…

How I Received the LORD

I grew up in a dysfunctional home. My mother had a severe mental illness, but was wholesome and loving. Meanwhile my father was a good provider and regularly took the family on outings (hikes, skiing, movies, camping and vacations), but he was aloof, brooding and verbally abusive.

Being verbally cursed by my father on a regular basis (e.g. "You're no good," "You're gonna turn to $#!%," etc.), I gravitated toward the wrong crowd during my teen years and wasted my time & talents on the party lifestyle and delinquency. During those lost years I collected gospel tracts, like those by John T. Chick, and had a handful of Christians share the gospel or their testimony with me. Every now and then I would break out those tracts and read 'em. On a few occasions I prayed the "sinner's prayer" at the end because I strongly sensed that I needed an inward overhaul. I suppose I was expecting some great epiphany that would suddenly change the course of my life for the positive, but nothing changed inside when I said these prayers.

Between the ages of 15-19 I searched for the truth in what I saw was a really screwed-up world. I looked into hedonism, the occult and science, but was left discontented by the hollow non-answers they offered. Despite my collecting of the tracts and reading them from time to time, I didn't seriously consider what the Bible had to say on the grounds that I pretty much wrote it off as myth, e.g. Adam & Eve and the "talking snake" or Noah's Ark. The few times I did seriously try to read the Scriptures—like the Psalms—the passages struck me as incomprehensible.

Four months after my 20th birthday, I was working alone one night as a janitor at a nice fitness center. It was after midnight and I was cleaning the female shower room. Suddenly something 'clicked' inside me while I was in a particular stall and I *believed*. It was awesome! I rode home that night excited with a newfound sense of peace. The next morning, I informed my mother & sister that I was now a Christian. Later that day I went to The Point, which was a personal favorite spot on the huge lake behind my parents' house. It was there that I officially prayed a "sinner's prayer" from memory in those tracts I collected, although it was definitely expressed from my heart.

The reason I bring up my salvation testimony is because a couple important points crop up: The first one is that this was my initial altar call experience and it didn't happen at a church assembly. We have to get away from this idea that God and the things of God are only experienced at a building where Christians gather a couple times a week. This is so far from the truth & Scripture that it's incredible some people actually think this way (more on this in a moment).

The second point has to do with the question of *when* I was technically "saved." The three possible answers are: **1.** When I first *believed* in the shower room, **2.** when I confessed Christ to others the next morning or **3.** when I "officially" prayed the sinner's prayer at the lake.

The answer is when I first *believed*. The other two are the automatic *fruits of* believing. Let me explain…

The Moment of *Faith* Is the Point of Salvation

The fact that the moment of genuine faith is the point of personal salvation can be verified by several passages:

> **"For God so loved the world that he gave his one and only Son, that <u>whoever believes</u> in him shall not perish but have eternal life."**
>
> **John 3:16**

> **"Whoever <u>believes</u> in the Son <u>has eternal life</u>, but whoever rejects the Son will not see life, for God's wrath remains on them."**
>
> **John 3:36**

> **"<u>Believe</u> in the Lord Jesus, and <u>you will be saved</u>—you and your household."**
>
> **Acts 16:31**

> **For it is by grace you have been saved, <u>through faith</u>— and this is not from yourselves, it is the gift of God— [9]not by works, so that no one can boast.**
>
> **Ephesians 2:8-9**

One of the most obvious passages to prove that the point of faith is the point of salvation can be observed when the thief crucified next to Christ obviously *believed*—acknowledging his Lordship with the statement

"Jesus, remember me when **you** come into **your kingdom**"—and so the Lord immediately recognized the man's salvation (Luke 23:39-43).

Repentance (Changing Your Mind) *Is* Consecration

Repentance means to **change one's mind in response to the truth**— whatever that truth might be—which naturally has an impact on one's actions. For instance, I heard & read the message of Christ several times throughout my teen years but didn't really believe it (even though I said the sinner's prayer on a few occasions). That is, *until* that one day in the women's shower room where I **changed my mind in response to the truth**; in short, I *believed.* I thus confessed Christ to others and started to commune with my Creator (meaning, I began a prayer life).

This reveals something important, previously stressed in chapters **2** and **4**: **Repentance & faith are two sides of the same coin,** which explains why they're the first two doctrines of the six basic doctrines of Christianity (Hebrews 6:1-2). It also explains why Christ and the apostles linked **repentance and faith** together:

> **"The time is fulfilled, and the kingdom of God is at hand; <u>repent and believe</u> in the gospel."**
> **Mark 1:15** (ESV)

> **"I have declared to both Jews and Greeks that they must turn to God <u>in repentance</u> and <u>have faith</u> in our Lord Jesus."**
> **Acts 20:21**

The moment a person *believes* in a particular potent truth can be referred to as a revelation or epiphany (a sudden realization) and repentance is the natural response—changing one's mind with the corresponding actions. This moment of belief/repentance is also a point of *decision* and *consecration.*

- **Decision** has to do with the individual's God-given power of volition (Deuteronomy 30:19 & Psalm 119:30).
- **Consecration** has to do with the corresponding *setting oneself apart* to live according to the revelation/directive in question. The Hebrew word for 'consecrate' means to "to set apart," which we are instructed to do in the New Testament (2 Corinthians 6:14-7:1).

In other words, when you have an "altar experience" you'll perceive a fresh revelation or directive from the Lord, but you have to *decide* to comply, which includes making the necessary sacrifices. This might be eliminating a piece of flesh (including thought issues) or a particular hindrance, either of which will prevent believers from fulfilling their commission (Hebrews 12:1-2). God is calling you (and me) to throw out these "idols," which is a part of consecrating yourself. Suddenly your mind and your time are freed-up and you have a *fire* for God and the things of God that was not there before (or maybe it was there and you lost it due to preoccupation with an "idol").

Recent Examples From My Own Life

On May 24th and July 17th of 2019, I had a profound double-whammy altar experience involving pruning, revelation & directive. It was a stunning realization where I needed to eliminate certain things from my life forever—both mentally and physically—in order to effectively fulfill God's call and the corresponding regular assignments.

Several months later, during the December holidays, I was led to take a 40-day fast of certain things for the new year to clear my mind and increase sensitivity to the Spirit. This led to another "altar experience" in mid-January. Just to be clear: Being led to give up some things for 40 days was not the altar experience—that was just "business-as-usual"—but this paved the way for my altar experience a couple of weeks later. Anyway, I decided to comply with the LORD's instructions (which is always the wisest choice, of course) and made the necessary sacrifices. I'm glad I did because I've been *so* blessed ever since with my relationship with the Lord and my service for the Kingdom!

Every altar experience will involve compliance and consecration. *You* have to decide to comply and set yourself apart accordingly to fulfill your particular mission. Compliance always results in blessing—even if it's "just" inward blessing, like a renewed spiritual fire or intimacy with the Lord—whereas stubborn stiff-neckedness will lead to frustration and ruin.

I should add that these three "altar experiences" didn't occur in a church facility. Speaking of which, let me close with a relevant story…

Close

I was in a Christian band in the early 90s and at one of our practice sessions a friend of the soundman visited and brought her serious boyfriend. They were complete strangers to the rest of us. During the halftime break the man shared his story: He was an unbeliever, but recently experienced some creepy things that revealed to him there was a spiritual realm. Long story short: He desperately *wanted* saved and so we prayed together and he received the Lord. Awesome, right?

The next day he & his girlfriend visited the assembly that most of us attended and he promptly went up to the front during the altar call. None of the band members & Co. were at this particular service because there were four different services every weekend (one on Saturday night and three on Sunday).

Shortly later, the man's girlfriend called Carol (who would become my wife a year later) and informed her of her boyfriend's altar call experience, which was wonderful. Yet she curiously made sure to emphasize that he was actually saved at the altar call at the facility (implying, of course, that he didn't really receive salvation at the band meeting). When Carol informed the rest of us, we just laughed it off and basically said "Whatever."

What was going on here? This woman couldn't grasp that her boyfriend believed & was saved at the band meeting, which was his first "altar experience." In her mind—for whatever reason—to truly be saved a person had to receive the Lord and say the sinner's prayer at an altar call at an official church service with the proper oversight of authorized clergy. Neither of these is true, of course, and it's sad that some people think this way.

It's one of the reasons this chapter exists.

<u>8</u>

HEALING BY FAITH:
For Yourself and Others

One of the challenges that the Spiritual Warrior will face is the attack of sickness & disease on yourself or others. How should you effectively tackle this obstacle and overcome?

Many times, the Lord said to people who received healing, "**your faith has healed you**" (e.g. Mark 5:34 & Mark 10:52). All this means is that they **believed** it was God's will for them to be healed and they received from the conduit of God's healing power, which was Jesus Christ. In the case of James 5:14-15, the conduit would be the elders of an assembly (an "elder" would refer to the fivefold ministers within a fellowship and, arguably, any anointed mature believer). Yet the believer can also receive healing by faith without any conduit. Remember, Jesus said: "whatever you ask for in prayer, **believe** that you have received it, and it will be yours" (Mark 11:24).

I had an irritating skin rash on the back of my hand for over two years. I showed it to my doctor and he referred me to a dermatologist. I had no desire to waste time on a skin doctor so I continued to put up with the viral infection until I got righteously angry over it one day. The Spirit impressed me to curse the rash repeatedly and speak healing over the back of my hand until it was gone, so that's what I did. I cursed the rash, commanded it to die and leave my body; and blessed my hand, loosing healing (this is explained in chapter **18** in the section *"Your Kingdom Come, Your Will Be Done on Earth"*). Guess what happened? It completely disappeared, but it took a while—9 weeks, in fact—and I had to be stubbornly tenacious, especially when it would reoccur after starting to die out. This is **perseverance** or following through.

As emphasized in chapter **4**, faith and the Word of God are not enough in such cases; we must add **perseverance**, which is **patience** (2 Peter 1:5-6). The Bible emphasizes that it's through **faith and patience** that we inherit what is promised, **not just faith** (Hebrews 6:12). Faith without perseverance isn't really faith because true faith *doesn't* believe for a little bit and then give up. **True faith *continues to believe no matter what.***

It's also important to understand that speaking in faith can be canceled out by speaking in unbelief because words have "the power of life and death" (Proverbs 18:21). Unbelief cancels out faith and vice versa; it's a common sense principle. So when you're speaking in faith for something never contradict your faith with words of doubt because, if you do, you won't receive that for which you're believing. Contradicting your faith with words of unbelief is tantamount to being double-minded, and the Bible emphatically declares that the double-minded person "should not think that he will receive anything from the Lord" (James 1:6-8).

Put a guard on your tongue after you speak in faith so that you don't succumb to words of doubt and grumbling, which is especially tempting when it's taking a while for your miracle to manifest.

Should You Get the Surgery or *Believe* for Healing?

Whether a person should seek physicians for a healing or go to the LORD is an ancient conundrum. King Asa dealt with the issue 2900 years ago (2 Chronicles 16:12). So, if you're facing this dilemma, it's nothing new.

The answer to this question is entirely dependent upon the individual. Healing is a core benefit of the gospel of Christ (1 Peter 2:24) and so you can believe in faith and receive your healing directly from the Lord, as observed in the Gospels (Mark 5:34 & Mark 10:52). I've done this on several occasions. I stress again: Combining your faith with **perseverance** is necessary to receive and maintain your healing (Hebrews 6:12).

'But Why Not Just Get the Surgery?'

This is certainly an option and you can do this if you so choose. It's entirely up to the individual.

I suggest healthy living and building up your faith to receive healing when necessary; only turning to medical professionals and drugs (aka medicine) when absolutely necessary. Regular checkups with an honest, trustworthy doctor are of course beneficial as they will provide necessary info in regards to what to believe for when you pray and so on.

The Bible says that the woman who was subject to bleeding for twelve years "had suffered a great deal under the care of many doctors and had spent all she had, yet instead of getting better she grew worse" (Mark 5:26). At that point she was fed up and desperate because she had blown many years of her time and "spent all she had"; so she went directly to the Lord for healing and received it because she *believed* (Mark 5:34). Obviously if she *didn't* believe, she wouldn't have received.

It is true that people with little faith or even no faith can receive a powerful healing, but they have to wait for a gift of the Spirit for healing to manifest (1 Corinthians 12:4-11). Gifts of the Spirit function as the Spirit wills and can only operate through a vessel that boldly believes and ministers accordingly, like the Messiah & the apostles did in Scripture. A good example is Christ's amazing healing of the high priest's servant with a cutoff ear (Luke 22:50-51); another is Paul's healing of Publius' father of fever and dysentery (Acts 28:7-8).

But these kinds of healings are hard to come by in this era of gross unbelief. In other words, finding an assembly/ministry where gifts of the Spirit regularly manifest isn't easy, yet they're out there, if you search. It's for this very reason that I encourage simply learning to receive healings directly from the Lord. Interestingly, the Pool of Béthesda was a type of the gifts of the Spirit and, specifically, the gift of healing (John 5:1-15).

Getting back to the woman who suffered feminine bleeding for twelve years while under the care of physicians, this explains why Carol & I don't use doctors unless absolutely necessary: Why blow time & money when you can get your healing directly from the Lord? Again, healing is a core benefit of the gospel (Isaiah 53:4-5) and so Carol & I take advantage of it. We'd be fools not to. At the same time, we value doctors for cases where they're needed and effective. For instance, I fell off a cliff when I was a teen, breaking my thigh bone and cracking my pelvis. I sure am thankful for my doctor & the medical staff that treated me! So please don't think that I'm anti-doctor or anti-healthcare. I'm not.

Of course, doctors and medical technology have improved exponentially in the 2000 years since the account of the woman with the issue of blood. This is absolutely true. Again, if you want to utilize the services of doctors & medical technology to (hopefully) cure whatever ails you then do so. But it's going to take time & money (traveling to medical facilities, long waits in rooms, etc.), plus—keeping it real—there *are* legitimate concerns even in our day and age of medical expertise and advances:

- The doctor can botch the surgery. For instance, my mother went 'under the knife' for foot surgery in 1985 and the doctor bungled the job. For the last twenty years of her life, she had a malformed foot with an unresponsive big toe. More recently, a popular 18 years-old young man in my area, a healthy star athlete, underwent minor surgery and never woke up from it. His funeral was attended by many fellow students and it was heartbreaking. In another infamous case, a man underwent surgery, but the doctor misidentified the patient and unnecessarily amputated his leg. Imagine waking up from the anesthesia with a missing leg! Sure, these are the exceptions and not the rule, but they're still very real possibilities when choosing surgery. Ask my mother.

- Doctors tend to push unnecessary surgeries and medications (drugs) because healthcare—when it comes down to it—is a **business**, which *needs* patients to exist. For instance, doctors are often linked to Big Pharma and so they rashly prescribe some medication (drug) for the patient's ailment, which of course costs time & money. Then there's often a side-effect to the medication (drug) and you have to take another drug to treat it. On-and-on it goes. Some people are on myriad "medications." It's absurd. Personally, I refuse to be a guinea pig to support the extravagant lifestyles of medical professionals & the people of the institutions that back them, like Big Pharma. But if you or anyone else wants to spend time & money on such procedures or "medications," that's your choice. It's not my business.

- You're more apt to get a staph infection—MRSA—at healthcare facilities, such as hospitals. A friend of mine visited a hospital for something routine several years ago and got MRSA. Not only did he almost die, he lost sight in one of his eyes, and had to start visiting the hospital a couple of times a week, every week, for dialysis. It even led to his death a few years later at the premature age of 59.

For all of these reasons, it's best to focus on healthy living/eating and learn to receive any healings you might need directly from the LORD. But to do this you have to **build up your faith**, otherwise you won't be able to believe to receive, which brings up...

Building Up Your Faith

How do you build up your faith? By adding knowledge—the Word of God—to your current level of faith on the topic in question (2 Peter 1:5-7), in this case **faith for healing** (Romans 10:17). For example, meditating on verses like Mark 11:24, John 14:14, John 16:24, Mark 1:40-41 and Matthew 8:1-3 will certainly beef up your faith in this area.

Feed on the relevant healing passages contained in this chapter (Matthew 4:4), plus receive from other anointed ministries who teach/preach faith & healing, as Christ's ministry did (Matthew 4:23). Stay away from ministries that preach unbelief/doubt and, in essence, advocate sickness/disease. Then start walking in faith to receive healing when you need it for relatively minor things before tackling bigger issues. For instance, if you don't have the faith to receive healing for a skin rash or back pain, you're probably not going to have the faith to tackle cancer. Before David had the faith to face Goliath, he built up his faith taking on the lion and the bear (1 Samuel 17:34-37). Like anything else, there are **stepping stones** to walking in victorious faith.

I should add that, just because someone believes in receiving healings by faith and walks in it as much as possible, it doesn't necessarily mean that s/he has the faith to receive healing for *everything* on *every* occasion. For example, a minister with a powerful healing ministry needed some serious dental work. This guy had led formidable healing crusades, but he discerned the LORD instructing him to get the work done because the Spirit said he didn't have the faith to receive on this occasion.

Perhaps it was a case where it would've taken *time* to build-up his faith to receive in the area in question and it needed immediate attention. I don't know. But we need to be honest with ourselves and God concerning what we have the faith to receive for and what we don't at any given time. In any case, the minister got the dental work done. There's **no condemnation** here for people who decide to go this route, whatever the reason. It's their decision and their right.

'But Is It God's Will That I Be Healed?'

Christ was Immanuel, which means "God is with us (in the flesh)" (Matthew 1:23). As such, what the Messiah did during his ministry on Earth **reveals God's will** to us. For instance, people needing serious healings would approach Yeshua and ask "*if* you are willing." The Lord *never* responded "No, it is not my will"; rather he plainly said it *was* his will (Mark 1:40-41 & Matthew 8:1-3).

Again, healing is part of the gospel of Christ (1 Peter 2:24), which is one of several reasons why it's "good news." The Bible promises a minimum of 70-80 years of life (Psalm 90:10) so, if you're under that age, you can claim this promise by faith (2 Corinthians 1:20). Even if you're over 80 you can believe and receive in faith in your awesome covenant with God simply based on your righteous desire (Mark 11:24, John 14:14 & John 16:24).

Don't Wait till the Last Minute to Build Up Your Faith

When people are in their 20s-40s they're in generally good health, so it doesn't really matter if the assembly/sect they're hooked up with emphasizes faith & healing. But in later decades it literally becomes a matter of life or death. For instance, when you're in your 50s-60s your body's 'check engine light' might start coming on.

Let me share a recent example of what I'm talking about: Carol has a healing anointing and so a woman around 50 years-old asked to meet with her for prayer because she was scheduled for surgery in a couple days. This presented a conundrum that I pointed out: Should Carol simply pray for the woman's surgery to go well, including praying for the medical professionals who would be treating her, or should she pray that the woman receive healing, which would of course make the surgery irrelevant (assuming she received it)? Carol was led to do the latter and so the woman's scheduled surgery would then be dependent on if she received healing by faith or not.

When they met, Carol wisely had this woman watch a teaching video on healing, which gave the scriptural basics about receiving healing by faith (this video was from a proven ministry that was anointed to minister in this area). This was necessary because, in order for the woman to receive a lasting healing, she was going to have to have faith to receive and strong belief like this is **a result of** hearing the Word (Romans 10:17). At that point Carol laid hands on her and prayed, to which the woman said her pain was gone and they praised the Lord. Carol suggested that she postpone the surgery and get retested.

Meanwhile the husband was curiously silent the entire time. Carol & I suspected that he would talk his wife out of receiving healing by faith and sticking with the scheduled surgery, which is what happened. The good news is that the operation was successful. There's nothing wrong with doing this if that's where the person's faith is. But God's best is to receive healing by faith rather than go under the knife, which can be costly to your body, time and finances. Yet, to do this, you *shouldn't* wait until the proverbial last minute (a mere couple days before a scheduled surgery) to build up your faith in this vital area. Are you following?

Of course, believing for a healing and not actually having the faith to receive it can also be costly. It's no secret that people have *died* doing this. That's why responsibility rests with the individual needing the healing and no one else.

If you choose to receive healings by faith—or walk the faith life in general—you're going to have to develop a righteously stubborn spirit in response to the lies/attacks of the Enemy, like Shadrach, Meshach and Abednego did (Daniel 3:16-18). You're going to have to righteously *hate* any curses the enemy tries to put on you to hamper (or end) your life & productivity in service of God's kingdom.

I should add that, in cases where your child needs medical attention, please take them to a physician. Never experiment with *your* faith when it concerns *someone else's* health needs (unless, of course, you have no other recourse in the situation, like pioneers in the Old West).

FIGHT the Good Fight of Faith!

The Bible says the believer is to **fight the good fight of faith** (1 Timothy 6:12). If there's a *fight* to faith, then there are *enemies* to faith. Sickness/disease is one of those enemies.

To build up your faith and develop a spirit that ardently fights the good fight of faith, master the principles & passages covered in chapter **20**.

Let's close this chapter with the relevant topic of…

Are Christians Commissioned to RAISE THE DEAD?

Christ raised three people from the dead during his earthly ministry:

- The widow's son at Nain (Luke 7:11-17).
- Jairus' daughter (Matthew 9:18-26, Mark 5:21-43 & Luke 8:40-56).
- Lazarus (John 11:1-44).

Because the Lord said "Very truly I tell you, whoever believes in me will do the works I have been doing, and **they will do even greater things than these**, because I am going to the Father" (John 14:12), some understandably argue that believers should be raising the dead as well. Here are two things to keep in mind on this:

1. Since one could hardly do greater works than Christ when he ministered on Earth, such as raising the dead, he was possibly referring to *volume* of works, particularly since he notes that he would be going to the Father and proceeds to emphasize that the Holy Spirit would come down and live inside believers as their Helper (John 14:16). When this occurred, it wouldn't be just one man doing the awesome works of Christ in one location, but rather believers all over the world because the spirit of Christ is in all of them (Romans 8:9).
2. The "greater things" Jesus was referring to would certainly include evangelizing people whereby they receive spiritual regeneration by the Spirit (Titus 3:5), which was not available during Christ's earthly ministry until *after* he died for our sins and was raised to life for our justification (1 Corinthians 15:1-4 & Romans 4:25). This would be raising the dead in a spiritual sense (Ephesians 2:4-5) and would definitely be a greater work than what Christ did during his 3½ years of earthly ministry. Another "greater work" would be laying hands on converts and their receiving the baptism of the Holy Spirit & and benefits thereof, as detailed in chapter **4**.

After Christ's death & resurrection, there are two cases in the New Testament where believers prayed for dead people and they were brought back; and one instance of a mortally-wounded person being fully healed:

1. Tabitha, who died after falling ill, but was raised from death after Peter prayed for her (Acts 9:36-42).
2. The boy, Eutychus *(YOO-too-kus)*, who fell from a window and died while Paul was preaching, but was raised to life via Paul's Spirit-led service (Acts 20:7-12).
3. Paul was mortally wounded after being stoned by religious zealots in Lystra and left for dead, but the believers gathered around him in prayer and he was fully healed (Acts 14:19-20).

While these believers were led of the Spirit to pray for the dead or dying and they were miraculously raised up, believers are not technically commissioned to raise the dead, as observed in the two passages that relay the Great Commission and the corresponding signs:

> He said to them, "Go into all the world and preach the gospel to all creation. [16] Whoever believes and is baptized will be saved, but whoever does not believe will be condemned. [17] And these signs will accompany those who believe: In my name they will drive out demons; they will speak in new tongues; [18] they will pick up snakes with their hands; and when they drink deadly poison, it will not hurt them at all; they will place their hands on sick people, and they will get well."
> [19] After the Lord Jesus had spoken to them, he was taken up into heaven and he sat at the right hand of God. [20] Then the disciples went out and preached everywhere, and the Lord worked with them and confirmed his word by the signs that accompanied it.
>
> **Mark 16:15-20**

> Then Jesus came to them and said, "All authority in heaven and on earth has been given to me. [19] Therefore go and make disciples of all nations, baptizing them in the name of the Father and of the Son and of the Holy Spirit, [20] and teaching them to obey everything I have commanded you. And surely I am with you always, to the very end of the age."
>
> **Matthew 28:18-20**

The Great Commission involves going out and making disciples from all over the world, baptizing them, and teaching them the New Covenant truths of Holy Scripture. In the passage from Mark 16, Christ also lists the *signs* that will accompany believers carrying out this commission, which includes exorcizing demons and laying hands on people to heal them. Yet nothing is said about raising the dead nor are there any instructions in the epistles concerning believers going out to raise the dead. Instead, this is what is taught:

> **Is anyone among you <u>sick</u>? Let them call the elders of the church <u>to pray over them and anoint them with oil in the name of the Lord</u>. [15]And <u>the prayer offered in faith will make the sick person well; the Lord will raise them up</u>. If they have sinned, they will be forgiven.**
> **James 5:14-15**

This corresponds to one of the signs Christ said would accompany believers—they will place their hands on sick people and they will get well. But please note the key element in releasing God's power to heal the sick in verse 15—FAITH. This is what the believers did when they gathered around the near-dead Paul in prayer and he miraculously received a full healing (Acts 14:19-20).

So, believers are not commissioned to run around laying hands on dead people in the hope of raising them to life. Can you imagine the awkwardness and embarrassment of a zealous believer trying to raise someone from the dead at a funeral and nothing happens, not to mention the serious legal ramifications?

That said, if you are led of the Spirit to lay hands on the freshly dead in a tragic situation, like Peter did with Tabitha and Paul with Eutychus, do as you are guided; the same if you're dealing with someone near-death, like Paul after being stoned and left for dead. Since raising someone from the dead or healing someone who is mortally wounded are *great* works, you'll at least have to be a great man/woman of faith to be effective; and you'll likely need one of the gifts of the Spirit to be flowing in you at the moment, like **special faith**, **healing** or **working of miracles** (1 Corinthians 12:4-11).

I stress being led of the Spirit because God does not automatically want someone brought back from physical death. For instance, when my father passed away at the hospital after suffering a series of strokes for several years and slowly deteriorating, including his leg being amputated on his final visit, I had zero leading to lay hands on him and pray for him to be brought back. Why? Because God was done with him on Earth and it was time for him to pass on.

Tabitha, by contrast, needed to be brought back so that she could continue her notable ministry to the poor and Eutychus was brought back because he was just a boy with a whole life in front of him. Meanwhile Paul was fully healed after being left for dead because he had years of world-reaching service to conduct, including two more missionary journeys and the writing of vital scriptural epistles.

<u>9</u>

MIGHTY SAMSON:
Was He Ungodly?

As pointed out in chapter <u>1</u>, historical accounts in the Old Testament were chronicled to teach or warn future believers, meaning you and me (Romans 15:4 & 1 Corinthians 10:11). With this understanding, let's consider the controversial example of Samson.

Samson was called by the LORD before his mother even conceived to "begin the deliverance of Israel from the hands of the Philistines" (Judges 13:3-5). He led Israel for 20 years after 20 years of oppression by the Philistines (15:20), not as a king, but as a 'judge' in the sense of a fierce warrior who judged Israel's foreign rulers as evil and boldly delivered them. The entire account of Samson is just four chapters, Judges 13-16.

The extraordinary thing about Samson, of course, is that he was anointed by God with great strength on occasion to slay a lion and 30 men with his bare hands, kill a thousand soldiers with just a jawbone of a donkey, tear loose the formidable gates of a city and carry them a long distance away, not to mention collapse an entire Philistine temple and execute the multitudes therein.

It should be added that Samson didn't necessarily look like a body builder since his great strength didn't come from his muscles but rather his divine anointing, an anointing—by the way—that he knew *wouldn't* manifest to oppose the very people he was called to deliver, the Israelites (Judges 15:12). Meanwhile, Samson had his own form of 'Kryptonite'—if his hair was shaved, he'd become only as strong as a normal man his size (16:17). In short, as great as Samson was, he wasn't invincible.

Common Criticisms of Samson

Samson was a Nazarite from birth. A 'Nazarite' referred to a Hebrew who was exceptionally consecrated unto the LORD, abstaining from alcoholic beverages, grape products, unclean foods, haircuts and contact with human corpses (Numbers 6:2-8). What we want to examine here are Samson's proclivities & practices, which have caused him to be denounced and slandered over the centuries, such as:

- His reoccurring desire for foreign women, all Philistines, which include: A woman from Timnah of whom Samson's parents disapproved because she wasn't a Hebrew (Judges 14:1-3), as well as a prostitute in Gaza (16:1) and Delilah (16:4).
- His gambling before possessing the very items he wagered, which happened to be thirty sets of clothes (14:12-13).
- His anger & violence issues (14:19 & 15:6-8).
- His enlisting the services of the aforementioned prostitute in Gaza (16:1).

While sleeping with the prostitute was definitely a sin, the others can be explained:

- Although Samson's choice for the woman from Timnah as a wife was questionable since the Philistines were Israel's foreign rulers at the time, the Philistines were not among the seven nations of Canaan that the Hebrews were forbidden to marry (Deuteronomy 7:1–6). If it was a sin for the Israelites to simply marry a foreign person, then Boaz sinned by marrying Ruth, a Moabite (Ruth 4). Obviously he didn't sin and neither did Samson. As far as the disapproval of Samson's parents concerning his choice of a wife, Samson did not dishonor them since **1.** they didn't *forbid* him from marrying her and **2.** choosing a lifelong mate was ultimately *his* decision as an adult and not theirs. Lastly, the text plainly states that Samson's desire to marry this particular woman was "from the LORD" (Judges 14:4).
- As for Delilah, the text says that Samson "fell in love" with her and he was obviously blinded by her beauty since he must have known

that she was being used by the Philistines to extract strategic information from him (similar to the situation with his former wife in 14:15). Yet there's no indication that he was fornicating with Delilah (16:4). While some commentators insist that he fornicated with her, the Scriptures don't mention it. Let's be silent where the Bible is silent and not *assume* Samson lived in sin with Delilah.

- Regarding Samson lacking the items to back up his wager with the Philistines, he knew he could easily acquire them if it came down to it because he had faith in God's anointing to take on Israel's oppressors. This faith is why Samson is acknowledged in the "Hall of Faith" chapter of the New Testament (Hebrews 11:32). For those who argue that making the wager in the first place was a sin because it's gambling, I can find no command in the Bible against making such a wager. Since this is the only occasion in Samson's account in which he did this—a time period spanning 20 years—it cannot be argued that he was addicted to gambling.

- As for Samson's anger & violence issues, there's a place for *righteous* anger, like when Christ was angry with the legalists who objected to his healing a man's shriveled hand on the Sabbath (Mark 3:1-6) or when he cleansed the Temple like a holy terror (Mark 11:15-18). In short, you can be angry and not sin (Ephesians 4:26). There's also something called righteous enmity (Psalm 5:4-7). Since the LORD rose up the judges in order to deliver the Israelites from their abusive foreign rulers (Judges 2:16), we can conclude that Samson's anger & violence toward the oppressive Philistines was righteous. As such, God didn't have a problem with his waylaying thirty Philistine men for their clothing, (14:19) or striking down a thousand men with the jawbone of a donkey (15:14-15). In both cases the text plainly says that "the Spirit of the LORD came upon him in power" *before* carrying out the violence. Neither did the LORD mind when Samson slaughtered many Philistines after they wickedly burned to death his former wife and her father (15:6-8). So Samson's supposed anger issues are examples of *righteous* anger rather than being carnally short-tempered; meanwhile his violence toward the Philistines was actually his divine calling and purpose.

Two other things we need to keep in mind about Samson's aggressive attitude toward the Philistines:

1. In the Old Covenant the Israelites were instructed to *fight* their human enemies (Deuteronomy 20:1-3).

2. In the New Covenant believers are commissioned to fight the spiritual forces of darkness as opposed to fighting "flesh and blood," aka people (Ephesians 6:12). (Please don't take this to mean that believers can't serve in the military; John the Baptist's instructions to some penitent Roman soldiers in Luke 3:14 are relevant).

In other words, God's directive in the Old Covenant has essentially flipflopped for believers in the New Covenant. Why is this? Simple: In the inferior Old Covenant (Hebrews 8:6) the Hebrews didn't have the advantage of spiritual regeneration (Titus 3:5) and therefore they didn't have authority over the devil & filthy spirits as believers do in the superior New Covenant (Colossians 2:15). As such, Old Testament saints only had authority to fight people *misled* by the spiritual forces of darkness. In the New Testament, by contrast, believers have authority to conduct spiritual warfare against the root cause of deception and evil, the devil & his wicked spirits, not to mention the grace to love our human enemies, including walking in tough love when necessary.

Please understand that no person on Earth had access to spiritual rebirth and the indwelling of the Holy Spirit *until* Christ died for our sins and was raised to life for our justification (Romans 4:25 & 1 Corinthians 6:19). This explains why the Lord said there was no one on Earth greater than John the Baptist and yet the *least* in the kingdom of God—the Church— was greater than him (Matthew 11:11). As great as John the Baptist was, he didn't have the benefit of spiritual rebirth and therefore the Holy Spirit was *on* him, but didn't live *in* him in the sense that only New Covenant believers experience. Likewise, the Spirit "came on" Samson, but he was not born-again spiritually (John 3:3,6) and therefore he was not a temple of the Holy Spirit, like we are today.

Samson's situation was compounded by the fact that he lived in a time of spiritual decline in which "everyone did as he saw fit" (Judges 17:6 & 21:25). As such, you'll observe the Israelites in the book of Judges engaging in some morally dubious actions, like Jephthah's rash vow which cost him his daughter's life (11:31 & 11:39).

With these things in mind, perhaps we should cut Samson some slack.

A Few Other (Undeserved) Criticisms of Samson

Some commentators accuse Samson of drinking wine, eating food that wasn't kosher and having contact with a corpse, all of which were against the Nazarite vow (Numbers 6:2-8). But these are dubious accusations since the account of Samson **1.** never says he drank wine or ate non-kosher food, even though he participated in a wedding feast in Philistia (Judges 14:10). And **2.** the prohibition against contact with a corpse referred to human beings, not animals, plus the lion in question was freshly slain by Samson and when he came back later all he did was scoop honey from a bees' nest in the carcass (14:5-9).

'Samson Was Ungodly'

Another accusation is that Samson was "ungodly," which suggests that he *wasn't* in communion with God, yet the biblical account plainly shows Samson praying *to the LORD* and never an idol (Judges 15:18 & 16:28). Furthermore, as already noted, God himself rose Samson up to lead Israel for 20 years (13:5 & 15:20) and the man is cited in the Hall of Faith Chapter of the Bible as a hero of faith (Hebrews 11:32). Would this be so if he were truly ungodly?

'Samson Lies to Delilah'

Yet another allegation is that Samson lied to Delilah three times about the secret of his strength (Judges 16:7, 16:11 & 16:13). However, these weren't malevolent or selfish lies, but rather *justifiable* untruths since he knew the rulers of the Philistines—Israel's enemies—were using Delilah to manipulate him into revealing the secret of his power in order to defeat the Hebrews (16:5), similar to how his wife in Timnah was earlier used (14:15).

If the Philistines took down Samson they'd have Israel under their thumb. So, naturally, Samson didn't divulge the truth to Delilah. The fact that he eventually did reveals Samson's flesh weakness for the fairer sex in general and Delilah in particular.

For anyone who thinks there's no such thing as a justifiable lie, that's simply not true. While **lying for selfish, evil purposes is *always* a sin**

(Leviticus 19:11 & Colossians 3:9), a *justifiable* lie is **not** a sin for the precise reason than **it's *justified*** and done with the greater good in mind. In other words, a justifiable lie is not evil, it's **good**.

One obvious example in the Bible is the Hebrew midwives lying to Pharaoh because his command was evil and it saved the lives of innocent babies, "So God was kind to the midwives… because the midwives feared God" (Exodus 1:15-21). Another one is Rahab the prostitute who lied to the officials of Jericho about the whereabouts of the Hebrew spies, for which she's commended in the Hall of Faith chapter (Joshua 2:1-6 & Hebrews 11:31).[6]

Samson's error was that he caved to the Philistines' manipulations by foolishly telling Delilah the truth about his anointing of strength, obviously due to his weakness for beautiful foreign women. Yet having a penchant for alluring Philistine women wasn't a sin in-and-of itself; it's what one does with such a proclivity that determines whether it's immoral or not. For instance, being attracted to and deciding to marry the woman from Timnah wasn't a sin; it was "from the LORD" (14:4).

'But What About His Sleeping With a Prostitute?'

Aside from the folly of surrendering to his enemies' manipulations due to his love for Delilah, this is the sole transgression we can lay on Samson from what is written in the text. It's only chronicled that he did it on one occasion (Judges 16:1). While this is bad, it's not as bad as King David committing adultery with Bathsheba and indirectly murdering her husband (2 Samuel 11) and, yet, David is constantly praised for his greatness.

It is true that David was "a man after God's own heart" (Acts 13:22) and thus he humbly confessed his sin after Nathan's rebuke (Psalm 51 & 2 Samuel 12). Yet what about Samson? Did he repent afterward? The text doesn't say but, clearly, he still had God's anointing to take hold of the massive city gates, tear them loose, and carry them to the top of a nearby hill (16:1-3).

What can we get from this all of this? How is it relevant to the Spiritual Warrior? Simply that "God's gifts and his call are irrevocable" (Romans

---

[6] For details, see my book *QUESTIONS & ANSWERS From the Bible* or the free article *Does the Bible Support a JUSTIFIABLE LIE?* at the FOL site.

11:29). For instance, I could be totally out of fellowship with the LORD and still effectively teach the Scriptures. How so? Because God gave me the gift of a teacher (Ephesians 4:11). It's a *gift*. This explains how an itinerate preacher can travel the landscape and have anointed services, but commit sexual immorality at his hotel in his off time.

Of course such sins will eventually draw God's judgment if they're not dealt with and removed from one's life (Numbers 32:23, Galatians 6:8 & 1 John 1:8-9). In other words, where God's gracious mercy ends, God's judgment begins, and this can be observed in Samson's very account: The impenitent lust of the eyes led to Samson's downfall (1 John 2:16) and so judgment ultimately fell and his eyes were gouged out in captivity wherein he spent the rest of his life grinding at a mill (16:21). The moral of the story is: If a sinful weakness is ignored, it will master you (Genesis 4:7)— first it will bind you, then it will grind you (Proverbs 5:22 & 29:6).

So, based on what is actually written in Samson's scriptural account, enlisting the services of a prostitute on one occasion and obviously having lust issues for beautiful Philistine women in general are the 'only' sins we can pin on the man. Otherwise, Samson is depicted as a mighty national leader and hero of faith (Judges 15:20 & Hebrews 11:32).

For those determined to denounce him, which is tantamount to faultfinding & slander, honestly ask yourself this question and be honest: In your life, as a believer, have you ever lusted after an attractive member of the opposite sex and had sex with them, if not physically, in your mind? (Matthew 5:28). If so, you've sinned in a similar fashion to Samson even with the advantage of spiritual rebirth and the indwelling Holy Spirit, both of which Samson did not have the benefit. In short, have some compassion for the man!

To close, Samson was called and anointed of God to fight against Israel's #1 enemy at the time, the tyrannical and ruthless Philistines. By keeping relations between the Hebrews and Philistines in a constant state of upheaval, he helped prevent the Israelites from being absorbed into their pagan culture.

<u>10</u>

IS CLEANLINESS NEXT TO GODLINESS?

You've probably heard the saying "cleanliness is next to godliness." A friend of mine lived on campus at Liberty University, the Baptist college founded by Jerry Falwell, and he said the staff would cite this proverb to motivate the students to keep things tidy and clean, including their personal hygiene. Is this saying true? Why is it important to the Spiritual Warrior?

Let's start with this passage:

> **But just as he who called you is holy, so <u>be holy</u> <u>in all</u> <u>you do</u>; [16]for it is written: "<u>Be holy, because I am</u> <u>holy</u>."**
>
> **1 Peter 1:15-16**

Peter was quoting the book of Leviticus:

> **"I am the LORD your God; consecrate yourselves and be holy, because I am holy. Do not make yourselves unclean by any creature that moves along the ground. [45]I am the LORD, who brought you up out of Egypt to be your God; therefore be holy, because I am holy."**
>
> **Leviticus 11:44-45**

120

<blockquote>
"Speak to the entire assembly of Israel and say to them: 'Be holy because I, the LORD your God, am holy.' "
</blockquote>

Leviticus 19:2

While the context of the first passage is in reference to the Hebrews staying away from unclean foods, the second verse was a general instruction, which corresponds to Peter's exhortation to "be holy in *all* you do."

So, we're to be holy in everything we do, but what does 'holy' mean?

The Greek word for 'holy' is *hagios (HAG-ee-os)*, which means "different, sacred, due to being set apart (consecrated) to the LORD." The corresponding Hebrew word is *qadosh (kaw-DOHSH)*.

Because God is absolutely pure, holiness refers to absolute purity, which can be observed in several passages where holiness is cited as the *opposite* of what is impure and indecent:

<blockquote>
For God did not call us to be <u>impure</u>, but to live <u>a holy life</u>.
</blockquote>

1 Thessalonians 4:7

<blockquote>
Such a high priest truly meets our need—one who is <u>holy</u>, blameless, <u>pure</u>, set apart from sinners, exalted above the heavens.
</blockquote>

Hebrews 7:26

<blockquote>
Therefore, since we have these promises, dear friends, let us <u>purify ourselves from everything that contaminates</u> body and spirit, <u>perfecting holiness</u> out of reverence for God.
</blockquote>

2 Corinthians 7:1

Notice how we're to purify ourselves from everything that contaminates (dirties) **the body** and not just the inner self. Speaking of which…

Bodily Cleanliness (Personal Hygiene)

Since we—believers—are temples of the Holy Spirit (1 Corinthians 3:16 & 6:19) and we are instructed to "be holy **in all we do**," be attentive keeping your body clean, which houses the Holy Spirit. Everyone naturally gets dirty & sweaty after physical labor, like yardwork, but then you shower or bathe. What is unacceptable is to go *days* without bathing and thus stinking like a trash dump. (The obvious exception would be people in rare situations where they *can't* bathe because they don't have access to water, soap and so forth, which is perfectly understandable). Those who refuse to regularly bathe get used to the smell and therefore don't think they stink, but everyone else can smell the odor, especially people in public who don't live with them and therefore aren't used to the stench.

If gross body odor is offensive to random people, how about the Holy Spirit who has to *live* in the 'house' of the person who reeks?

Notice how the Bible describes the noble king of Israel, which is applied to the King of Kings, the Anointed One (Messiah):

> **All your robes are <u>fragrant with myrrh and aloes and cassia</u>;**
>> **from palaces adorned with ivory**
>> **the music of the strings makes you glad.**
>>> **Psalm 45:8**

Both the earthly Hebrew king and the heavenly King of Kings had a pleasant aroma, not the foul stench of body odor! If you are a believer then *you* are a child of the King (John 1:12). So do likewise—regularly bathe and keep yourself smelling good. As it is said, "cleanliness is next to godliness."

This aligns with the Spiritual Warrior's commission to spread "the fragrance of the knowledge of him"—"the pleasing aroma of Christ"—which is "the fragrance of life" as opposed to the stench of death (2 Corinthians 2:14-16).

Keeping Your "Camp" Clean

Notice what the LORD instructed the Israelites when they were camping out in the desert wilderness before conquering the Promised Land:

> **For the LORD your God moves about in your camp to protect you and to deliver your enemies to you. <u>Your camp must be holy</u>, so that he [God] will not see among you anything <u>indecent</u> and <u>turn away from you.</u>**
>
> **Deuteronomy 23:14**

God wanted the camp of the Hebrews to be kept holy so that it would not hinder his actions in the camp. This would of course include keeping the area cleansed of filth of any kind.

The other day I was working out in our humble gym in the basement when I noticed that one of our cats vomited on a gym towel. I took it to the sink in the dark corner to wash it and noticed how dirty the sink had gotten due to neglect. Naturally I took the time to wash the whole sink. After all, if the LORD wanted the Israelite's camp clean, he'll want the neglected areas of our abodes clean as well.

We shouldn't get legalistic about this, of course. Genuine love in the home is far more important than it being perfectly clean and ordered, the latter of which can create a sterile atmosphere. Healthy homes are "lived in," if you know what I mean.

Spiritual/Moral Cleanliness

Another piece of the puzzle is that demons are referred to as *unclean* or *impure* spirits:

> **Jesus called his twelve disciples to him and gave them authority to drive out <u>impure spirits</u> and to heal every disease and sickness.**
>
> **Matthew 10:1**

The Greek word for "impure" here is *akathartos (ak-ATH-ar-tos)*, which simply means unclean or impure. It reveals that evil spirits are filthy. This makes sense in light of the fact that the LORD is absolutely pure—holy—and so anyone consecrated unto God must likewise be purified. Thus anyone who rejects the Almighty and is cast from his presence becomes the opposite—*un*holy, *im*pure. Since you can't get further from God than the irredeemable fallen angels, they're utterly unholy—unclean, impure, filthy.

Being filthy, there's a stench to unclean spirits in the spirit realm. This explains why one spiritually-sensitive minister said he could always recognize someone who was walking in sexual perversion when they came up for prayer at his meetings. He said there was a *foul* odor in the spirit.

One of my relatives married a literal witch and she wasted no time in getting her new husband to totally separate from his family. My nephew met her when he was a child and he kept curiously asking "What's that smell? Something stinks!" He was just a little kid at the time and said the odor smelled like vomit. No one present knew what he was talking about, so he was obviously picking something up in the spirit. Children are more sensitive to the spiritual realm and are therefore apt to pick up things that hardened adults can no longer perceive.

All this explains why the Bible instructs us:

> **Therefore, <u>get rid of all moral filth</u> <u>and the evil that is</u> <u>so prevalent</u> and humbly accept the word planted in you, which can save you.**
>
> **James 1:21**

While believers are *born* holy in their spirits when they receive spiritual regeneration (Titus 3:5 & Colossians 1:22), **practical** holiness only occurs as you learn to put off your flesh—the "old self "—and live according to your new righteous nature—the "new self "—with the help of the Holy Spirit (Ephesians 4:22-24). This is what theologians refer to as the process of sanctification—*purification*—and part of this process includes doing what James instructed: "get rid of all moral filth and the evil that is so prevalent."

Impure spirits are naturally attracted to that which is morally impure. Just as flies are attracted to doo-doo and rats are drawn to garbage, so filthy spirits are attracted to that which is morally filthy. So get rid of all moral filth and you'll stop attracting filthy spirits! It's not rocket science. We'll look at this in more depth in chapter <u>17</u>.

11

BLAMELESS NOT SINLESS

The apostle Paul *prayed* that the Philippian believers would be **blameless** and *encouraged* it:

> **And this is my prayer: that your love may abound more and more in knowledge and depth of insight, [10]so that you may be able to discern what is best and may be pure and <u>blameless</u> for the day of Christ, [11] filled with the fruit of righteousness that comes through Jesus Christ—to the glory and praise of God.**
>
> **Philippians 1:9-11**

> <u>**Do everything without grumbling or arguing,**</u> **[15] so that you may become <u>blameless</u> and pure, "children of God without fault in a warped and crooked generation." Then you will shine among them like stars in the sky [16]as you hold firmly to the word of life. And then I will be able to boast on the day of Christ that I did not run or labor in vain.**
>
> **Philippians 2:14-16**

David is hailed in Scripture as "a man after God's own heart" (Acts 13:22) and he put an emphasis on keeping himself blameless before the LORD:

> **[22]All his laws are before me;**
> **I have not turned away from his decrees.**
> **[23]I have been <u>blameless</u> before him**
> **And <u>have kept myself from sin</u>.**
>
> **Psalm 18:22-23**

> **Keep your servant also from <u>willful sins</u>;**
> **may they not rule over me.**
> **Then I will be <u>blameless</u>,**
> **innocent of great transgression.**
>
> **Psalm 19:13**

Obviously being blameless is linked to keeping oneself from sin and, specifically, "willful sins," but how exactly can Spiritual Warriors keep themselves blameless when other passages clearly show that even the best of us will miss it now and then? Here are three examples:

> **Indeed, there is no one on earth who is righteous, <u>no</u> <u>one who does what is right and never sins</u>.**
>
> **Ecclesiastes 7:20**

> **"...for there is <u>no one</u> who does not sin..."**
>
> **1 Kings 8:46**

> **If we claim to be without sin, <u>we deceive ourselves</u> and the truth is not in us.**
>
> **1 John 1:8**

These passages show that we're all going to miss it here and there, even those of us who are spiritually mature and walk in the spirit on a day-to-day basis (although of course spiritual leaders should be freed-up from the bigger sins, as observed in 1 Timothy 3:1-7). That's why 1 John 1:8 goes on to say:

> **If we confess our sins, he is faithful and just and will forgive us our sins and purify us from all unrighteousness.**
>
> **1 John 1:9**

This is the key to keeping yourself blameless before the LORD. When you inevitably miss it, be honest about it and 'fess up to your Creator. And God will be faithful & just to forgive you and cleanse you from *all* unrighteousness, which means you'll once again be righteous in the Lord's sight and even "free from accusation" (Colossians 1:22). This is what the Bible calls "keeping with repentance" (Matthew & Luke 3:8). It's crucial to keep yourself blameless before your Maker in this manner.

Interestingly, only *humble* people can do this because it takes humility to honestly admit that you've missed it and confess accordingly. Proud people, by contrast, have a very difficult time admitting that they've made a mistake, how much more so disclose that they've sinned? This explains something that Scripture emphasizes repeatedly: "God **opposes the proud** but **shows favor** [grace] **to the humble**" (James 4:6, 1 Peter 5:5 & Proverbs 3:34).

Put simply, **arrogance *repels* God** while **humility *attracts* God** (Isaiah 66:2).

You could say that the LORD is only close to the humble and this explains why only humble people are greatly used of God, like Moses (Numbers 12:3) and David (1 Samuel 18:23). While humility is meekness, it's *not* weakness.

If you know someone who's involved in ministry that **1.** constantly boasts, **2.** regularly puts people down (to elevate himself/herself) and **3.** refuses to ever admit making a mistake, you can be sure that he/she is *not* close to God regardless of the airs they put on.

Understanding "Willful Sins" and Keeping Blameless

As noted above, David prayed:

> **Keep your servant also from <u>willful sins</u>;**
> **may they not rule over me.**
> **<u>Then I will be blameless,</u>**
> **innocent of <u>great transgression</u>.**
>
> **Psalm 19:13**

You cannot be blameless before the Lord if you're walking in "willful sins," which David equals to "great transgression." You see, there's a difference between a person struggling with a certain sin, yet humbly keeping with repentance, and a person who regularly engages in willful sin. The word 'willful' in the Hebrew is *zed (ZAYD)*, which means arrogant, proud, presumptuous or insolent. In other words, people who commit a willful sin *know* it's a sin but still do it and aren't sorry about practicing it. This is "great transgression" in God's eyes and will eventually incur judgment if the individual continues to walk in it with no care of repentance.

Let me stress that the LORD is greatly merciful and compassionate (Psalm 145:8, 103:8 & Jonah 4:2). In other words, God sympathetically understands the human struggle with the flesh—relapsing—and *wants* to set people free. If you're struggling with a certain sin, rejoice, there *is* deliverance. Yet Scripture also says:

> **Do not be deceived: God cannot be mocked. A man reaps what he sows. ⁸Whoever sows to please their flesh, from the flesh will reap destruction; whoever sows to please the Spirit, from the Spirit will reap eternal life.**
>
> **Galatians 6:7-8**

The LORD knows the difference between someone struggling with a sin, missing it, and getting back up with a penitent heart (Proverbs 24:16) as opposed to someone brazenly walking in willful sin. The former person keeps the flow of God's grace pouring into their lives while the latter individual will eventually reap divine judgment in the form of some manner of destruction. We saw this in Samson's life last chapter.

You see, God treats us according to the light we have (John 9:39-41, John 15:22 & John 15:24). The Creator expects us to parallel the level of knowledge and understanding we've attained. If you're a pint, live up to being a pint; if you're a gallon, live up to being a gallon. The Pharisees & other Judaic leaders were very learned in the Holy Scriptures that existed up to that point (John 5:39) and so the LORD expected them to parallel that great knowledge and understanding. This explains why Christ openly rebuked them on appropriate occasions, calling them "hypocrites" (fakes), "blind fools," "snakes" and "brood of vipers" (Matthew 23:13-33). Someone who's steadily growing spiritually, even while missing it on occasion and honestly keeping with repentance, is a different story.

Walking in willful sins and not keeping oneself blameless before the Lord explains Paul's statement to the believers at Corinth, some of whom were partaking of the Lord's Supper while engaging in willful sins, which brought judgment in the form of ailments and even premature death:

> **Everyone ought to <u>examine themselves</u> before they eat of the bread and drink from the cup. [29] For those who eat and drink without discerning the body of Christ <u>eat and drink judgment on themselves</u>. [30] <u>That is why many among you are weak and sick, and a number of you have fallen asleep</u>. [31] But if we were more discerning with regard to ourselves, <u>we would not come under such judgment</u>. [32] Nevertheless, when we are judged in this way by the Lord, we are being disciplined so that we will not be finally condemned with the world.**
>
> **1 Corinthians 11:28-32**

You'll rarely hear passages like this taught at church services for obvious reasons, but it ties into keeping oneself blameless before God.

Earlier we saw how Paul linked walking blameless before the LORD to doing "everything *without* **grumbling** or **arguing**" (Philippians 2:14-16). Grumbling means "to mutter, whisper or murmur with smoldering discontent." Here's what the apostle said about grumblers when writing to believers at Corinth (*believers,* not unbelievers):

> **<u>And do not grumble, as some of them did—and were killed by the destroying angel</u>.**
> **[11]These things happened to them <u>as examples</u> and were written down <u>as warnings for us</u>, on whom the culmination of the ages has come.**
>
> **1 Corinthians 10:10-11**

Those "killed by the destroying angel" refers to Numbers 16 where Korah, Dathan & Abiram and their 250 followers grumbled against God and his chosen leaders (verse 11). It also includes the thousands of Israelites who grumbled the day after these rebels were slain by the LORD, which brought about the death of 14,700 more Israelites. These **complaining** rebels "were killed by the destroying angel" and Paul said that these examples were chronicled "**as warnings to <u>us</u>**." Obviously, if a believer wants to be blameless before God s/he *can't* be a constant grumbler. Of course this *does not* mean ignoring legitimate issues in relationships and the Christian community that should be brought up and corrected when appropriate (Proverbs 9:7-9 & 27:5-6).

Paul linked blamelessness to not being a contentious person as well (Philippians 2:14-16). A contentious person is someone who likes to quarrel about anything and everything on a regular basis. These are angry, miserable souls who lack godly peace and constantly try to drag others into the darkness of unprofitable arguments (1 Timothy 6:4, 2 Timothy 2:14, Proverbs 20:3 & 27:3).

Also consider the issue of gossip/slander. At some point in spiritual growth, God expects us to remove this sin from our walk. It's a matter of keeping oneself blameless. If a believer knows the truth yet continues to arrogantly engage in two-faced talebearing & backbiting you can be sure s/he will reap judgment (James 5:9). Paul says "This is why many among you are weak and sick." Why? Because they were engaging in willful sins with no concern of penitence; thus they reaped judgment. These people no doubt prayed for healing concerning their weakness/sickness, but their faith didn't 'work.'

This explains why Paul encourages believers to "examine themselves" in the above passage (1 Corinthians 11:28) and elsewhere (2 Corinthians 13:5). When a curse comes upon you (Deuteronomy 28), the first thing you should ask is if *you* brought it upon yourself through a willful sin. If so, then honestly 'fess up and God will forgive you, then **fight the good fight of faith** and receive your healing or deliverance (1 Timothy 6:12).

Let me close by reemphasizing how David—"a man after God's own heart"—was diligent to keep himself blameless before the Lord:

> **⁹Hide your face from my sins**
> **and <u>blot out all my iniquity</u>.**
> **¹⁰<u>Create in me a pure heart, O God</u>,**
> **and renew a steadfast spirit within me.**
> **¹¹Do not cast me from your presence**
> **or take your Holy Spirit from me.**
> **¹²Restore to me the joy of your salvation**
> **and <u>grant me a willing spirit, to sustain me</u>.**
>
> **Psalm 51:9-12**

> **<u>Teach me your way, LORD</u>,**
> **that I may rely on your faithfulness;**
> **<u>give me an undivided heart</u>,**
> **that I may fear your name.**
>
> **Psalm 86:11**

12

FASTING

Fasting is a spiritual discipline in which the individual goes without food for a period of time to, ideally, humble themselves and focus on spiritual things. You could say it's **denying the needs of the outer man to attend to the needs of the inner man**.

The Messiah insinuated that the Church would fast after he was crucified:

> **Then John's disciples came and asked him, "How is it that we and the Pharisees fast often, but your disciples do not fast?"**
> **[15]Jesus answered, "How can the guests of the bridegroom mourn while he is with them? The time will come when the bridegroom will be taken from them; <u>then they will fast</u>."**
> **Matthew 9:14-15** (see also Mark 2:20 & Luke 5:35)

As such, Christ *expected* believers to fast, with these instructions:

> **"<u>When you fast</u>, do not look somber as the hypocrites do, for they disfigure their faces to show others they are fasting. Truly I tell you, they have received their reward in full. [17]But when you fast, put oil on your head and wash your face, [18]<u>so that it will not be obvious to others that you are fasting, but only to your Father, who is unseen; and your Father, who sees what is done in secret, will reward you</u>."**
> **Matthew 6:16-18**

So it's assumed that believers will fast, but this is a personal matter between the believer and his/her Creator. And notice that nothing is said about how long or how often one should fast. Furthermore, believers are not *commanded* to fast anywhere in the New Testament. Hence, you have to be led of the Holy Spirit regarding both, keeping in mind that the Spirit is the believer's Counselor and Teacher (John 16:13 & John 14:26). This of course requires relationship, which develops as you mature spiritually.

What Are the Benefits of Fasting?

There are several profitable things about fasting assuming it's not used to manipulate God into answering prayer or devolves into a legalistic work that fuels religious arrogance (Luke 18:12):

- It's a way of humbling yourself before the LORD and, as repeatedly emphasized in this book, humility attracts God's favor (James 4:10, 1 Peter 5:6, Psalm 35:13 & Ezra 8:21).
- It helps you focus on the needs of your inner self and honestly look at areas that need improvement (Matthew 4:4 & 2 Corinthians 13:5).
- It naturally provides extra time to devote to God and the things of God since you're not preoccupied with preparing or consuming food.
- By coming nearer to the LORD in this manner, the LORD comes nearer to you and you will be *blessed* because of it, one way or another (James 4:8 & Hebrews 11:6). It's an *axiom.*
- It thus increases faith (2 Corinthians 10:15).
- It keeps the flesh under via the practice of **self-control**, which is a fruit of the spirit (2 Timothy 1:7, 1 Corinthians 9:25, Proverbs 16:32 & Galatians 5:22-23); and a virtue that needs *developed* (Titus 2:6).
- It gives a needed break to your digestive system, not to mention **cleans out** your system (stomach/bowels). Speaking of which…
- It activates the bodily process of autophagy *(uh-TAA-fah-gee)*, which literally means "self-eating." This is the body's way of purging old, dysfunctional cells in order to regenerate fresher, healthier cells. It recycles and cleans at the same time, which is like pressing the reset button to your physical system. Basically, autophagy takes damaged or excessive materials and converts them into energy, which is all-around healthy for your body.
- It naturally helps prevent you from becoming massively overweight—which isn't healthy—since fasting shrinks your stomach and so you won't need as much food to feel full.

If you're not used to fasting, I suggest starting with skipping a meal or doing a one-day fast once a week for a few weeks—assuming your medical condition can handle it—and then be led of the Spirit from there. You can add another one-day fast a week or consider a two-day fast now & then; then maybe an occasional three-day fast or what have you. It may take a while to develop a personal plan that works for your current season.

Please keep fasting a positive discipline in your life. Don't allow it to become physically harmful or bog you down in religious drudgery. Get plenty of rest when you fast. Speaking of which, I don't recommend fasting when your work demands a lot of pressing activity (since this would naturally require regular sustenance to be effective on the job).

Imperative Closing Words

Again, the Scriptures expect that New Covenant believers will fast, but nothing is said about how long or how often; and neither is fasting commanded. Whether you fast or not, how often and how long, is between you and your personal Counselor. Every believer's situation is different.

Speaking of which, I know strong believers filled with the Word & wisdom who *don't* fast on a regular basis, although they have fasted on particular occasions in the past and will fast if the LORD leads them to do so. I know other believers who fast on a regular basis, e.g. weekly.

One devout woman my wife knows *said* she fasted for 40 days to concentrate on a spiritual breakthrough regarding her husband, and she was victorious, but I can't in good conscious recommend taking such a looong fast—40 days—seeing as how 43-70 days without food is the point that people will die of starvation, depending on their weight and state of health. Meanwhile people can only survive without water for about 3-7 days, sometimes a few days longer.

Sure, Moses did it, but he was on his face **in the supernatural presence of the Almighty** on Mount Sinai (Exodus 34:28 & Deuteronomy 9:18). So please don't consider an extraordinarily looong fast without the very certain confirmation of your divine guide and helper, the Holy Spirit.

A mighty minister who flowed in the gifts of the Spirit and has positively influenced people all around the globe for decades said he was bent on taking extremely long fasts when he was a young man in Christ and suffered some health problems due to it (he had a history of medical issues going back to when he was a kid). He recovered quickly, thankfully, but the Lord instructed him to never again put his physical health at risk by engaging in dubiously lengthy fasts. He said the Spirit counseled him from then on to live what he called the "fasted life," which was to never eat to the point of being full. This worked for *him* and his global calling.

I point this out because how often you fast and how long you fast—not to mention what precise *kind* of fast you take—**is between you and the LORD**, corresponding to your unique situation and calling. Whatever you decide, make sure the peace of Christ governs your heart (Colossians 3:15). Don't do anything you don't have a *peace* about.

Lastly, fasting is not the all-and-end-all spiritual discipline and so believers have to be careful to not allow it to become a legalistic ascetic practice, which fuels religious arrogance (Colossians 2:23 & Luke 18:12). If you fast, keep it between yourself and your heavenly Father, as Christ plainly instructed (Matthew 6:16-18).

And, please, don't allow any spiritual discipline to go to your head and think you're better than others since "**God *opposes* the proud** but shows favor to the humble" (James 4:6). Actually, as noted above, one of the purposes of fasting is to ***humble* oneself before the LORD** (Psalm 35:13 & Ezra 8:21).

NOTE: Matthew 17:21 is not covered here because it cannot be found in the earliest, most reliable manuscripts of Scripture, which explains why some versions of the Bible don't include it, such as the New International Version (although it *does* include it in the footnotes). How do we explain this verse's inclusion in later manuscripts? Evidently an overzealous scribe foolishly added it to the text at some point, evidently due to Mark 9:29, perhaps thinking he could make God's Word better (Proverbs 30:6).

Speaking of Mark 9:29, it features a similar scenario to Matthew 17:21 (although not necessarily the same occasion) where "and fasting" was *added* in later manuscripts. This explains why these words are absent in translations that are based on prior, more dependable manuscripts, like the NIV, ESV and BSB.

There are two other occasions in the New Testament where the word "fasting" was wrongly added to the text at some later point: Acts 10:30 and 1 Corinthians 7:5. Again, "fasting" is not included in these verses in the earliest, best manuscripts.

<u>13</u>

THE PRAYER OF JABEZ

It's a good idea for Spiritual Warriors to be up on the biblical prayer of Jabez and utilize it regularly. Why? Because if you aren't blessed first, you can't very well bless anyone else. This isn't an issue of selfishness; just a fact. Here's the prayer from the two most popular English versions:

> **Jabez was more honorable than his brothers. His mother had named him Jabez, saying, "I gave birth to him in pain." [10]Jabez cried out to the God of Israel, "Oh, that you would <u>bless me</u> and <u>enlarge my territory! Let your hand be with me</u>, and <u>keep me from harm so that I will be free from pain</u>." And God granted his request.**
>
> **1 Chronicles 4:9-10** (NIV)

> **And Jabez was more honourable than his brethren: and his mother called his name Jabez, saying, Because I bare him with sorrow. [10]And Jabez called on the God of Israel, saying, Oh that thou wouldest <u>bless me indeed</u>, and <u>enlarge my coast</u>, and that <u>thine hand might be with me</u>, and that thou wouldest <u>keep *me* from evil, that it may not grieve me</u>! And God granted him that which he requested.**
>
> **1 Chronicles 4:9-10** (KJV)

This passage is all we know about Jabez in the Bible. Because his mother bore him in pain & sorrow, she gave him a name that originated from the Hebrew word for 'pain.' Yet Jabez chose not to lead an unjustifiably cursed life and so turned to the LORD. As such, Jabez is cited as "more honorable than his brothers" in Holy Scripture.

This shows that, whatever raw deal has been handed you in life, you can turn it around to the positive with God's assistance (Romans 8:28 & 2 Peter 3:18). After all, isn't the LORD the "Fountain of Life" who pours abundant life into the lives of those who humbly seek & honor the Creator of All? See Psalm 36:9 and John 10:10.

Jabez' prayer had four general points:

1. He sought the Creator's blessing on his life.
2. He sought for God to enlarge his "territory" and therefore his influence.
3. He sought the LORD's hand of support, help and favor.
4. He sought the Almighty to keep him from harm or evil and the corresponding pain & grief; in other words, he wanted protection from the life-altering hurt of unnecessary tragedies.

These four requests are the general ones that any noble soul desires in this life (in contrast to the *ignoble* soul obsessed with carnal things, like Mammon, fame and foolish sexual gratification). Because Jabez diligently pursued the LORD in faith, God granted his requests (Hebrews 11:6).

The Jabez passage does not exist by accident. It's there to show us that— no matter how cursed our lives might be—we have the option to turn to the Almighty for succor and blessing, for God is no respecter of persons (Romans 2:11). **The LORD can turn *any* ship around**, so to speak, **no matter how bad it is**.

Recently, I took a 40-day fast from a couple things and prayed the prayer of Jabez every day corresponding to the specifics of my life in association with Carol. Since it's a general prayer—a *skeleton* prayer—you can of course tweak it to apply to *your* situation.

For a good commentary on this topic, I recommend Bruce Wilkinson's (short) book *The Prayer of Jabez: Breaking Through to the Blessed Life*.

<u>14</u>

WHY GOSSIP & SLANDER ARE SO EVIL

Spiritual Warriors do not engage in faultfinding and the corresponding gossip & slander, otherwise known as backbiting. While this topic has surfaced in a few previous chapters, it's an important enough issue to warrant a whole chapter. You'll see why.

What is gossip? Gossip *can* refer to trivial talk, which is generally harmless, but when it involves talking about others behind their backs in either a derogatory fashion or concerning personal matters, it's definitely wrong. This includes putting a negative spin on what the person in question says and does. Although there are sometimes legitimate reasons for discussing a person's possible flaws and questionable character, like work or ministry situations (hiring, promoting or demoting, etc.), outside of these obvious exceptions it becomes gossip.

Why is gossip wrong? For one thing, because the victim of the condescending talk isn't present to defend himself or herself. The first person to present a case against another always sounds right with enough bluster; that is, until you hear an honest account of the other side (Proverbs 18:17).

Secondly, because speaking badly of people behind their back smacks of arrogance, which is a superiority complex. When individuals tear others down or make fun of them, they're in essence lifting themselves up.

Thirdly, gossip is just plain ignoble and suggests a "two-face" personality. Gossipers will usually put on friendly airs in the presence of their victims, but then proceed to destroy them behind their backs with the "sword of their mouth" (Proverbs 25:18).

Fourthly, whether the gossiper realizes it or not, the gossip will poison people's minds against the victim. In other words, it *contaminates* a person's perspective of someone who's not present, which causes **division**.

Lastly, gossip is wrong because the information might not even be true. It might only be partially correct or wholly false. When this happens, the gossip becomes slander or false testimony! Even if the gossip starts out as accurate it becomes less accurate the more people it goes through, meaning it devolves into **slander**. As such, those who engage in this kind of gossip are breaking one of the moral commandments: "You shall not bear false witness against your neighbor"!

For all these reasons, God *hates* gossip, which can be observed in the book of Proverbs and its list of seven sins that the Creator especially hates:

> **There are six things the LORD hates,**
> **seven that are detestable to him:**
> **[17]haughty eyes,**
> **a lying tongue,**
> **hands that shed innocent blood,**
> **[18]a heart that devises wicked schemes,**
> **feet that are quick to rush into evil,**
> **[19]a false witness who pours out lies**
> **and a person who stirs up conflict in the community.**
> **Proverbs 6:16-19**

Three of these seven are directly linked to gossip and another is indirectly linked. A "lying tongue" and a "false witness who pours out lies" bespeak of a gossiper because, again, gossip naturally devolves into slander. A "person who stirs up conflict in the community" also points to gossip because **hostility and division are the *results* of gossip** (Proverbs 16:28).

Lastly, "haughty eyes" is indirectly tied to gossip because haughty eyes stem from a proud heart (Proverb 21:4) and pride is the root cause of gossip. Pride gives birth to envy, jealousy and rivalry, and the result is gossip—defaming the person in question.

Gossips Are Fools Who Hurt and Cause Dissension

Proverbs is the book of **godly wisdom**; notice what it blatantly says about those who gossip and slander:

> **…whoever spreads slander is <u>a fool</u>.**
>
> **Proverbs 10:18**

> **With his mouth <u>the godless</u> destroys his neighbor…**
>
> **Proverbs 11:9**

> **A person who lacks judgment derides his neighbor…**
>
> **Proverbs 11:12**

> **A <u>perverse person</u> stirs up conflict,**
> **and a gossip <u>separates close friends</u>.**
>
> **Proverbs 16:28**

Gossips & slanderers are **fools** who destroy others with their tongue, which is the "sword" of their mouth. People who regularly engage in gossip & slander are "perverse" because they naturally stir up conflict and destroy relationships. They destroy relationships because, on some level, they're jealous or envious of the bond in question. For instance, they might be envious of the loyalty someone has toward their rival and so they naturally gravitate toward destroying that relationship with gossip & slander.

It has been said that small minds talk about people, average minds talk about things and great minds talk about ideas. People who are gossips & slanderers reveal how small they are—they're small-minded fools.

By contrast, *godly* people—those who are "like God"—build others up with their tongues through encouragement, knowledge and appropriate correction:

> **The tongue of the righteous is choice silver,**
>
> **Proverbs 10:20**

> **The lips of the righteous nourish many,**
>
> **Proverbs 10:21**

> **Let a <u>righteous man</u> strike me—that is a kindness;**
> **let him rebuke me—that is oil on my head.**
> **My head will not refuse it,**
>
>

Psalm 141:5

> **The mouth of the righteous is a fountain of life,**
> **but the mouth of the wicked conceals violence.**
>
>

Proverbs 10:11

That last one reveals something about gossip & slander: It's **verbal violence** which attacks people with words behind their backs. As such, the tongue of gossips & slanderers is their **weapon**:

> **Like a <u>club</u> or a <u>sword</u> or a <u>sharp arrow</u>**
> **is one who gives false testimony against a neighbor.**
>
>

Proverbs 25:18

It's natural to think of "false testimony" in the sense of a witness in a court trial but, really, anytime someone shares information about another person that isn't accurate it's a form of false testimony—it's testifying to other people against that person and, consequently destroying his or her reputation. People who do this are utilizing their tongue as a "club," "a sword" or a "sharp arrow." In other words, gossips & slanderers may not be wielding a literal weapon, like a gun or knife, but they have their tongue and they use it as a weapon to covertly destroy others and their relationships. In essence, they *murder* people with their lips. This explains why Christ associated being angry with a brother or sister without cause to murder (Matthew 5:21-22).

We see evidence of this repeatedly in God's Word:

> **You who practice deceit,**
> **your tongue plots destruction;**
> **it is <u>like a sharpened razor</u>.**
>
>

Psalm 52:2

> **I am in the midst of lions;**
> **I am forced to dwell among ravenous beasts—**
> **<u>men whose teeth are spears and arrows</u>,**
> **<u>whose tongues are sharp swords</u>.**
>
>

Psalm 57:4

> **See what they spew from their mouths—**
> **<u>the words from their lips are sharp as swords,</u>**
> **and they think, "Who can hear us?"**
>
> **Psalm 59:7**

A lot of gossips & slanderers will put on an innocent act—like they're unaware of the harmful effects of their talebearing words—but, make no mistake, they realize the destructive power of their tongues and relish using it as a weapon to destroy, even if it's on a subconscious level.

What's their motive? Hatred since "A lying tongue *hates* those it hurts" (Proverbs 26:28).

Gossips & Slanderers Are Two-Faces

Those who regularly badmouth others with their tongues are typically **two-faces** who smile to your face, but destroy you behind your back:

> **...they flatter with their lips**
> **but harbor deception in their hearts.**
>
> **Psalm 12:2**

> **Do not drag me away with the wicked,**
> **with those who do evil,**
> **who speak cordially with their neighbors**
> **but harbor malice in their hearts.**
>
> **Psalm 28:3**

> **His talk is smooth as butter,**
> **yet war is in his heart;**
> **his words are more soothing than oil,**
> **yet they are drawn swords.**
>
> **Psalm 55:21**

It goes without saying that once someone proves they're a two-face—a verbal backstabber—it's almost impossible to be close with him or her. As such, gossips & slanderers are their own worst enemies; they destroy their own potential for genuine, close relationships. True, they might be able to hide their backbiting proclivities with their charm for a time but, if they don't honestly change their heart and actions, they'll eventually be found out and no one in their right mind will want to be close to them, particularly anyone who's remotely godly.

Speaking of repentance, I don't have a problem having relationships with **ex-gossips** & **ex-slanderers**—those who have had a humbling life-changing encounter with the LORD and so have honestly 'fessed up and changed. But that's not who I'm talking about here; I'm talking about those who gossip & slander year after year, decade after decade with no concern of penitence, even professing Christians and ministers. Such people are *hypocrites,* which literally means "actors." In other words, they're phonies or **fakes**.

"Put to Silence" Gossips Within Your Social Sphere

David is described as "a man after God's own heart" in the Scriptures and he wouldn't even badmouth his enemy, King Saul, who was trying to kill him! When David later became king of Israel, he made it clear that gossip & slander would not be tolerated in his kingdom:

> **Whoever slanders their neighbor in secret,**
> **him will I <u>put to silence</u>;**
> **whoever has haughty eyes and a proud heart,**
> **<u>I will not tolerate</u>.**
>
> **Psalm 101:5**

Like David, we need to make sure that gossip is not tolerated in our "kingdom." This means **your sphere of influence**—your house, your neighborhood, your friends & family, your workplace, your school or class, etc.

I've come to really hate gossip. A couple of years ago someone said something defamatory about an enemy of mine. I guess he thought I'd welcome the information since the man was an adversary, but he was wrong. I knew what he said wasn't true, so I corrected it on the spot and the gossip was snuffed out. Even in cases where the information is correct it's wrong to condone the talk.

Speaking of which, it's wrong to overlook active gossip. I'm talking about hearing people gossip and allowing them to continue, even though you're not technically engaging in it. Hence, you're *absorbing* their wicked words. How is this wrong? For one, because your mind will be poisoned by the negative information, whether you realize it or not. Secondly, by giving ear to the gossiper you fuel the gossip and are encouraging its spread. You're also encouraging the gossiper to continue in his/her immoral speech.

> **If a ruler listens to lies,**
> **all his officials become wicked.**
>
> **Proverbs 29:12**

When a leader absorbs the lies of a talebearing slanderer, it's not just him or her that's corrupted, but those within the inner circle as well. Carol & I witnessed this at an assembly we attended for 7 years. A relative of the pastor would concoct stories about godly people and gossip about it. The pastor gave ear to her lies and thus it soiled the leadership of that fellowship in general.

The best way to deal with someone who starts gossiping in your presence is to either immediately excuse yourself (which speaks volumes by itself) or counteract the gossip with something positive about the absent victim. For instance, someone might say, "Pastor John's not aging well at all." Counteract it with "He's such a great man of God and has so blessed my life." Someone says, "Jill's such an alcoholic!" Counteract it with, "Maybe, but she's one of the kindest persons I've ever met."

If the people gossiping are believers, you can stop them in their tracks by suggesting prayer for the victim and then do it—bow your head and start praying. If the gossiper is an elder in the Church, like a pastor, teacher, deacon or worship leader, you should correct him/her on the spot. Why? Because elders are leaders who **should know better** and are *supposed* to set a godly example. Be as gentle or stern as the situation calls for, as led of the Holy Spirit. If they're truly spiritual they'll appreciate your correction and commend you for it; if not, they'll hate you for it (Proverbs 9:7-9).

Although I was never a problem gossiper, I've of course fallen into it simply because it's so easy to do. The way the LORD dealt with me was to convict me if I engaged in gossip, meaning the Holy Spirit made me feel bad about it. I felt like I was being unfaithful to the person in question; like I was sinning against him or her.

On one occasion a person's name came up to which Carol & I started focusing on her flaws and I immediately felt bad about it. I said, "I don't want to be like this, Carol." So Carol & I have gotten in the habit of correcting each other if a conversation starts to devolve into gossip. Instead of gossiping about people we humbly pray for them, just be careful that the prayer doesn't turn into gossip-with-the-airs-of-prayer; that is, a "gossip prayer." Unsurprisingly, this "buddy system" has helped purge gossip from our lives.

Titus 3:2 instructs: "**speak evil of no one**." Chew on that!

I should add that political candidates in a democracy are a unique category. If they're evil, foolish or incompetent and you have clear evidence of this, it's *your duty* to inform the citizenry of the truth because voters are the ones who will determine whether or not such politicians are in power or remain in power. This naturally has an impact on the quality of your life and how freely God's Word is spread in your community (1 Timothy 2:1).

Gossips & Slanderers *Cannot* to Be Close to God

Consider this fascinating insight from one of David's psalms:

> ¹**LORD, who may dwell in your sacred tent?**
> **Who may live on your holy mountain?**
> ²**The one whose walk is blameless,**
> **who does what is righteous,**
> **who speaks the truth from their heart;**
> ³**whose tongue utters no slander,**
> **who does no wrong to a neighbor,**
> **and casts no slur on others;**
> ⁴**who despises a vile person**
> **but honors those who fear the LORD;**
> **who keeps an oath even when it hurts,**
> **and does not change their mind;**
> ⁵**who lends money to the poor without interest;**
> **who does not accept a bribe against the innocent.**
> **Whoever does these things**
> **will never be shaken.**
>
> **Psalm 15**

Verse 1 asks the question: "Who may dwell in your sacred tent?" The "sacred tent" refers to the Old Testament **Tabernacle** that was used to house the Ark of the Covenant before Solomon built the Temple; God's presence dwelt on the cover of this Ark between the sculptured cherubim. The second half of the verse asks: "Who may live on your holy hill?" The "holy hill" refers to Mount Zion, which was the site of the Jerusalem Tabernacle and Temple, God's dwelling back then.

This psalm features a form of Hebrew poetry called synonymous parallelism where the second part of the verse says the same thing as the first, but in different words. In essence, verse 1 is asking the question: Who may be close to God? or Who hangs out in God's presence? The psalm answers by listing several attributes of those who are close to God and hang out in his presence. Notice what verse 3 says:

> **<u>whose tongue utters no slander</u>,**
> **who does no wrong to a neighbor,**
> **and <u>casts no slur on others</u>;**

In short, **only those who "utter no slander" and cast "no slur on others" can be close with the LORD**. This means that anyone who's an unrepentant gossip & slanderer is *not* close to God, no matter what they claim or what position they hold in a fellowship, including pastors, apostles, evangelists, teachers, prophets and those involved in praise & worship.

People who regularly and impenitently engage in gossip & slander might as well be holding a blow horn announcing, *"I'm NOT close to God; I DON'T hang out in the presence of the LORD!!"*

Christ said, "By **their fruit** you will know them" (Matthew 7:16,19-20). Speaking of which…

Those Who Engage in Gossip Are Like the Devil!

The name 'satan' means "adversary" or "enemy," which explains why he's often referred to as "the enemy" by Christians. Satan is also called the devil, which is translated from the Greek *diabolos (dee-AB-ol-os)*, meaning "**slanderer**." The term comes from the verb *diaballó (dee-ab-AL-loh)*, meaning "to slander, accuse, defame, complain." The Bible plainly describes satan as "the accuser of our brothers and sisters, who accuses them before our God day and night" (Revelation 12:10). Moreover, Christ called the devil a "**murderer** from the beginning" and "the father of **lies**" (John 8:44).

Do you know a (supposed) brother or sister in the Lord who regularly accuses and smears believers? They're behaving like satan which, needless to say, is not a good thing. Either they're a child of the devil and therefore a counterfeit believer (Matthew 7:15-23) or they're grossly ignorant and misled of the enemy (2 Timothy 2:24-26). The fact that there are "leaders" in the body of Christ acting like this is a sad commentary. Please pray for them and correct them as led of the Spirit. Don't allow them to poison your mind against people—usually *innocent* people—who aren't present to share their side of the story (Proverbs 18:17).

Let's close this chapter with the linking topic of…

Faultfinding

While gossip/slander is rooted in envy, jealousy and rivalry (a spirit of competition), it's also linked to a faultfinding spirit.

Jude warned believers in the 1st century about false teachers; notice how he describes them:

> **These people are grumblers and <u>faultfinders</u>; they follow their own evil desires; they boast about themselves and flatter others for their own advantage.**
> **Jude 1:16**

The one description we want to focus on is 'faultfinder.' A faultfinder is someone who tends to find fault in others—usually a rival—and then murmurs & complains about it to others, which naturally *poisons* the minds of the listeners against the victim and thus creates **division**. This is something the LORD "hates," as observed in the afore-cited Proverbs 6:16-19. Such criticisms are usually of a vague, petty nature voiced in a mocking manner; that is, with an air of scorn, condescension, insult and chortling.

James commented on faultfinding in his epistle:

> **Brothers and sisters, do not slander one another. Anyone who speaks against a brother or sister or judges them speaks against the law and judges it. When you judge the law, you are not keeping it, but sitting in judgment on it.**
>
> **James 4:11**

> **Don't grumble against one another, brothers and sisters, <u>or you will be judged</u>. The Judge is standing at the door!**
>
> **James 5:9**

Wow, impenitent faultfinding *draws* divine judgment! Beware.

Of course, when a brother or sister *sins* against you, they should be confronted & corrected as led of the Spirit (Luke 17:3 & Matthew 18:15-17), but that's not what we're discussing. We're talking about the tendency to pick out the faults in others—typically a person the critic is envious/jealous of—and then regularly murmuring about it in a mocking manner to other people, which spurs division and strife.

Everyday Examples of Faultfinding

People can easily slip into a faultfinding spirit, usually influenced by a carnal ringleader. For instance, Carol & I were hanging out with a few believers several years ago and one person started mocking a certain man not present who happened to be involved in ministry. We all ended up joining-in with mocking comments, except for my wife, who later said she didn't feel right about it. It was easy for me to get in on the act since I was at odds with this particular man at the moment (a former best friend). The next Sunday I was scheduled to give a sermon and had *no* anointing; it was a struggle from beginning to end. Convicted by the Spirit, I knew what the issue was and humbly repented.

A more recent example took place on X. A man posted a video of a well-known minister and ridiculed him as a con man. I'm not a big fan of this particular minister, but I've read a couple of his books and heard a handful of his sermons. While I don't agree with every jot & tittle of what he says, he's a formidable man of God and I respect him. Dozens of others on the thread joined in with disparaging comments regarding the preacher, all trite criticisms.

So I watched the video to see what the issue was and all it depicted was the minister illustrating how to put on the armor of God and, specifically, use the sword of the Spirit, which is the Word of God implemented as an offensive weapon (elaborated on in chapter **19**). I pointed this out to the man who posted the video and he responded, "Did you see the look in his eyes? He's obviously demon possessed. The Bible says 'The eye is the lamp of the body' in Luke 11:34."

I replied, "He was simply illustrating **how to conduct spiritual warfare**, which you shouldn't approach as Howdy Doody. You have to mean business." I then asked him: How did Christ look when he astonishingly cleared the Temple of fools (Mark 11:15-18)? How did Paul look when he radically confronted a meddling magician on Cyprus (Acts 13:8-12)? These were mere *physical* confrontations; consider Jesus and Paul's demeanor in serious *spiritual* confrontations during spiritual warfare.

A couple of others chimed in, but I pointed out how all the criticisms on the thread were **vague accusations** regarding the minister's eyes or what have you. There was no meat to their carping. I asked, "Since he overtly preaches *against* sin and hasn't been involved in a scandal, the issue must be doctrine. What doctrine do you think he's teaching falsely? Be specific." One person—only one—said that the man preached giving and receiving back. I pointed out how the Bible actually supports the principle of giving & receiving (Luke 6:38, 2 Corinthians 9:6 & Philippians 4:17), not to mention God's provision (Philippians 4:19 & Proverbs 10:22).

So, I asked again, what specific doctrine does this minister embrace that unquestionably makes him a *false* believer? The only thing the critic could come up with was to say that there are videos about the minister that prove he's a false teacher. In other words, backed against a wall, she couldn't even voice the particular doctrine that proved he was a false believer, such as denying Christ as LORD.

An additional criticism of the minister was that he supposedly preached that believers will experience nothing but peaches and cream on Earth. I countered that I've never heard him say this; on the contrary, he plainly teaches that believers will face persecutions and trials—and all the more as one matures—but, thankfully, he also instructed *how to overcome* by fighting the good fight of faith (1 Timothy 6:12).

All I got back was crickets, which is good. The believers on the thread were hopefully ashamed of their faultfinding and penitent.

What David Said About a Gossiper He Knew

Observe what God's Word says about a faultfinding slanderer:

> <u>**¹⁷He loved to pronounce a curse**</u>—
> **may it come back on him.**
> <u>**He found no pleasure in blessing**</u>—
> **may it be far from him.**
> <u>**¹⁸He wore cursing as his garment;**</u>
> <u>**it entered into his body like water,**</u>
> **into his bones like oil.**
> **¹⁹May it be like a cloak wrapped about him,**
> **like a belt tied forever around him.**
> **²⁰May this be the LORD's payment to <u>my accusers</u>,**
> **to <u>those who speak evil of me</u>.**
>
> **Psalm 109:17-20**

There are people who love to badmouth others so much that it covers them like their clothes. It flows through their bodies like water. You could say it's in their blood.

Spiritual Warriors must not be like this. On the contrary, your noble character will actually attract the gossip & slander of such people. This is why the Lord said, "Blessed are you when people insult you, persecute you and falsely say all kinds of evil against you because of me" (Matthew 5:11).

The Spiritual Warrior's life must be *so* opposed to the carnal way of this lost & dying world that your very existence is an act of rebellion against the darkness of this world—a *righteous* rebellion.

15

GROWING IN GIVING / SHUNNING GREED

All believers will stand before the Lord and give an account of their lives for what they do or don't do at the Judgment Seat of Christ (2 Corinthians 5:10-11). This includes what you do with **your income**. More is expected of those with greater knowledge, talents and spiritual maturity. As Christ said, "To whom much is given, much will be required" (Luke 12:48).

As covered in chapter 4, New Covenant believers are not *under* the Mosaic law, rather we fulfill the moral law by walking in the spirit (Romans 7:6).

Christians are under the law of Christ, which is the **law of love**—loving God and loving people as we love ourselves. If we are walking in love toward the diligent ministers & ministries that we receive from and are blessed by, we'll support them from our income, whatever form that may be, and with our time & talents, not to mention respect (1 Timothy 5:17 & 1 Thessalonians 5:12-13).[7]

It's important to realize that roughly 50% of people in any given country don't earn money in the conventional sense, so they'll have to give in different ways. Another vital thing to keep in mind is that God honors giving based on the amount the giver possesses. For instance, the poor

---

[7] That said, we **shouldn't** support or tolerate *abusive* ministers & ministries (Matthew 15:14). Christ didn't, as observed in Matthew 23:13-36. Abuse is the misuse of power.

widow in the Bible gave *more* in the Lord's eyes than all the wealthy contributors at the Temple even though she gave what amounted to pennies (Mark 12:41-44).

We are instructed in the New Testament to "grow in the grace of giving" (2 Corinthians 8:7 & Luke 6:38), but no amount is set because it will be different for each believer according to their means & talents, as well as how the Spirit leads. For instance, in the book of Acts, some believers were selling whole properties and giving the money to the Church (Acts 4:33-36). This was way beyond 10% of their income.

However, 10% is a good starting place because Abraham gave Melchizedek 10% of the booty (Hebrews 7:1-2). Abraham is the Father of Faith and New Covenant believers are Abraham's children of faith (Romans 4:16). Secondly, Melchizedek was a type of Christ and this was *before* the Mosaic law, which required 10% of the Israelites' earnings to support the Levites (Numbers 18:21) and they, in turn, gave 10% of that back to the LORD (18:25-26).

As such, if a believer is part of a ministry and receiving from it, 10% of one's income is a good place to start in regards to giving. If you have 10 eggs, give one. If you have a 100, give 10. From there you can "grow in the grace of giving" as led of the Spirit. Again, New Covenant believers are not under the Mosaic law, but giving 10% to support genuine ministries is considered "tithing" because the word for tithe in the Hebrew, *maasar (mah-as-AYR)*, simply means 10%.

But, please, it's important to understand that the LORD only wants believers to give out of a giving heart that's happy to give. He doesn't want believers to give reluctantly or under compulsion—which includes being coerced by ministers preaching condemnation, aka 'condo.' There's no condo in Paul's request for funds for needy Christians in Jerusalem, as chronicled in 2 Corinthians 8-9. (This offering, by the way, would've been a contribution above and beyond the believers' regular support for the church in Corinth). Paul shares the need, encourages the believers to give, stresses that they'll be rewarded, and then adds that they should only give what they decide to *gladly* give (2 Corinthians 9:7). This is the only way they would be blessed for their giving; otherwise, they'd be giving from the flesh to earn salvation or whatever, which is what Hindus, Muslims and other religionists do.

Another thing we can get from this passage is that Paul didn't view believers as pawns to fund ministry projects which the apostle considered important, including altruistic ones. He respected and loved the believers where they were spiritually and permitted them to make up their own minds as led of the Spirit (or not led of the Spirit).

Something else important to keep in mind was previously noted in chapters **3** and **7**. It's the fact that believers "are not their own" because we were "bought at a price" (1 Corinthians 6:19-20), which explains why we're instructed to be "**living sacrifices**" (Romans 12:1-2). In other words, *our whole lives* are God's possession already, not just 10% of our financial earnings. Our bodies, our thoughts, our material possessions, our earnings—they're all God's already. This frees us up to happily "grow in the grace of giving."

Thus the principle of giving 10% of one's resources is, at best, a starting point in the New Covenant. The LORD wants believers to become **living sacrifices** every day wherein we grasp that everything we are & everything we own has already been purchased by our Mighty Maker. "You are not our own." Your tongue belongs to God (i.e. what you say), not to mention your hands (what you do), your feet (where you walk), your eyes (what you look at) and your ears (what you listen to)

Of course you have to grow into this powerful revelation, which is where the day-to-day process of sanctification comes into play (1 Thessalonians 5:23).

The Proper Attitude in Giving and Receiving

The Lord said:

> **"Give, and it will be given to you. A good measure, pressed down, shaken together and running over, will be poured into your lap. For with the measure you use, it will be measured to you."**
>
> **Luke 6:38**

This is a general principle. Those who give, will receive back, which is also taught in the Old Testament's book of wisdom:

> ²⁴**One person gives freely, yet gains even more;**
> **another withholds unduly, but comes to poverty.**
> ²⁵**A generous person will prosper;**
> **whoever refreshes others will be refreshed.**
>
> **Proverbs 11:24-25**

> ⁹**Honor the LORD with your wealth,**
> **with the firstfruits of all your crops;**
> ¹⁰**then your barns will be filled to overflowing,**
> **and your vats will brim over with new wine.**
>
> **Proverbs 3:9-10**

So, as you grow in the grace of giving, you can expect to receive in return, one way or another. However, you shouldn't give a gift to a person expecting the same from him/her, which Christ commented on:

> **"And if you lend to those from whom you expect repayment, what credit is that to you? Even sinners lend to sinners, expecting to be repaid in full."**
>
> **Luke 6:34**

Let's say you treat someone out to eat as a gift. If you insist that this person reciprocate down the road then what you gave wasn't a gift, but an exchange. So, when you give a gift to someone, let it go. Don't expect him/her to pay you back at some point and be angry if they don't.

Provision, Money and "Prosperity"

The Bible distinguishes that poverty is a curse and prosperity is a blessing (Deuteronomy 28). Poverty is not having enough to make it while prosperity is the opposite. It's God's will to **provide for you** so that you can effectively fulfill your assignment & call, whatever they may be (Philippians 4:19). The individual has a part to play in this, of course. For instance, you can't be lazy and prosper (Proverbs 13:14) and we are called to "grow in the grace of giving" (2 Corinthians 8:7, 2 Corinthians 9:6-8 & Luke 6:38); in other words, you can't be ungenerous and expect financial blessing (Proverbs 11:24-25). God is your *helper,* not your do-everything-for-you-so-you-don't-have-to-do-anything-at-all-er (Psalm 54:4).

As far as money goes, Christ emphasized that you cannot serve God and Mammon (Matthew 6:24) while Paul said that the *love of* money is the root of all kinds of evil (1 Timothy 6:10). Please notice that money itself isn't evil, but rather the *love of* money. Nor is money the root of *all* evil, but rather the root of "all kinds of evil." For instance, money isn't the root of sexual immorality, but rather carnal lust. Needless to say, make sure that you're loving God & serving the LORD and not money. This is a given. But this doesn't negate the importance of finances or provision in your life. For instance, you can't help provide for others if you aren't first provided for yourself. In other words, you can't bless others materially unless you are first blessed materially.

The Bible Has a Lot to Say About Money

Some believers freak out when the topic of money is brought up in the context of a Christian teaching because of hang-ups. Yet the Bible actually has a lot to say on the subject. One in five verses address the issue of wealth one way or another, whether finances, property, possessions, inheritance or otherwise. One third of Christ's parables address the topic. It's only right that believers have a *balanced* understanding of what the Holy Scriptures say on wealth and provision otherwise we'll develop an erroneous perspective stemming from the world or religion:

- The world basically teaches that money is god and therefore worships wealth. As such, peoples' worth is evaluated on how much money & possessions they have. This is a *worldly* viewpoint (2 Corinthians 5:16-17).
- Religion—including counterfeit "Christianity"—teaches two lies from opposite extremes: **1.** Poverty is godly and so ministers of certain sects take a vow of poverty; or **2.** Christianity is about being as filthy rich as possible and poor people should be regarded as if they have the plague.

Concerning taking a "vow of poverty," Deuteronomy 28 makes it clear that poverty is a curse along with other curses, like mental illness, physical sickness & disease, defeat to enemies and premature death. So taking a vow of poverty is as absurd as taking a vow of sickness & disease or a vow of premature death.

As for the other religious lie, that Christianity is all about being as financially prosperous as possible and anyone who isn't is (supposedly) cursed of God, Christ rebuked the believers at the Laodicean assembly thusly:

> **You say, 'I am rich; I have acquired wealth and do not need a thing.' But you do not realize that you are wretched, pitiful, poor, blind and naked.'**
>
> **Revelation 3:17**

Wow, what a reprimand! This shows that it's possible for believers to be financially wealthy but **thoroughly impoverished** in regards to more important things in God's eyes. This can be observed in the proverb: "better to be poor than a liar" (Proverbs 19:22). Think about what this verse is saying: According to God's Word, it is *better—superior—*to be an honest poor person than a financially rich liar.

In regards to the worldly lie that money is god and wealth should be pursued above all else, Christ said that there was no human greater than John the Baptist up to that point in time (Matthew 11:11), yet John dwelled in the lonely desert with clothes made of camel hair, living on locusts and wild honey (Matthew 3:4).

Believers overcome this world **through faith** (1 John 5:4)—which includes overcoming any *curses* the enemy throws at us, like disease, defeat and poverty—and **faith comes through hearing what God's Word says on any given topic** (Romans 10:17). We are to fight the good fight of faith to overcome the curses of the enemy (1 Timothy 6:12) and this explains why Christ regularly said things like "According to your faith be it done to you" (Matthew 9:29). Needless to say, it's important to increase our knowledge and build-up our faith in regard to God's provision and money in general.

Please don't stumble over the word "prosperity." **Prosperity is relative to your God-given mission and environment.** Joseph, for instance, was **a slave** in Potiphar's house and **a prisoner** in Egypt, but the Bible says he *prospered* in both environments despite the obvious limitations thereof (Genesis 39:2-6 & 39:20-23).

"Do Not Wear Yourself Out to Get Rich"

When I was in my early 20s, I was working for a small company when the supervisor suddenly quit and I was offered his job. I was excited because the position offered an impressive salary. I took the job but suddenly found myself running around like a headless chicken and no longer had the time to spend with studying the Scriptures or prayer/meditation, things that were dear to my heart. After a few weeks I went to the remote corner of a dark stockroom and literally wept. I had inadvertently made money my god and was pursuing it at the expense of more important things.

This brings to mind this wise Scripture:

> **Do not wear yourself out to get rich;**
> **be wise enough to restrain yourself.**
>
> **Proverbs 23:4** (BSB)

The verse corresponds to what Christ said about how the deceitfulness of wealth—which includes the obsessive pursuit of it—can "choke the word, making it unfruitful" (Mark 4:19). This is what happened to me on the occasion described above.

Needless to say, we have to be careful *not* to fall into the mindset of the world where everything revolves around how much you make and the respect/privileges thereof. The world says that if you make *under* a certain figure, you're in "poverty," and if you make *over* a certain figure, you're "prosperous," but this is irrelevant to true prosperity. Again, the Scriptures say that Joseph was prosperous as a slave in Potiphar's house and when he was in prison. Chew on that.

We'll look at the definition of prosperity and what to do when you're hit with a financial attack in chapter **20**.

Why Wasn't God Pleased With Cain's Offering?

Here's the passage in question:

> **Now Abel kept flocks, and Cain worked the soil. [3]In the course of time Cain brought some of the fruits of the soil as an offering to the LORD. [4]And Abel also brought an offering—fat portions from some of the firstborn of his flock. The LORD looked with favor on Abel and his offering, [5]but on Cain and his offering he did not look with favor. So Cain was very angry, and his face was downcast.**
> **[6]Then the LORD said to Cain, "Why are you angry? Why is your face downcast? [7]If you do what is right, will you not be accepted? But if you do not do what is**

> right, sin is crouching at your door; it desires to have you, but you must rule over it."
>
> [8]Now Cain said to his brother Abel, "Let's go out to the field." While they were in the field, Cain attacked his brother Abel and killed him.
>
> [9]Then the LORD said to Cain, "Where is your brother Abel?"
>
> "I don't know," he replied. "Am I my brother's keeper?"
>
> [10]The LORD said, "What have you done? Listen! Your brother's blood cries out to me from the ground."
>
> **Genesis 4:2b-10**

Abel was a shepherd while **Cain was a farmer**. Thus when they presented offerings to the LORD, Abel sacrificed some of the choice firstborn of his flock whereas Cain naturally gave an offering of the fruits of the soil. God looked favorably on Abel & his offering, but not Cain, why? We know it wasn't Cain's offering itself that the LORD took issue with since:

1. "Cain worked the soil" (4:2) and therefore his sacrifice to God would be based on the fruits of his work.
2. Grain offerings and harvest offerings would later be revealed as legitimate expressions of worship under the Mosaic law (Leviticus 2:1-6, 19:23-24 & 23:9-14).

So what was God's issue with Cain's offering? It was not his offering, but the *attitude of his heart*, as revealed in the New Testament:

> **By faith Abel brought God a better offering than Cain did. By faith he was commended as righteous, when God spoke well of his offerings. And by faith Abel still speaks, even though he is dead.**
>
> **Hebrews 11:4**

Abel gave a "better offering" than Cain due to his faith, which refers to belief; and belief has to do with one's heart or mindset. We know that:

- The pure in heart are "blessed" and "will see God" (Matthew 5:8, Hebrews 12:14 & Proverbs 22:11).

- Yet Cain's heart was obviously not pure since he didn't hesitate to murder his brother due to jealous hatred and then brazenly lied to the LORD about it (verses 8-9).
- Thus Abel was "commended as righteous" and Cain wasn't.

You could say that Cain gave out of a spirit of religion: His heart possibly begrudged giving the offering, but felt he had to do it because it was the law; in other words, he gave out of an attitude of legal-ism. Abel, by contrast, gave out of a spirit of faith and therefore pure-hearted cheer (2 Corinthians 9:7). It is the people with this attitude who will experience closeness to the LORD and the favor (grace) thereof.

Top Levite musician Asaph recorded how the LORD rebuked the Israelites, but the problem was *not* their ceremonial sacrifices, as witnessed here:

> **I do not rebuke you for your sacrifices**
> **or concerning your burnt offerings, which are ever**
> **before me.**
>
> **Psalm 50:8**

So what did God take issue with? The rest of the psalm reveals:

> [14]**"Sacrifice <u>thank offerings</u> to God,**
> **fulfill your vows to the Most High,**
> [15]**and <u>call on me</u> in the day of trouble;**
> **I will deliver you, and you will honor me."**
> [16]**But to the wicked person, God says:**
> **"What right have you to recite my laws**
> **or take my covenant on your lips?**
> [17]**<u>You hate my instruction</u>**
> **And <u>cast my words behind you</u>.**
> [18]**When you see a <u>thief, you join with him</u>;**
> **You <u>throw in your lot with adulterers</u>.**
> [19]**You <u>use your mouth for evil</u>**
> **And <u>harness your tongue to deceit</u>.**
> [20]**You sit and <u>testify against your brother</u>**
> **And <u>slander your own mother's son</u>.**
> [21]**When you did these things and I kept silent,**
> **you thought I was exactly like you.**
> **But I now arraign you**
> **and set my accusations before you.**

> [22]"Consider this, <u>you who forget God,</u>
>   or I will tear you to pieces, with no one to rescue you:
> [23]Those who sacrifice thank offerings honor me,
>   and to the blameless I will show my salvation."
>
> **Psalm 50:14-23**

The LORD didn't have a problem with their religious sacrifices, but rather with the carnal attitude of their hearts:

- They were unthankful
- Ignored the Almighty
- Ignored God's instruction, i.e. God's Word
- Committed thievery
- Committed adultery
- Maliciously lied
- Falsely testified against innocent people
- Slandered their own brothers (physical or spiritual)
- Forgot about their Creator

Likewise, God didn't have a problem with Cain's ceremonial offering, but rather the sinful condition of his heart, which resulted in murder (1 John 3:12).

David commented on such things:

> [6]**Sacrifice and offering you did not desire—**
>   **but my ears you have opened—**
> **burnt offerings and sin offerings**
>   **you did not require...**
> [8]**I desire to do your will, my God;**
>   **your law is within my heart."**
>
> **Psalm 40:6,8**

It's not that the LORD didn't want David's offering, it's that God wanted genuine worship even more. Going through the motions of religious ceremony does not please our Creator. The desire to do God's will must come from the heart, as observed in verse 8.

Now let's consider the linking subject...

What Is Greed? What's Wrong With It?

Greed is the love of money—the idolization of lucre, the obsession with wealth—and any corruption that goes with it. As noted earlier, it's *not* money that's bad, but rather **the love of it**. (People often misquote 1 Timothy 6:10 based on the KJV's dubious translation of it).

Many righteous men and women in the Bible were wealthy or became wealthy or, at the very least, had ample money to live on, but that didn't make them guilty of greed. Examples include Abraham, Job, David and Solomon. Speaking of Solomon, he fell away from God later in life, but it wasn't due to his wealth, but rather his weakness for women (1 Kings 11:1-6).

Some people wrongly claim that Christ was poor, but he wasn't. Yes, he was born in a stable because there were no inns available, but during his life he was a carpenter who made good money, much like quality carpenters today. When he became a traveling minister at the age of 30, he wasn't poor either; one member of his ministry team was assigned the job of treasurer (John 12:6 & 13:29). Also, Jesus said, "The poor you will always have with you, but you will not always have me" (Matthew 26:11). Christ didn't become poor until he was unjustly apprehended and crucified, as shown in 2 Corinthians 8:9. Poverty is a curse (Deuteronomy 28) and "cursed is everyone who is hung on a pole" (Galatians 3:13).

It's significant to note that when Paul instructed the young pastor Timothy on rich people in the congregation, he didn't tell him to rebuke them for being wealthy or greedy, he simply told him to tell them **not to be arrogant**, to put their hope in God rather than their riches, and "to be rich in good deeds and to **be generous** and **willing to share**" (1 Timothy 6:17-18). Why did Timothy have to tell them not to be arrogant? Because the attainment of wealth tends to feed the fleshly ego and tempts people to look down on those with less. This is a form of greed. So is putting on airs to impress others. Needless to say, if you're wealthy don't let it go to your head.

Why did Paul want Timothy to instruct the wealthy to be generous? Because **giving with a cheerful heart is the proof that you've conquered greed**.

It should be emphasized that you can be dirt poor and be guilty of the love of money. I was a supervisor at a company decades ago and we hired a woman of modest means. She once took other people's pay envelopes because she thought there was cash in them, like hers, but when she discovered they had checks in them, she gave them back—ripped open, of course. Why did she do this? Because she loved money so much that she was willing to steal other people's earnings if the opportunity presented itself. In essence, money had become the god whom she obeyed, at least on this occasion. So the love of money—greed—is a form of idolatry.

Another obvious example of greed is when an employer hoards profits for his or her luxuries, but fails to pay the workers on payday. This is being a **rich oppressor** and it's condemned in the law of Moses (Deuteronomy 24:14-15). It's true that workers in that particular culture were paid at the end of each day but the principle holds true today in that workers are to be paid on payday. James 5:1-5 is a sobering passage that warns employers who hoard profits while failing to pay their workers. If they refuse to repent, they'll reap judgment and destruction!

One of the best verses on greed in the Bible is this one where Jesus said:

> **"Watch out! Be on your guard against all kinds of greed; a person's life does not consist in the abundance of his possessions."**
>
> **Luke 12:15**

Wow, write this on the tablet of your heart!

Neither Pastors Nor Deacons Can Be Lovers-of-Money

Notice some of the qualifications Paul gave for being an "overseer":

> **Here is a trustworthy saying: Whoever aspires to be an overseer desires a noble task. [2]Now the overseer is to be above reproach, faithful to his wife, temperate, self-controlled, respectable, hospitable, able to teach, [3]not given to drunkenness, not violent but gentle, not quarrelsome, <u>not a lover of money</u>.**
>
> **1 Timothy 3:1-3**

Overseers are not to be lovers of money, but what is an overseer? When the **elders** of the assembly of Ephesus met Paul in Miletus, he instructed them to "Keep watch over yourselves and all the flock of which the Holy

Spirit has made you **overseers**. Be **shepherds** [pastors] of the church of God, which he bought with his own blood" (Acts 20:28). This shows that elders *(presbuteros)*, overseers *(episkopos)* and pastors *(poimén)* are synonymous in the New Testament.

In other words, they refer to the same office, although "elder" could refer to another fivefold minister (or, arguably, any mature godly believer in the assembly). For instance, the apostle John was nicknamed "the elder" when he was mature in years (2 John 1:1 & 3 John 1:1). (A nickname is a nickname, not a title; for instance, one pastor I knew was called Butch, even though his name was Bob). Also, an overseer could refer to an apostle since apostles start out as pastors and eventually oversee several assemblies. Even prophets, evangelists and teachers are overseers of the inner circles of their ministries.

With this understanding, fivefold ministers in the Church cannot be lovers of money, aka Mammon worshipers. Why? Because obtaining money would be their primary goal and not serving the body of Christ & others. In short, if the minister is greedy, it would lead to corruption in leadership, such as manipulation and abuse.

This was one of the core problems of the Pharisees, as observed in Luke 16:14. Every Spiritual Warrior must ask himself or herself: Do I want to be a *Pharisaical* minister or a *godly* minister? You cannot be both.

Paul followed up these qualifications for ministers with qualifications for deacons, which means believers in helps-ministry:

> **In the same way, <u>deacons</u> are to be worthy of respect, sincere, not indulging in much wine, and <u>not pursuing dishonest gain</u>. [9]They must keep hold of the deep truths of the faith with a clear conscience. [10]<u>They must first be tested</u>; and then if there is nothing against them, let them serve <u>as deacons</u>.**
>
> **1 Timothy 3:8-10**

Not just anyone who says they're a Christian can be involved in helps ministry. They must first be evaluated by servant-leaders in the ministry and proven to be respectable, honest, not drunkards (or druggies), **not lovers-of-money who pursue dishonest gain**, faithful to his/her spouse and able to effectively manage his/her household. These general qualifications would apply to anyone functioning in a service-oriented position at an assembly. After all, would you want the sound operator or usher at your fellowship to leave the service and commit adultery or fraud on their off days? Obviously not.

16

DO YOU NEED A "SPIRITUAL COVERING"?

As covered in chapter **1**, Spiritual Warriors will take the initiative to step out in faith and do something in service of God's kingdom. This inevitably draws criticisms like:

- *"Who's your covering?"*
- *"Who are you accountable to?"*
- *"You're not one of us!"*

Those who voice such criticisms are curiously upset that someone's actively doing the work of God. In some cases, they're obviously rivalrous and envious. The diligent apostle Paul was familiar with these types of people in the early days of the Church, as observed in Philippians 1:15.

Such a faultfinding spirit can be observed with the disciples when Christ was on Earth:

> **"Master," said John, "we saw someone driving out demons in your name and <u>we tried to stop him, because he is not one of us."</u>**
> **[50]<u>"Do not stop him</u>," Jesus said, "for whoever is not against you is for you."**
>
> **Luke 9:49-50**

> "Teacher," said John, "we saw someone driving out demons in your name and <u>we told him to stop, because he was not one of us</u>."
> [39]"<u>Do not stop him</u>," Jesus said. "For no one who does a miracle in my name can in the next moment say anything bad about me, [40]for whoever is not against us is for us.
>
> **Mark 9:38-39**

The disciples saw someone exorcising demons in the name of Christ, but instead of praising the LORD for people being delivered from satanic oppression and the advancement of God's kingdom, they tried to stop the man because… he wasn't one of them.

In other words, he wasn't part of *their* group, *their* sect. Thus they assumed he didn't have the authority to do God's work and thought the Lord would agree with them, but they were wrong. Christ plainly instructed them *not* to stop the man since he clearly wasn't working against the kingdom of God, but rather *for* it.

When someone's knee-jerk response to your sincere service for the LORD is you're "not one of them," it's an indication of the infection of sectarianism, which is a work of the flesh and a form of religious legalism. (The list of works of the flesh in Galatians 5:20 includes "factions," which is *hairesis* in the Greek, meaning a religious or philosophical **sect** and the corresponding factionalism or contention).

Those who cop such an attitude are spiritually immature and tend to view people *outside* their group with a suspicious, rivalrous eye. What's absurd is that this man was doing an incredibly good work—driving out demons—but it didn't matter to John & the other disciples because they were blinded by their carnal factionalist spirit.

Christ put an immediate stop to this nonsense. His response was simple: "Do not stop him, for whoever is not against you is for you." Obviously it didn't bother the Lord that the man was operating outside their group. It didn't irk him in the least that this guy didn't go to Jesus' 'seminary.' The man was doing a good work in bold faith and he was clearly on their side, so what was the problem? There wasn't one, but those infected by rigid sectarianism will always create a problem when it concerns someone who operates outside the box with which they've put themselves and God.

Now please notice that…

Christ Did *Not* Stop Him, Saying "He Has No Covering"

I point this out because sincere believers who are actively serving the LORD and advancing the kingdom of God one way or another might occasionally hear the criticism: "Who's your covering?" The implication, of course, is that these Spiritual Warriors (supposedly) have no covering; or perhaps the critic doesn't approve of their covering.

So what do these rivalrous faultfinders mean by "covering"? The term can be traced back to the Shepherding Movement of the 1970s-80s, aka the "Discipleship Movement," which taught that submission to an elder authority—a fivefold minister—provided spiritual 'covering' for the believer by being aligned with God's delegated authority in the Church. Their support texts for this concept include 1 Thessalonians 5:12–13, 1 Corinthians 11:3 and 1 Peter 5:5.

While this principle is good and healthy **to a degree** in light of Paul being Timothy's mentor (Acts 16:1-3 & 1 Corinthians 4:17) and Elijah being Elisha's mentor (2 Kings 2), at some point the mentee should be mentored enough to strike out on his/her own in the field, like Timothy did. (This isn't to say that every protégé is called to the fivefold ministry, of course). The biggest problem with the Shepherding Movement is that it emphasized *total* submission to one's spiritual 'covering,' including getting permission for major decisions in life, such as career options and spousal choices, which, needless to say, is unhealthy, not to mention absurd.

There was a large assembly in my area back in the '80s, that subscribed to heavy shepherding wherein the congregants required permission to purchase major items, even a refrigerator (!). In these types of assemblies, if one family member decides to leave the fellowship, the remaining members are often instructed to cut all ties with him/her. While there may be times in your Christian walk where you might have to cut ties with someone for legitimate reason (like stubborn impenitence), such a strict, family-destroying attitude is Christianity-gone-wrong. In short, it's *toxic* religion.

Carol & I experienced this a dozen years ago after we decided to leave a certain assembly that we considered joining. We didn't do anything wrong, of course (in fact, we did everything *right*), but the pastor was evidently so offended by our decision not to join after two months of attending that he instructed the congregants to shun us if they ran into us in public (!).

So the Shepherding Movement was marked by cult-ish authoritarianism and the corresponding abuses—excessive oversight, absolute obedience, manipulation and intimidation—which explains why the movement justly fell into disrepute. Leaders of the coalition, like Derek Prince and Bob Mumford, publicly apologized for the harm it caused.

We shouldn't be surprised when abuses like this occasionally rear their ugly head in the Church today since the New Testament plainly warns of slick authoritarians in the ministry who are obsessed with "drawing away disciples after them" (Acts 20:29-30, Galatians 1:7, Galatians 2:4 & 2 Corinthians 11:3-4). Abuse, by the way, is the *misuse* of power.

To Whom/What Is Each Believer Accountable?

New Covenant believers are accountable in three ways:

1. Accountable to the LORD

All believers are ultimately accountable **to God** and will thus stand before Christ at the Judgment Seat to give an account of what we did in the body, whether good or bad (2 Corinthians 5:10-11). We'll even have to give an account for our *words* (Matthew 12:36). Unbelievers are also accountable to their Creator and will thus undergo the Great White Throne Judgment (Revelation 20:11-15).

It is the Mighty Christ who is the worthy infallible **Head** of the worldwide Church (Colossians 1:18, 2:10 & 2:19), as well as its **Foundation** (Acts 4:11-12 & 1 Corinthians 3:11). Thus the LORD is the "Chief Shepherd" while fivefold ministers—e.g. pastors and teachers—are *under*-shepherds who are to lead in a *servant-like* fashion, not as pompous authoritarians (1 Peter 5:1-5, Galatians 2:1-14, Ephesians 2:19-20 & 4:11-15). Yeshua spoke *against* authoritarian-styled leadership in the Church in no uncertain terms (Matthew 20:25-28).

Hence we are to seek *the Lord's* approval above human approval (2 Timothy 2:15). Remember, there's only *one* mediator between God and people and that's Jesus Christ (1 Timothy 2:5). While fivefold ministers, like pastors and teachers, are strategic to the spiritual growth of believers, they do not share this position with the Lord. We should certainly respect diligent, fruit-bearing ministers (1 Thessalonians 5:12–13), but we need to be careful about giving them *too* much weight—as if they're God Jr.—since doing so is foolish and will create strife or division in the Church, as observed in 1 Corinthians 3:3-9.

2. Accountable to Fellow Believers

In the worldwide Church—regardless of sectarian label—all genuine believers are to be submitted to one another (Ephesians 5:21), which means **we're accountable to each other**—young and old, male and female, spiritually mature and immature, fivefold minister and congregant. Holding each other accountable is relevant to **A.** how we're living and **B.** the accuracy of the doctrines—the teachings—we spread (James 3:1). The effectiveness of this corrective principle is explained in the book of Proverbs: "As iron sharpens iron, so one person sharpens another" (Proverbs 27:17).

While believers are accountable to those *over them* in the Lord, accountability naturally works both ways (1 Thessalonians 5:12-13). For instance, if your pastor or worship leader is committing adultery or sneaking finances from the ministry fund, should you remain silent? Obviously not. Anyone who thinks these types of things never happen is naïve. I know pastors who have done both (but thankfully repented).

Speaking of pastors, it should be emphasized: The true ministerial spirit that fivefold ministers (should) have is for **building believers up** and *not* tearing them down (2 Corinthians 10:8 & 13:10). Paul also stressed this in Ephesians 4:11-13 wherein he detailed the purpose of all ministers: "to prepare God's people for works of service, so that the body of Christ may be **built up**."

3. Accountable to God's Word

Believers are accountable to the LORD and each other based on what? Obviously **God's Word**, which informs us **A.** how to live and **B.** what to believe. All Christians—whatever sectarian tag they choose to go by (or not go by)—are to honestly meet at **the blueprint for Christianity, the Word of God**, regarding all matters of morality, practice and doctrine (2 Timothy 3:16-17 & 1 Corinthians 4:6). We all must be humbly willing to concede to the authority of **the God-breathed Scriptures** and what they clearly & consistently teach from a New Covenant perspective based on sound hermeneutics, such as "Scripture interprets Scripture" and "context is king."

We can all legitimately claim ignorance now and then—and the LORD deals with us according to the light we currently possess (John 9:41 & 15:22-24)—but once scriptural revelation is provided, we are obligated to make corrections accordingly.

Examples of Accountability

A minister from America who was working on the other side of the world wrote me in response to one of our extended articles and asked by what authority I'm doing this teaching ministry. Isn't this reminiscent of the disciples' criticism in Luke 9:49?

I humbly answered that I gave the article in question (and our other works) by the authority of the rightly-divided Word of God. He then had the opportunity to respond by explaining what he specifically disagreed with and proving his case from the Holy Scriptures, but he didn't. I'm assuming he investigated the topic further and saw that the article wasn't in error, as he initially thought.

On another occasion a minister from another state wrote and corrected me on a biblical theory featured in a footnote of one of my books. I examined his scriptural support and realized that he was correct and so immediately changed the info in the corresponding articles but, unfortunately, couldn't change the footnote in the book since it was already in print. However, I will fix it if the book is ever rereleased in revised form.

These are examples of two believers meeting at God's Word to settle a matter.

In light of all this, please be careful about denouncing certain believers because they're teaching something you might never have heard before, or their calling is different, or they're not part of *your* group (Romans 14:4). One minister I know was actively trying to reach those involved in sexual perversion and was criticized for it—even slandered—by seasoned believers in ministry positions. Wow, God forbid that anyone would try to reach those most lost amongst us! (Obvious sarcasm). Remember what the

Messiah said to his judgmental disciples: "Do not stop him, for whoever is not against you is for you."

Of course, you should correct sin or false doctrine, as led of the Spirit, assuming you can scripturally back up your case. Yet there's a right way to confront & correct and a wrong way.[8]

'What About Hebrews 13:17?'

This is an understandable question in light of what the verse says:

> **Have confidence in your leaders and <u>submit to their authority</u>, because they keep watch over you as those who must give an account. Do this so that their work will be a joy, not a burden, for that would be of no benefit to you.**
>
> **Hebrews 13:17**

Submission to spiritual authority is good assuming the minister in question consistently bears fruit of the spirit (Matthew 7:15-23) and walks blamelessly before the LORD, which is different from being sinless, since no one on Earth is sinless (1 John 1:8-9, Ecclesiastes 7:20 & 1 Kings 8:46). In other words, there's *healthy* submission and *unhealthy* submission to a spiritual authority.

Obviously you shouldn't obey and submit to any minister in the absolute sense. If your spiritual leaders told you to jump off the roof of a building, should you do it? Of course not. If they instructed you to do something immoral, should you? Clearly not. So these instructions have parameters or limitations, which can be observed throughout the rest of the New Testament.

The exhortation here to submit to spiritual leaders is akin to other appeals in the Epistles for wives to submit to husbands, children to obey parents and believers to submit to governing authorities (Ephesians 5:22-6:9 & Romans 13:1-6). Such instructions are only applicable when the authority gives good or neutral instructions. Otherwise "we must obey God rather than human beings" (Acts 5:29).

---

[8] This is covered at length in my book *How to Handle OFFENSES: Personal & Criminal* or see the corresponding FOL article for free.

The Greek word translated as "obey" in most English versions of Hebrews 13:17 is *peithó (PAI-thoh)*, which means to be persuaded of what is trustworthy. For instance, the Lord *persuades* the yielded believer to be confident in his preferred-will. (Observe how *peithó* is translated as "I am confident" in Galatians 5:10 and as "I am convinced" in 2 Timothy 1:12; this explains the NIV's rendering of the verse in Hebrews as "Have confidence in your leaders"). This involves obedience, yes, but it is **the result of** God's persuasion through **1.** the proper instruction/interpretation of the Word of Truth and **2.** the leading of the Spirit.

So—by all means—be sure to obey what your spiritual leaders **have proven to be true** from God's Word as confirmed in your own study time with the help of your Counselor (1 John 2:27). But never blindly obey anyone, especially if you sense they're putting on big-headed airs to impress or intimidate, which is bluster.

So, Do Believers Need a "Covering" or Not?

If having a 'covering' means believers need to receive from mentors in order to learn to minister effectively then, yes. After all, a 'disciple' is a *learner* since that's what the word actually means, as explained in chapter **4**.

Take the man from Luke 9:49 who was driving out demons and thus stirred up the disciples' envy/rivalry, he obviously heard Christ's public teachings on the believer's authority & faith and so took the initiative to go out and minister to people suffering from demonic oppression. As such, the Messiah was his mentor and this shows that you don't have to know someone personally to be mentored by them. Learn from the person and put what you learn into practice as you have the opportunity and leading.

However, if having a 'covering' means to submit to a human being in ministry in the absolute sense then, no, the Bible does not support this. To do so wouldn't just be questionable, it's unhealthy since it fuels arrogance in the mentor and paves the way for potential abuse. Believers are only to submit to the LORD in the absolute sense (Acts 5:29).

Unhealthy submission to a human mentor can result in *over*reliance and a *dependent* spirit, which will actually hinder the disciple's productivity and prevent him/her from fulfilling their God-given call. For instance, an associate minister in the Midwest informed the senior pastor of his fellowship that he had decided to leave and pursue other ministerial endeavors, led of the Spirit. The pastor sternly told him that it wasn't God's will for him to go and, if he did, he'd "come back crawling on his hands and knees." Can you believe it? No wonder the LORD was calling him out of that shepherd's 'covering.' He followed the Spirit's leading, rather than this pastor who was obviously infected by arrogance, and ended up producing great fruit in ministry in the years to come.

The lesson? Don't allow a flawed human 'covering' (mentor) to prevent you from fulfilling your God-given calling and the many fruit-bearing works thereof. Be guided by your Helper and Counselor.

<u>17</u>

HOW TO DEFLECT DEMONIC SPIRITS

These next five chapters feature the heaviest material of this manual. A lot of it was originally featured in my book *ANGELS*, but I'm including the info here in edited form because the topics are mandatory for the Spiritual Warrior. (For details on peripheral issues, please see that book).

A basic understanding of human nature is necessary to grasp how evil spirits negatively influence people and destroy their lives. This will help the Spiritual Warrior to understand the simple measures we need to take in order to prevent this from happening. These are *simple* actions and they're easy as pie to master.

Let's first establish the essentials of human nature and then observe some key passages that show how malicious spirits negatively sway people.

Human Nature and Spiritual Influence

Human beings are made up of three basic parts: **spirit**, **mind** and **flesh**. Your mind is the center of your being and it's flanked by two opposing natures—spirit and flesh. Your spirit is your higher nature whereas your flesh is your lower nature. Put another way, your spirit is your godly nature while your flesh is the sinful nature. Your spirit is the part of you that inclines toward what is positive, productive and godly because it's the side of you that "delights in God's law" (Romans 7:22). Your flesh, on the other hand, is the part of you that veers toward what is negative, destructive and *un*godly because it's the side of you "where nothing good dwells" (Romans 7:18).

These two natures regularly transmit impulses, images and desires to your mind. The mind is the center of your being; it's the part of you that thinks (intellect), feels (emotion) and makes decisions (volition). Your mind is caught between these opposing natures (Galatians 5:17). In other words, you regularly experience the *conflict* of these two natures in your mind. This diagram helps picture all of this:

While it's not fun being caught in a conflict between two opposing natures, there's good news: Because your mind possesses volition—*will*—you have the God-given **power of decision** and therefore the ability to **DECIDE** which nature you're going to receive from and follow—your godly nature (spirit) or your sinful nature (flesh).

Assuming you're a believer, the Holy Spirit gave birth to your new regenerated spirit (John 3:6 & Titus 3:5), which was "created to be like God in true righteousness and holiness" (Ephesians 4:24). On top of this, you are a temple of the Holy Spirit—a **temple of God**—because the Spirit of God resides *in* you. Exactly what part of your being does the Holy Spirit inhabit? Your spirit, of course, since your spirit was made holy through regeneration (Ephesians 3:16). In fact, it's only *because* your spirit has been reborn **holy** that the *Holy* Spirit is able to indwell you! With this understanding, your spirit—your "new self"—is indwelt and led by the Holy Spirit. So when you follow the impulses of your regenerated human spirit you are simultaneously following the leading of the Holy Spirit.

By contrast, if you follow the impulses of the flesh—the sinful nature—you are automatically following the leading of the devil and filthy spirits because the flesh *is* the sinful nature, which is the satanic nature. In other words, all a person has to do in order to fulfill the devil's will on Earth is to live according to his/her fleshly impulses.

What I'm getting to is this: **The Holy Spirit (God) works with you through your spirit—your godly nature—while demonic spirits work with through your flesh—the sinful nature.**

In light of this, it's imperative that you learn to distinguish spiritual thoughts from fleshly ones. Both types of thoughts will be transmitted to your mind on a regular basis. Once you can distinguish these two kinds of thoughts you simply need to learn to discard the negatives impulses and feed positive ones.

Doing so naturally keeps demonic spirits from being attracted to you and setting up house, so to speak. How so? Because, as we saw at the end of chapter **10**, demons are *impure* spirits and are therefore attracted to what is morally dirty (Matthew 10:1). So keeping moral filth far from your "house"—your mind & body—automatically keeps filthy spirits at bay.

Distinguishing Spiritual Thoughts From Fleshly Ones

To accomplish this, you'll have to learn to differentiate thoughts that originate from your godly nature from impulses that proceed from your sinful nature. The former are positive and productive whereas the latter are negative and destructive. Distinguishing the two is easy.

The Bible offers fairly detailed descriptions of what these conflicting natures produce:

> **<u>The acts of the flesh</u> are obvious: sexual immorality, impurity and debauchery; [20] idolatry and witchcraft; hatred, discord, jealousy, fits of rage, selfish ambition, dissensions, factions [21] and envy; drunkenness, orgies, and the like. I warn you, as I did before, that those who live like this will not inherit the kingdom of God.**
> **[22] But <u>the fruit of the spirit</u> is love, joy, peace, forbearance, kindness, goodness, faith-fulness,**

²³gentleness and self-control. Against such things there is no law.

Galatians 5:19-23

Every believer has to learn to recognize and throw off thoughts that stem from the flesh, like sexual immorality, hatred, discord, jealousy, rage, selfishness, envy and other obvious carnal traits, such as arrogance, deceit and slander (Proverbs 6:16-19). Don't feed these types of thoughts. Instead feed thoughts that stem from your spirit, your higher nature, which is why Paul said:

> **Finally, brothers and sisters, <u>whatever is true</u>, whatever is <u>noble</u>, whatever is <u>right</u>, whatever is <u>pure</u>, whatever is <u>lovely</u>, whatever is <u>admirable</u>—if anything is <u>excellent</u> or <u>praiseworthy</u>—<u>think about such things</u>. ⁹ Whatever you have learned or received or heard from me, or seen in me—put it into practice. <u>And the God of peace will be with you.</u>**

Philippians 4:8-9

The more you "feed" positive, productive thoughts like these, the more you'll live out of your higher nature. It's simple. The Bible puts it like this:

> **Those who live according to <u>the flesh</u> set <u>their minds</u> on the things of <u>the flesh</u>; but those who live according to <u>the spirit</u>⁹ set <u>their minds</u> on the things of <u>the spirit</u>.**

Romans 8:5

So learning to set your mind on things of the spirit rather than things of the flesh is key to walking free of the satanic nature and the influence of evil spirits.

---

⁹ Because there is no capitalization in the biblical Greek, translators must determine if "spirit" should be capitalized in reference to the Holy Spirit or not capitalized in reference to the human spirit. Many translations capitalize "spirit" in these passages and some do not (for example The New English Bible). Since these passages (and other such passages) are plainly referring to the human spirit, "spirit" should not be capitalized because the context is contrasting the conflicting parts of human nature, as indicated in Matthew 26:41. In a way it makes no significant difference since the believer's born-again human spirit is indwelt and led by the Holy Spirit (Ephesians 3:16).

Also, as verse 9 of the Philippians passage instructs, get in the habit of observing genuinely spiritual believers (not religious people) and put into practice the positive things you observe. When you practice these two things, notice what results: "and the God of peace will be with you." Needless to say, filthy spirits will *not* be attracted to you when you do this (which is *not* to say that they won't attack you for righteousness' sake when permitted, which is explained in chapter **20**).

Managing the Soil of Your Heart

It helps to understand the biblical concept of **the heart** and how it fits into the model of human nature.

"Heart" is *kardia (kar-DEE-ah)* in the Greek, which is where we get the English 'cardiac.' Like the English word 'heart,' *kardia* literally refers to the blood-pumping organ but figuratively to the **core thoughts or feelings of a person's being or mind** (Strong 39). Greek scholar E.W. Bullinger describes the heart as **"the seat and center** of man's personal life in which the distinctive **character** of the human manifests itself" (362). The heart could therefore be described as the core of the mind. It is *part* of the mind, but specifically refers to the deepest, most central part; that is, **the core**.

What dwells in your heart is determined by which nature you have *decided* to live by, whether spirit or flesh (Romans 8:5-6). Jesus said, "The good man brings good things out of the good stored up in his heart, and the evil man brings evil things out of the evil stored up in his heart" (Luke 6:45). What does this mean? Simple: If you, in your mind, *decide* to dwell on carnal thoughts, then carnal, negative, destructive things will naturally store up in your heart over time. If, on the other hand, you *choose* to focus on spiritual thoughts, then good, positive, productive things will store up in your heart. Whatever's *in* your heart then determines your actions and therefore the course of your very life. This is why the book of wisdom says: **"Be careful what you think for your thoughts run your life"** (Proverbs 4:23 NCV). Take heed—truer words have never been spoken!

Here's our diagram of human nature with the heart added:

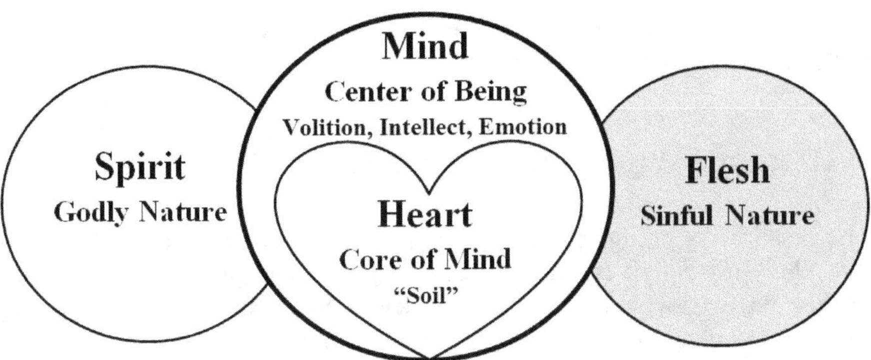

Notice that the heart is the core of your mind and is figuratively called "soil." Why? Because the Bible likens the heart to **soil** (Luke 8:15). Soil in the natural is a neutral substance that grows whatever seed is planted in it. This is the way it is with the soil of your heart, except that it grows non-physical "seeds," whether spiritual or *un*spiritual. By "seeds" I mean thoughts, impulses, desires, images or impressions. Dwelling on these "seeds" waters them, so to speak, and thus enables them to grow. In short, your meditation *feeds* them; and that is how they grow. Whatever grows in your heart is what eventually fills your heart and produces the desires thereof. These desires of your heart then determine your actions, good or bad.

Has someone ever offended you and you dwelt on it so much that you made more of it than what it was? When the issue was finally resolved, you realized you made a mountain out of a mole hill. How did this happen? Simple: You fed the offense with your thought life and thus it grew. As you kept thinking about it, the bigger it got. This principle goes into motion with any impulse you choose to focus on and give life to, whether of the spirit or of the flesh.

In regards to fleshly impulses, the Bible details the scenario like so:

> **but each person is tempted when they are dragged away <u>by their own evil desire</u> and enticed. [15] Then, after desire has conceived, it gives birth to sin; and sin, when it is full-grown, gives birth to death.**
>
> **James 1:14-15**

People are tempted by evil desires that stem from their flesh, the sinful nature. Once they grab ahold of the bad impulse and feed it with their thought life, desire is conceived in their hearts, which eventually gives birth to the action, the sin itself.

Demons Work With People Through Their Flesh

The reason I'm going into detail about human nature is so you'll grasp how **the Holy Spirit (God) works with you through your spirit, your higher nature, whereas evil spirits work to destroy you (and those linked to you) through your flesh, the sinful nature**.

Because the flesh is the satanic nature, all a person has to do in order to be "of the devil" is to habitually live out of his/her sinful nature. For instance, envy, jealousy, rivalry, hatred and strife are works of the flesh. If a person regularly lives out of these fleshly impulses, he or she will automatically carry out the Devil's will in whatever environment s/he operates.

Take a woman at an assembly who embraces thoughts of envy and jealousy. This naturally gives birth to rivalry and hostility toward the people with whom she's envious and jealous. Hostility is hatred. There are degrees of hostility, of course, but—whatever the degree—hatred always eventually morphs into unjust attacks, starting with malevolent gossip, which is slander. This of course poisons people's minds against their maligned brother or sister in the Lord, which then produces discord in the assembly and robs the fellowship of peace and unity. Every Christian assembly on Earth has experienced this scenario and the root problem can always be traced to an individual who gave-in to the fleshly impulses of envy, jealousy & rivalry and then spread the resulting hostility to others.

Or consider the example of a married Christian man who meets an alluring woman on the job and it stirs up fleshly interest. The more he *thinks* about her, the more desire grows in his heart until it manifests into adultery when the opportunity presents itself.

In both of these cases, neither the woman who gossiped and created strife at her assembly nor the man who committed adultery were possessed by evil spirits. They simply ignored the leading of their higher nature (and the corresponding guidance of the Spirit) and surrendered to their fleshly desires by feeding them with their thought life, which made the corresponding desire grow in the soil of their hearts. And then they eventually acted on these desires.

Allow me to point out that the word 'spirit' does not always refer to a spiritual entity; it can simply refer to a person's character, as in Joshua had "a different spirit" than other Hebrews and thus served the LORD wholeheartedly (Numbers 14:24). Neither the woman who engaged in hostile gossip, which created strife in her fellowship, nor the man who committed adultery was possessed by demons to do what they did. They simply gave their hearts over to the destructive impulses of their flesh, fed those desires, which then grew in their hearts, and ultimately acted on them. As such, the woman had a spirit of gossip and strife—a *character* of gossip and strife; and the man had a spirit of adultery—a *character* of adultery.

Yet neither was possessed by a demon to do what they did. They have no one to blame but themselves for their foolish decisions. Remember, we all have **the power of decision** and therefore we *decide* which nature we're going to live out of, whether flesh or spirit, sinful nature or godly nature. It's our choice every day.

However, this is not to say that demonic spirits didn't "whisper in their ears," so to speak (which we'll look at momentarily). Not to mention, once they started engaging in their particular sin, it no doubt attracted evil spirits because filthy spirits are drawn to that which is morally impure, much like flies are attracted to dog poop and vermin to garbage.

In chapter **10** I shared how an anointed minister would pick up a stench in the spirit when sexual perverts came up for prayer as he was ministering. I also shared how a boy, my nephew, smelled vomit when he was around a practicing witch who married into the family. People who take paths that are morally dirty like these—sexual perversion and witchcraft—naturally attract filthy spirits. This results in demonic bondage to the sin, at best; and demonic possession, at worst. I'm not saying this with Pharisaical condescension or condemnation, but rather godly compassion and the desire to see people set free, whatever their transgression is, whether sexual immorality, witchcraft, adultery, gossip/slander, religious legalism, drunkard-ness or what have you.

Needless to say, don't entertain impulses of the flesh. Learn to put into motion the law of displacement by focusing on impulses of your higher nature (Ephesians 4:22-24). Concentrating on spiritual thoughts naturally displaces carnal desires. This keeps evils spirits at bay because they're not attracted to that which is pure, godly and spiritual. And when they observe that a person is stubbornly single-minded, they'll give-up and seek easier prey. Remember: sloth is a trait of the satanic nature and so impure spirits are lazy by nature.

How Does satan "Fill a Person's Heart"?

All of the above helps us to interpret a couple cases in the Bible where it says that satan filled a person's heart.

Let's start with the case of Ananias from Acts 5:1-11. This was the era of the early Church where believers were selling land and extra houses to provide money for the needy in the fellowship (Acts 4:32-37). Ananias followed suit by selling a piece of property and giving the proceeds to the church, but he kept a good chunk for himself. There was nothing wrong with this and Peter even said so (Acts 5:4). It was Ananias' property and his money; and he could do whatever he wanted with it, as led of the Spirit. The problem was that Ananias and his wife deceptively said they gave *all* the proceeds to the church, evidently to appear exceptionally generous and spiritual. Thus Peter asks: "Ananias, how is it that <u>Satan has so filled your heart</u> that you have lied to the Holy Spirit and have kept for yourself some of the money you received for the land?" (verse 3).

How did satan fill Ananias' heart? Did he literally possess him? No, he filled his heart in the sense that Ananias gave his mind over to the fleshly impulses of the sinful nature, which is the satanic nature. Ananias wanted to impress others by appearing more generous than he actually was, so he lied about giving all the profit of his sale when he only gave part.

This is the typical way the devil fills a person's heart, which we observed in the examples from the previous section: satan filled the heart of the woman who succumbed to envy and hostility, which resulted in gossip and produced strife in the assembly. The married man surrendered to his carnal lust for a flirtatious female at work and allowed desire to build in his heart until it manifested in adultery. The devil "filled their hearts" in the sense that they gave themselves over to the cravings of the satanic nature, but they weren't possessed by satan or demons. Are you following?

How Did satan Fill Judas' Heart?

The case of Judas Iscariot shows that satan or demons can fill people's hearts more literally. Judas, of course, was the fake disciple who betrayed

Christ for 30 pieces of silver. This reveals that his main problem was greed (that is, his main problem beyond not actually *knowing* the Lord). The Bible blatantly describes him as a thief who regularly pilfered from the treasury of Jesus' ministry (John 12:6). The Lord knew what was going on, of course, because he functioned in the gifts of the Spirit, one being the word of knowledge (1 Corinthians 12:4-11).

Thus Yeshua indirectly referred to Judas as "a devil" well before this incident (John 6:70-71). Why? Not because Judas was literally possessed by an evil spirit at the time, but because he walked in the flesh without repentance and therefore wasn't a genuine follower of Christ. Anyone who chooses to live out of their flesh will automatically perform the will of the devil because the flesh is the sinful nature, the satanic nature. This is why the Lord called Judas "a devil"—his allegiance was clearly to the devil, even though he wasn't likely aware of it.

That said, a couple of other passages reveal that satan literally possessed Judas on two separate occasions over a year later:

> **Then Satan entered Judas, called Iscariot, one of the Twelve.**
>
> **Luke 22:3**

> **As soon as Judas took the bread, Satan entered into him.**
> **So Jesus told him, "What you are about to do, do quickly."**
>
> **John 13:27**

The verse from Luke is talking about when Judas skulked away to the chief priests to agree to betray the Lord for a monetary reward. The verse from John takes place over a day later during the Last Supper, which is when Christ discharged Judas from the celebratory meal to betray him.

The texts do not contradict one another because John acknowledges the first occasion where Judas was possessed in verse 2 of the same chapter (John 13): "The evening meal was in progress, and **the devil had already prompted Judas**, the son of Simon Iscariot, to betray Jesus." This refers to the events of the Luke passage.

We can glean a few important facts from both verses:

- Satan possessed Judas not once, but twice
- There was an interim period between the two possessions in which Judas was not possessed. This fact indicates a *partial* possession.
- Even though Judas' will was not under the direct control of the devil during the interim, he did not 'fess up or seek to undo Christ's unjust arrest which he had set in motion.

No doubt the Sovereign LORD insisted on the interim so that Iscariot had time to reflect on what he had done, graciously providing him the opportunity to repent.[10] Since Judas didn't have a change of heart, however, he was without excuse. In other words, Judas couldn't justify his actions on the grounds that "the devil made him do it."

A fourth point is that this kind of demonic possession does not come out of nowhere. A person isn't just morally heading one way one day; then is suddenly possessed by a demon and proceeds to go in a totally different direction. No, possession of this nature occurs when a person has *already* given in to the sinful nature and is therefore *already* habitually fulfilling the devil's will, which naturally attracts wicked spirits. If the person is eventually possessed by demons, he or she simply goes deeper down the same fleshly path s/he was going.

We see this with Judas: He was *already* habitually stealing from the treasury because of his greed. Jesus knew this early on due to the word of knowledge and thus thoroughly interceded for the thief. Christ even made it known that he was on to him outright (John 6:70-71). Unfortunately, Judas remained impenitent. His eventual succumbing to the temptation of blood money for Christ's arrest was simply deeper down the same dark road. *It wasn't until **then** that satan possessed him.*

Of course, Judas' possession was a special case that warranted the devil's direct involvement. When satan possesses the Antichrist during the future Tribulation it's likewise a special occasion (2 Thessalonians 2:9 & Revelation 13:2). In the vast majority of cases, however, satan prefers to kick back and allow his filthy underlings to perform hands-on work like this (i.e. possess people).

---

[10] God reigns supreme, which includes reigning over the devil who's the temporary "god of this world" (2 Corinthians 4:4). Thus even satan has to have permission to carry out his wicked attacks, as shown in Job 1:6-12 and 2:1-7. That said, this is a general truth and it's uncertain how far and detailed it extends concerning any given satanic strategy and the target(s) thereof.

It's important to distinguish between demonic possession that occurs due to increasing immoral activity (as was the case with Judas) and demonic possession by a spirit of infirmity, which results in some kind of mental/physical malady. This latter type of possession may have nothing to do with a person participating in immorality. For instance, the boy who had a mute, deaf spirit (Mark 9:17-29) and the woman with the crippling demon (Luke 13:10-16). There is zero indication that either of them suffered possession and the corresponding maladies due to increasing, unrepentant immorality.

This shows that living a morally blameless life (which, of course, requires keeping in repentance[11]) is not enough to walk free of demonic possession as far as spirits of infirmities are concerned. Having a close relationship with God is not enough either. Why? Because these kinds of spirits prey upon **the ignorant**. Hosea 4:6 comes to mind. The only antidote to ignorance is knowledge; and knowledge is power, assuming it is implemented (Proverbs 24:5). Any believer who knows and practices the scriptural truths detailed in this chapter & the following four will protect themselves from spirits of infirmities.

This illustrates the difference between:

- The Person of God.
- The wisdom principles of God's kingdom.

It's possible to genuinely know God, but be ignorant of the principles of God's kingdom, including spiritual warfare. Likewise, it's possible to grasp principles of godly wisdom and yet not know the LORD whatsoever. For instance, an atheist doesn't know God—and possibly hates God—but because he lives by the principle that "diligent hands will rule" (Proverbs 12:24) he prospers in his occupation.

The ideal, of course, is to walk in *both:* **1.** Develop a relationship with the Person of God and **2.** learn the wise principles of God's kingdom.

This brings up the question of…

---

[11] See Matthew & Luke 3:8. Keep in mind that being blameless is not the same as being sinless, as covered in chapter **11**.

Can Believers Be Possessed?

The answer is no and yes. Let me explain…

True believers can never be *totally* possessed because they're already indwelt by the Holy Spirit (Romans 8:9). Of course, evil spirits are assigned to believers to try to oppress them and ruin their lives—the very opposite of what heavenly angels are commissioned to do (which is to serve people, as observed in Hebrews 1:14). This shows why learning and mastering spiritual warfare is vital as we grow in Christ.

Genuine believers cannot drink of the cup of the Lord and the cup of demons as well (1 Corinthians 10:21). To be *fully* possessed of a demon or demons, a believer would have to first fall away by denying Christ, whether literally or through incorrigibly wicked actions. For proof that a Christian can indeed fall away, see Hebrews 6:4-9, 2 Peter 2:20-21, 2 Timothy 2:11-13 and Titus 1:16. I want to emphasize that **God's Word supports the doctrine of eternal security 100%** and this is verified by Christ himself in John 10:28-29. However, the Bible clearly does not support the doctrine of *unconditional* eternal security, as verified by these crystal-clear passages and numerous others.[12]

Although genuine believers cannot be fully possessed, they can fall prey to *partial possession*. Here are two types of partial possession observed in the Scriptures:

1. A person suffers possession by a spirit of infirmity, which causes some type of ongoing physical disorder. In this scenario, a spirit of infirmity induces a malady, but the person is otherwise uncontrolled by the spirit. The woman from Luke 13:10-16 whose crippling condition was caused by a demon and required exorcism is a good example. There's no evidence that she *wasn't* in control of her faculties. Thus this demon caused her crippling state, but it did not control her mind and will. It had power over her physically, but not mentally. It was thus a *partial* possession.

2. Another kind of partial possession is when a spirit takes control of a person's mental faculties one way or another, but **the spirit comes and goes** and thus it's not a perpetual condition. This was the case with a woman I personally knew. She was decidedly a Christian, but

---

[12] For details see the section in chapter **20** *The Enemy WILL Attack these God-Given Blessings*. Also see the article *Once Saved Always Saved?* at the FOL site.

an evil spirit would come on her now and then, with two different manifestations—a depressed, worried state or a mean, stubborn state. Both of these manifestations were thoroughly demonic and she occasionally committed self-harm in one form or another. Yet she was her normal, pure, loving self about 50% of the time. Since the evil spirit came and went it wasn't a total possession, but rather a partial one. This is evidence that a true believer can suffer partial possession where a demon comes on him or her from time to time and wreaks havoc. It's not a total possession, but such people need exorcized nevertheless, like the boy in Mark 9:18 and Luke 9:39.

In cases where believers suffer partial possession, the demon attacks their body or mind, but it cannot afflict their spirit because they are indwelt by the Holy Spirit (Ephesians 3:16).

Satanic Head Games

It was pointed out earlier that fallen angels are able to "whisper in a person's ear," that is, shoot thoughts into people's minds, obviously corresponding to the desires and weaknesses of their flesh. Consider Christ's temptation after the Spirit led him to fast in the wilderness for 40 days and nights:

> **Then Jesus was led by the Spirit into the wilderness to be tempted by the devil. [2] After fasting forty days and forty nights, he was hungry. [3] <u>The tempter came to him and said</u>, "If you are the Son of God, tell these stones to become bread."**
> **[4] Jesus answered, "It is written: 'Man shall not live on bread alone, but on every word that comes from the mouth of God.' "**
> **[5] <u>Then the devil took him to the holy city and had him stand on the highest point of the temple.</u> [6] "<u>If you are the Son of God,</u>" he said, "<u>throw yourself down.</u> For it is written:**
> **'He will command his angels concerning you,**
> **and they will lift you up in their hands,**
> **so that you will not strike your foot against a stone.'"**
> **[7] Jesus answered him, "It is also written: 'Do not put the Lord your God to the test.' "**

> [8] Again, <u>the devil took him to a very high mountain and showed him all the kingdoms of the world and their splendor.</u> [9] <u>"All this I will give you,"</u> he said, <u>"if you will bow down and worship me."</u>
> [10] Jesus said to him, "Away from me, Satan! For it is written: 'Worship the Lord your God, and serve him only.' "
> [11] Then the devil left him, and angels came and attended him.
>
> **Matthew 4:1-11**

This occasion warranted satan's direct involvement. He knew that the Mighty Christ came to destroy his work[13] so he personally tried to stop the Messiah by tempting him to succumb to the weaknesses of his flesh and therefore sin. This, of course, would've made Jesus unacceptable as a substitutionary curse for humanity since the sacrifice had to be innocent.

Notice that verse 3 says "The tempter came to him and said…". Did the devil actually *appear* to the Lord or did he come to him and 'whisper in his ear,' so to speak? In other words, did he come to him invisibly and simply transmit the tempting words to his mind? The Greek word for "came to" doesn't necessarily mean appear visibly, but simply 'to come to, come near to, approach.' Since satan is a spiritual being, not physical, it's more likely that he came to the Messiah spiritually and therefore invisibly, although Christ no doubt discerned his presence through the gift of discerning of spirits (1 Corinthians 12:4-11).

I'm not saying that satan *didn't* appear to Yeshua in some physical form, just that it's very possible that he simply came to him spiritually— invisibly—and spoke to him by shooting flesh-based suggestions into his head. This is how evil spirits try to negatively influence you and me, why wouldn't it be the same in this situation?

Someone might understandably argue that verses 5 & 8 show the devil taking Christ to the highest point of the Temple in Jerusalem and then to a high mountain, but satan could've taken him there in a mental sense, relaying his temptation in thought form or perhaps a vision. After all, have you ever been tempted wherein an evil spirit *physically appeared* to you or *physically transported* you to the applicable environment or did you

---

[13] See Hebrews 2:14, 1 John 3:8 and Acts 10:38.

simply experience the temptation through thoughts, impulses and the imagery thereof? The latter, of course.

The Sword of the Spirit and the Law of Displacement

Christ counteracted these temptations by simply **speaking the truth**. On all three occasions Jesus responded with a quote from the Scriptures. This is what we need to do when we encounter temptation: When you experience an inner carnal impulse, perhaps combined with the corresponding imagery, recognize it for what it is—a negative, destructive, ungodly temptation rooted in the flesh. **Then** boldly speak the counteractive truth. Repeat as necessary until the temptation lifts. This is one of our God-given spiritual weapons; it's called **the sword of the spirit** (Ephesians 6:17). It's simply speaking the Word of God in bold faith as a defensive or offensive tool. Use it! This "sword" does you no good if you don't take advantage of it. It guarantees victory over temptation.

You'll notice in the second temptation that the devil quoted a Scripture verse. Please understand that satan & evil spirits know the Scriptures and will sometimes use them to tempt people to take a wrong path, just as the devil did here with Yeshua. The Messiah recognized that satan's usage of this verse conflicted with other truths, of course, and so he cited *another* passage that gave balance to the matter, which is in line with the hermeneutical guideline "Scripture interprets Scripture."

You can only do this *if* you're familiar with the Scriptures, so I encourage you to acquaint yourself with God's Word more and more by developing a daily reading (or audio) program. Try different reading (or audio) plans until you find one that fits your lifestyle and schedule. Change your plan every now and then so it doesn't get predictable and boring. Also switch translations from time to time; and consider plans based on topical studies. *Pray for* knowledge, understanding and wisdom on a regular basis and the LORD will bless you (Proverbs 2:1-7).

It's important as well to understand that the enemy can tempt you **through a person or group** who cite Scripture (2 Corinthians 11:13-15). The Jehovah's False Witnesses are a relevant example. Yet such a temptation can very well come through people functioning under the tag of whatever camp you favor (Baptist, Evangelical, Charismatic, Reformed, Mainline, Pentecostal, Independent, etc.). Thankfully, it's easy to recognize these fakes, if you know for what to look. Speaking of which…

Christ said that false prophets can be recognized **by their fruit** (Matthew 7:15-23). A false prophet is simply a minister who falsely speaks for God and you can identify them by the fruit they bear. Do they produce fruit of the spirit on a regular basis or works of the flesh? (Galatians 5:19-23). No one is perfect, of course, but what do they *habitually* produce? And are they willing to humbly 'fess up and apologize when they miss it (1 John 1:8-9). Do they have a spirit of love or a spirit of abuse? Do they build up or tear down? Genuine ministers are called to build up, not tear down (2 Corinthians 10:8 & 13:10). After giving appropriate correction, they build-up and encourage, not condemn. Needless to say, if you observe consistent bad fruit and an unwillingness to keep with repentance in a "minister" then **head for the hills** (Matthew 15:14).

One last thing on this matter: When you 'swing' your sword of the spirit by speaking the truth in bold faith, it doesn't have to be a word-for-word verse or even a Scripture text at all. It simply has to be **truth**, which is **the way it really is**. Say, for example, a wicked spirit whispers in your ear that you're a no-good piece of excrement who can't do anything right. You don't have to quote an *exact* Scripture to counteract this lie, just speak the truth: "I'm a child of God born of the seed of Christ by the power of the Holy Spirit; I was *born* righteous and can do all things through him who strengthens me!" If you're familiar with the Bible, you know this is a personalized paraphrase of several verses.

But, again, you don't have to cite from Scripture at all to counteract a temptation—whether word-for-word or paraphrasing—as long as what you say is **the truth**. For instance, we earlier considered the example of a married man who was tempted by a coquettish lass at work. All he has to say to thwart the temptation is the truth: "I am a *married* man of the Most High God! I *love* my wife and am faithful to her and God!"

When you do this, you're putting into motion **the Law of Displacement**, which means that two things cannot occupy the same space at the same time. It applies to your thought life in this particular case: When you experience a tempting thought, you counteract it by simply speaking (and thinking) the counteractive truth, which displaces the negative thought. Repeat as necessary. When you do this, you're swinging your sword of the spirit and slicing down the lies of the enemy.

Another thing you can do is sing praise & worship songs. Blast some music and have a praise & worship session; or do it yourself, like David did in the Psalms (e.g. Psalm 8 and 65). Praise & worship is a powerful spiritual weapon because praise ushers in God's manifest presence and there's fullness of joy in the presence of the LORD (Psalm 100:4 & 16:11).

Examples of Demonic Head Games

The Bible repeatedly shows that the LORD *knows* our thoughts, which of course includes the Holy Spirit (1 Corinthians 2:11, Psalm 94:11 & Proverbs 20:27). But the devil and his loser minions lack this power. All they can do is determine your weaknesses by observing you; and tempt you by shooting ideas into your mind corresponding to the weaknesses of the flesh, like lust, greed, pride, envy, jealousy, fear and doubt.

We know that angels are assigned to people to serve them (Hebrews 1:14). It's the same thing in the kingdom of darkness, except that demons *disservice* people through misleading, hindering, oppression or possession. In short, they want to ruin people's lives.

With this in mind, say a demon is assigned to a woman. This spirit cannot read her thoughts, but it can observe her actions and words day & night and so ascertain her fleshly weaknesses. The demon then transmits thoughts into her mind accordingly in the hope of ruining her one way or another. The spirit can also lure into her life the 'right' people to assist in the diabolic plot; that is, the *wrong* people.

This is likely what happened with a teenage girl who embraced demonic thoughts and became convinced that she was going to be "taken" one day and her mother & sister would never see her again. She repeatedly shared this curious belief with her mother & sister. Once the (presumed) evil spirit manipulated her into using the power of her mind in conjunction with the power of her tongue (Proverbs 18:21), the next step was to inspire the right psychopath to meet her at the wrong time and place. Thus she was apprehended, raped and tragically wiped off the face of the planet. This case was featured on Unsolved Mysteries.

Now consider the hypothetical woman we talked about earlier who caused strife in her fellowship due to her envies and jealousies. The demon (or demons) assigned to her would observe that she had issues with envy/jealousy/rivalry and so it would draw into her life the right person or persons who would stir up these fleshly impulses. Meeting these people would produce hostility in her—that is, hatred—and so she would start gossiping and slandering, which would in turn produce discord in the assembly, the precise opposite of what the Lord wants (Psalm 133).

It's the same thing with that hypothetical married man who was enticed by an alluring woman at work. The wicked spirit (or spirits) assigned to him would notice his penchant for a certain type of female and then lure into his environment the fitting candidate. The man would experience unwholesome impulses from his flesh, particularly when the woman flirts with him. The demon might assist in the temptation by transmitting thoughts into his mind. In other words, this spirit "whispers into his ear" corresponding to the evil desires of his flesh. Once he grabs ahold of the idea and feeds it with his thought life, desire is conceived in his heart and keeps growing as he feeds it. He eventually falls into adultery when the opportunity presents itself.

This is how evil spirits work behind-the-scenes in regards to any type of sin.

A Real-Life Story

Let me share an actual example. When I was a young man, shortly out of high school, I hooked up with this singer who was still in school for the purpose of starting a band. I'll call her Laura. We attended the same megachurch.

While the band thing didn't work out, I was impressed by Laura's devotion to God and her genuine evangelistic spirit. She told me several stories about being a witness for Christ at her school and so forth. After graduating high school, she quickly went off to college and I fell out of touch with her. Unfortunately, her rock-solid Christian family experienced several serious blows within the course of a year, starting with her father, who was a respected deacon at the fellowship. He committed adultery and the marriage eventually fell apart. Around the same time Laura's younger sister, who was 17, died in a tragic car wreck. On top of all this, her first year at university didn't go well, to put it mildly. She was assaulted by the wave of ungodly humanism that secular colleges are known for and suffered sexual abuse, possibly date raped, I don't know. She dropped out of college and came home, but didn't return to her former assembly.

A close friend ran into her a couple years after these events and said she was palpably bitter. He brought up the Lord, but she didn't want anything to do with God or Christianity. That was over three decades ago and I'm unaware of what happened to her after that.

This tale shows that no one is exempt from satanic attack. If you're a threat to the devil's kingdom you *will* be attacked. If you fail to take advantage of the armor & weaponry that God has faithfully provided and "fight the good fight of faith" the enemy will take you out, just like this young woman.

Simply put, you can't half-buttocks it with the Lord. I've known several guys who got saved and went to church gatherings for a long season, but they never came to a point of taking the things of God seriously enough. They continued to flirt with the flesh and the world to some degree. I'm talking about things like boozing, porn, drugs, smoking, fornication and the like. They ended up losing their marriages, their jobs and basically becoming down-and-out. Three ended up in prison. A few have died.

But—and this is an important "but"—I'm confident that this will not be the case with *you*. If you've come this far in this book then you obviously have a thirst for knowing the LORD and what God's Word says about being a victorious Spiritual Warrior and your responsibility thereof as a New Covenant believer.

As insinuated, one of the keys to overcoming the enemy's attacks is to utilize God's armor & weaponry, which we'll address in chapter **19**. Here we're going to focus on a couple of other demonic strategies. The Bible instructs us to be aware of the devil's schemes so that we're not outwitted (2 Corinthians 2:11).

How the Enemy Blinds People's Minds

The Scriptures show that the enemy has the power to blind people's minds:

> **And even if our gospel is veiled, it is <u>veiled</u> to those who are perishing. [4] <u>The god of this age has blinded the minds of unbelievers,</u> so that <u>they cannot</u> see the light of the gospel that displays the glory of Christ, who is the image of God.**
>
> **2 Corinthians 4:3-4**

The devil & his loser minions don't want people to comprehend the awesome message of Christ because "it is the power of God that brings salvation" and sets them free (Romans 1:16). Evil spirits therefore veil it "to those who are perishing."

"Veil" means to hide, conceal or keep secret. How exactly do wicked spirits conceal the gospel to unbelievers? Do they unleash a spiritual fog around their minds? Not literally, but in a sense, yes: They blind people's minds by implanting an erroneous ideology, which is the result of embracing "deceiving spirits and things taught by demons" (1 Timothy 4:1). More traditional English versions refer to this as "doctrines of demons" or "doctrines of devils" (NASB & KJV). "Doctrines" is another word for teachings or instructions; so "doctrines of demons" simply refers to the *teachings* or *instructions* of unclean spirits.

While these false teachings originate from a demon whispering error in someone's ear, so to speak, they are passed to others through a human agent—someone who's already blinded by the warped indoctrination. The Bible describes such people as "hypocritical liars, whose consciences have been seared as with a hot iron" (1 Timothy 4:2). Although the context refers to false teachers in the Church, how much more so in the world? Lib college professors are Exhibit A. As people give ear to these warped teachings, they naturally develop an ideology; and this indoctrination— this perspective or mindset—blinds them to the good news of the gospel and the truths of the Word of God in general.

To understand how this works, let's look at…

Noémas—Mindsets, Ideologies

Notice what the Bible exhorts us to do:

> **We demolish arguments and every pretension that sets itself up against the knowledge of God, and we take captive every thought to make it obedient to Christ.**
> **2 Corinthians 10:5**

Christ is the living Word of God who is the truth (John 1:1 & 14:6). So we are to "take captive" thoughts and make sure that they comply with the truth. 'Truth' is *alétheia (ah-LAY-thee-ah)* in the Greek, which means "reality" or "the way it really is." So we are to take "thoughts" and make sure that they conform to **reality**. If they don't comply with the truth then they are 'weeds' of *un*reality and should be purged from the soil of our hearts.

The word 'thought' in this passage is *noéma* in the Greek *(NOH-ay-mah)*. While *noéma* can refer to thoughts, good or bad, it can also refer to **a person's perspective—mindset, attitude** or **ideology**—which is the result of indoctrination, positive or negative. Indoctrination is naturally determined by the doctrine—the teaching or instruction—to which you are regularly exposed. For instance, if you sit under a secular humanist professor long enough and don't counteract what s/he teaches with the truth of the rightly-divided Word of God (or the truth *period*) you'll naturally develop a secular humanist ideology. You'll then start to live out of this mindset, to one degree or another. The doctrine or teachings you're exposed to on a regular basis will determine your indoctrination, which is your mindset, good or bad. Such a mindset is a noéma.

The Greek word for "doctrine" is *didaskalia (did-as-ka-LEE-ah)*, which—as noted above—means teaching or instruction. It can be positive or negative depending on how true the teaching is or is not. The Bible speaks of sound doctrine (1 Timothy 4:6) and bad doctrine:

> **Now the Spirit expressly states that in later times some will abandon the faith to follow deceitful spirits and the <u>teachings</u>** *(didaskaliais)* **of demons,**
> **1 Timothy 4:1** (ESV)

Obviously the teachings of demons aren't good because demons are *deceitful* spirits.

The point is that a person's mindset or ideology—noéma—is determined by the teachings to which he or she is regularly exposed. Noémas formulate over the course of time as a person is fed information. The longer it takes for a noéma to develop, the more imbedded it is in the individual's psyche.

It is through negative noémas that the enemy "blinds the minds of unbelievers, so that they cannot see the light" (2 Corinthians 4:4). The devil has control of their minds—through demonic noémas—and the truth cannot penetrate the indoctrination. To help you visualize this, I went to the Facebook page of a Christian friend I hadn't seen for over 30 years and was surprised by his cover pic. It was a skull with a red dragon wrapped around its head. No doubt he chose this pic because he thought it looked 'cool' or whatever, but it's actually an excellent illustration of how the enemy blinds people's minds: The red dragon represents the devil and he has control of the person's mind, which is depicted as a skull and symbolizing death, the natural result of satanic misleading.

Notice how 2 Corinthians 10:5 (quoted above) says we are to "take captive" thoughts and mindsets. The Greek for 'take captive' literally means to "take captive as a prisoner and interrogate." The Bible is saying that we should take any perspective we have and honestly examine it, making sure it conforms to reality (the way it really is) rather than unreality (the way it really isn't). If we discover that the mindset does *not* comply with reality then it needs to be thrown out.

This can apply to any doctrine—*teaching*—you were taught during your formative years as a believer. Just because you were indoctrinated by a particular teaching in a relatively sound sect by a respected pastor doesn't make the doctrine true. So you need to "interrogate" it in light of reality. Does it comply with the rightly-divided Word of Truth and the Spirit of truth (John 17:17 & 16:13)? If not, it needs to be discarded in favor of whatever the truth is, which is reality.

As pointed out above, this applies to secular indoctrination as well, such as the godless humanism that's commonly taught at secular schools. Generally speaking, these professors teach that the idea of an intelligent Creator is absurd and thus life is meaningless; you're just an accident. There's nothing special about human beings, they say, and we're basically just animals. And, when ya die, that's it. The consequences of this kind of brainwashing are devastating—it produces moral rot and an attitude of no respect for life, including one's own; it encourages living with a temporal perspective (noéma) rather than an eternal one (noéma). Such a hedonistic philosophy can be summed up as: "Let us eat and drink, for tomorrow we die" (1 Corinthians 15:32).

One example of secular indoctrination is sexual perversion. While this was still a crime in much of the USA as of the new millennium, that's all changed. Now sexual perversion is taught to be innate and healthy in our secular culture and people are encouraged to experiment with perversion and embrace it as a legitimate alternative lifestyle. Our secular mentors are increasingly active perverts. Parents allow their children to sit under them where they're exposed to their smooth propaganda and then wonder why some of their offspring eventually embrace the lifestyle of sexual perversion. Notable people who publicly "come out" are commended by celebrities and governing officials alike. Those who refuse to approve, by contrast, are considered evil bigots and punished severely, socially speaking. The truth about sexual perversion, however, is that it's a damning sin and those who unrepentantly practice perversion will *not* inherit the kingdom of God. "Do not be deceived," the Bible warns (1 Corinthians 6:9-11).

A believer struggling with this kind of worldly indoctrination or degenerate desires can take these noémas (mindsets/thoughts) captive and interrogate them in light of the truth of Scripture and the leading of the Spirit of truth. Since these noémas don't comply with the truth they need to be purged out of one's mindset in favor of reality.

As you do this with every thought/impulse/attitude/ideology, you purge your heart of falsity and unreality. This is "being made new in the attitude of your mind" (Ephesians 4:22-24).

How to Prevent Demonic Oppression and Possession

There are three effective ways to deflect evil spirits and they're all taught in this passage:

> **Submit yourselves, then, to God. <u>Resist the devil, and he will flee from you</u>. [8] <u>Come near to God and he will come near to you</u>. Wash your hands, you sinners, and <u>purify your hearts</u>, you double-minded.**
>
> **James 4:7-8**

The three ways to keep evil spirits at bay are:

- Resist the devil and he will flee from you.
- Draw near to God.
- Purify your heart.

Let's look at all three:

Resist the Devil and He Will Flee From You

Resisting "the devil" doesn't mean resisting satan himself because the devil is, generally speaking, on his throne in the Underworld directing the activities of his dark kingdom. He only *personally* gets involved in matters that are of great magnitude to him, like tempting Christ to sin (Matthew 4:1-11) or moving Judas to betray the Lord (John 13:27). When James taught that we are to "resist the devil" he was speaking of the kingdom of darkness in terms of its leader much as historians speak of military aggression in relation to the aggressor nation's leader, like "Hitler invaded France," when, in fact, Hitler was nowhere near France. So resisting the devil means resisting the kingdom of darkness and, specifically, the evil spirits that are assigned to oppress you one way or another.

At the time that James wrote this passage he was addressing believers scattered across the nations, but his words apply to all believers scattered across the world throughout the Church Age. We're called to "resist" evil spirits and their oppression. This means we are to conduct spiritual warfare—confront and overcome enemy attacks by utilizing the armor & arms that God has faithfully supplied us, which we'll examine in chapter **19**.

Draw Near to God

This simply means to make a regular effort to come closer to the LORD and corresponds to the first and greatest command: "love the Lord your God with all your heart and with all your soul and with all your mind and with all your strength" (Mark 12:30).

More than anything else, to draw near to God refers to cultivating a close relationship. The gospel of Christ is called "the message of reconciliation" because it's all about *reconciling* to the Creator. To 'reconcile' means to turn from hostility to alliance. You must understand that God wants to be **your friend** (John 15:13-15). Of course, you can't have friendship without relationship; and relationship requires communion, which is genuine communication. So cultivating a close relationship with the LORD involves developing a prayer life.

Prayer is simply communion with God—talking with your Creator—and the foremost form of prayer is simple communion or fellowship. This is observed in Jesus' outline for prayer in Matthew 6:9-13, which we'll look at in detail next chapter.

Purify Your Heart

Demons are "unclean spirits" or "impure spirits," which means *filthy* spirits. As such, they're naturally attracted to that which is morally dirty. They are drawn to moral filth much as flies are attracted to excrement and rats to refuse. By contrast, the Holy Spirit and holy angels are attracted to that which is holy. "Holy" means purity, the natural result of being consecrated unto the absolutely pure Creator.[14]

This shows why the Bible instructs us to "get rid of all moral filth and the evil that is so prevalent and humbly accept the word planted in you, which can save you" (James 1:21). Doing this repels evils spirits because they're deterred by holiness and attracted to filthiness.

James didn't just say to get rid of moral filth and evil, he also said to "humbly accept the word planted in you, which can save you." He was talking about the Word of God planted in believers through the teaching & preaching of Holy Scripture, which includes James' very epistle. Remember, in the 1st century they didn't have Bibles in book form available to every believer and so they relied on the teaching & preaching of the apostles, pastors and teachers who ministered to them. This included copies of epistles or gospels that might pass through their assemblies.

Why does James say "humbly accept" the Word planted in you? Because it "can save you." 'Save' is a form of the Greek word *sozo (SOHD-zoh)*, which in this context means to rescue from the power of sin. James was teaching the "put off/put on" principle: Put off the moral filth and displace it with the truth. This corresponds to the law of displacement. As you do this you'll be transformed as you're "made new in the attitude of your mind":

---

[14] I was at a church Bible study 20 years ago where the associate pastor insisted that 'holy' doesn't refer to purity, but rather "consecrated unto God." I understandably asked: "So when God is worshipped by the seraphim and living creatures in Heaven with the words 'Holy, holy, holy is the LORD' (Isaiah 6:3 & Revelation 4:8) what these angels are really saying is 'Consecrated unto God, Consecrated unto God, consecrated unto God is the LORD'?" This of course is nonsensical and the pastor had no answer; he was upset that his definition of 'holy' was shown to be dubious. Today, he unsurprisingly advocates the sexual perversion movement.

> **You were taught, with regard to your former way of life, to <u>put off your old self</u>, which is being corrupted by its deceitful desires; [23] to be <u>made new in the attitude of your minds</u>; [24] and to <u>put on the new self</u>, created to be like God in true righteousness and holiness.**
>
> **Ephesians 4:22-24**

To "put off your old self" means to put off the sinful nature. The works of the flesh are obvious (Galatians 5:19-23). When you miss it, be quick to humbly 'fess up and the LORD will forgive you and cleanse you from all unrighteousness (1 John 1:8-9). John the Baptist called this "keeping with repentance" (Matthew & Luke 3:8). The repentance/ forgiveness dynamic is fundamental to your walk with God because it enables you to **1.** get back up when you inevitably miss it, **2.** receive God's forgiveness, **3.** have your slate wiped clean, and **4.** continue to progress forward.

However, James' admonition to "get rid of all moral filth and the evil that is so prevalent" shows that putting off the old self is more than just repenting of sins committed, it's also a matter of **getting rid of anything that contributes to falling into sin, which includes anything that attracts filthy spirits**.

For instance, I've thrown away secular album collections because I sensed some of their dubious lyrics and imagery were holding me back. I was being led by the Holy Spirit to consecrate myself to the LORD further than I already was at the time. I've likewise thrown away movies for this same reason. I encourage believers to regularly take inventory of their possessions—the items to which they expose their eyes and ears—and purge as directed.

When I was a young Christian, I had several posters on the wall of my bedroom at my parents' home that were 'sword & sorcery' in nature. I defended them on the grounds that the images were typically of warriors fighting demonic-type creatures. My brother-in-law, however, was visibly taken aback by them and argued that they could attract demonic spirits. While I didn't necessarily believe this—since they depicted mighty warriors *fighting* evil beings—I decided to take the dubious art down in favor of more agreeable works. I didn't regret the decision.

I know people who are essentially "stuck in a rut" of the past because they stubbornly refuse to move on from the art, music and accouterments with which they grew up. Please don't misunderstand me here because God's call on each person is different and the Lord often leads believers to stay within the culture or subculture with which they're familiar (1 Corinthians 7:17-24). Why? Because the best way to reach people in a culture is through believers *from* that culture who are familiar with it. They speak the same language and therefore people can more readily relate to them and hence receive from them. Nevertheless, if there are certain things that you sense are bogging *you* down spiritually you need to either remove them from your life or, at least, limit your exposure to them. Of course, if something's leading you into error or sin, it's necessary to get rid of it altogether.

Years ago, I read this book on ridding your home of spiritual darkness. The author argued that certain items can be cursed in the sense that impure spirits are attached to them and thus having such a cursed item in your house provides a door for that demon to oppress you one way or another. He didn't give much scriptural support and so I was skeptical—and still am—but *some* of it made sense in light of the fact that demons seek places that are dry of God and the things of God (Matthew 12:43). This makes sense when you grasp that the LORD is the Fountain of Life from whom rivers of living waters flow (Psalm 36:9 & John 7:38). Moreover, demons are attracted to that which is morally filthy, including occult-oriented objects or items that support the occult. They're also attracted to objects of literal idolatry. In fact, the Bible says that demons are the entities *behind* the 'gods' that idols represent (1 Corinthians 10:19-22). As such, those who worship idols are, in reality, worshipping demons! Needless to say, purge anything that has to do with idol worship from your household.

During the days of the early Church, articles that Paul touched, like handkerchiefs and aprons, "were taken to the sick, and their illnesses were cured and **the evil spirits left them**" (Acts 19:11-12). It was the same thing with Peter's shadow (Acts 5:15-16). These things had the anointing of God on them and thus physically or mentally ill people exposed to them **were healed and demons fled!** A good example from the Old Testament would be Elisha's bones (2 Kings 13:20-21). These various items were blessed as conduits of God's power. Could the inverse also be true? Could certain items be cursed with a demonic non-anointing? If the former is true with the kingdom of light, isn't it possible—even likely—that the reverse is true with the kingdom of darkness? Passages like Deuteronomy 32:16-17 and the aforenoted 1 Corinthians 10:19-22 suggest that demons can associate themselves with certain objects, in this case idols. So don't take chances with dubious items—purge yourself and your abode of anything questionable.

Let me share a couple of personal examples: In 2001 I purchased this wooden jungle mask while on vacation in Mexico and displayed it on our living room wall. Of course, I valued it as nothing more than an exotic piece of art, but I finally decided to discard it simply because I didn't want anything in my house to attract evil spirits, not that there was any evidence of the mask doing this. I just felt that biblically-oriented art would be more appropriate for my dwelling.

It was the same thing with these little elephant figurines that my sister innocently sent me from one of her trips abroad. My stepson informed us that they were actually idols in India, so I promptly threw 'em out. I realize that things like this come down to a person's heart and if the individual in question doesn't perceive the object in an occultist or idolatrous manner there's likely no problem (1 Corinthians 8:4 & 10:19-20). **But**, why even take the chance? As Paul said: "You cannot drink the cup of the Lord and the cup of demons too; you cannot have a part in both the Lord's table and the table of demons" (1 Corinthians 10:21).

Consider how Solomon decorating the Holy Temple in Jerusalem with godly art, like cherubim, (1 Kings 6:23-29). Fill your dwelling with items that attract the Holy Spirit & holy angels and repel filthy spirits. Get rid of anything morally dubious. Amen?

Now relate this principle to the abode of your body & mind. YOU are a temple of God—a living, breathing *house* of God (1 Corinthians 3:16). What's 'decorating' the walls of your mind & heart? This offers additional insight to James' admonition to purify your heart.

Shun Drugs, aka *Pharmakeia*

Drugs played a vital role in ancient cults with their lifeless prayers to their gods—that is, demons—at pagan shrines and the magic empowered by these lying spirits. Sorcerers and witches used drugs in their spells, which explains something about the words "witchcraft" or "sorcery" used in Paul's list of works of the flesh in Galatians 5:19-21. The original Greek term is *pharmakeia (far-mah-KIH-ah)* and is where we get the words pharmacy and pharmaceutical. It literally means "drugs" or "medication" and only refers to magic by extension due to witches and magicians using drugs in their spells. As a work of the flesh, *pharmakeia* concerns any and all drug-related sins, which includes drug experimentation, drug abuse, drug trafficking, etc.

Needless to say, we should shun drugs if we want to avoid demonic influence, oppression and possession. This includes doctor-approved meds that you don't really need, which doctors perpetually prescribe in order to keep the pharmaceutical biz thriving and support their ritzy lifestyles.

The enemy uses witchcraft (including supposed "white" witchcraft), sorcery, séances, Ouija boards, and all occult-oriented activities to open a person up to demonic influence on a more personal basis, with partial or total possession being the goal.

Are There Spirits of Certain Sins, Like Lust?

Christ said that some demons are more wicked than others (Matthew 12:45), but did he mean more wicked in general or more wicked in regard to a particular sin? I assume the former.

In any case, just as people are assigned heavenly angels (Matthew 18:10) so individuals are presumably assigned evils spirits on behalf of the kingdom of darkness. Just as angels are watchers (1 Corinthians 4:9 & Luke 15:10), so demons are watchers. And it wouldn't take long for an evil spirit assigned to a person to discern what his/her fleshly weaknesses are, whether envy, jealousy, hatred, arrogance, strife, greed, lust, perversion, alcohol, drugs, sloth, fear, doubt, depression, etc. Once a demon determines the carnal proclivity, it then "works with" the person to get him/her to live according to their carnal weakness, whatever that is.

It must be stressed, again, that devils never *make* a person sin except in cases where someone is wholly possessed, which—as covered earlier—is something that takes place down the road, after a person has *already* significantly conceded to the corrupt desires of the flesh. The Bible makes it clear that sin is the result of one's "own evil desire" and so no one can claim 'The devil made me do it' (James 1:14-15). Consider, for example, when satan tempted Christ: The enemy knew Jesus was weak & hungry from fasting so he slyly proposed that he turn the rocks into bread and partake, but the devil couldn't *make* him do anything (Matthew 4:1-4). All evil spirits can do is *tempt*. The decision to commit evil or not comes down to the will of the individual.

If a demon successfully tempts a person and gets him/her into the habitual practice of sin it would eventually attract other evil spirits because filthy spirits are naturally drawn to that which is morally filthy. While these spirits may be attracted to the specific sin in question, they may just as well be attracted to sin in general. Whatever the case, a satanic bondage to the sin thus develops.

Thankfully, there's freedom in Christ (John 8:36), but it doesn't come through rebuking a demon of a particular sin, like a "spirit of alcohol" or a "spirit of gossip" or a "spirit of homosexuality." Although there's nothing wrong with authoritatively saying "Away from me, foul spirit" if you discern you're under severe temptation; after all, Jesus did this (Matthew 4:10). Freedom from sin comes through **1.** being spiritually regenerated (if the person isn't saved, that is) and **2.** knowing and applying the relevant truths of God's Word, as detailed above—putting off the evil desires of the flesh and learning to live out of your new nature by the Holy Spirit, which includes renewing the mind (Ephesians 4:22-24).

Notice how the Lord said freedom is attained:

> **Then Jesus said to those who had believed in him, "<u>If you <u>continue in my word</u>, you are truly my disciples; ³² and <u>you will know the truth</u>, and <u>the truth will make you free</u>."**
>
> **John 8:31-32** (NRSV)

So acquiring the truth and putting it into practice is what sets people free, not verbally rebuking a demon of such-and-such sin. As the individual who is struggling with a particular sin acquires truth and puts it into practice any evil spirit oppressing him or her will eventually flee and seek easier game (James 4:7).[15] But the person has to be diligent with the things

---

[15] This brings up a question: If a demon is assigned to an individual, where would it flee to if it leaves that particular person? We can only theorize based on the biblical data: Obviously demons aren't assigned to one individual and that's it. For instance, people eventually die and new people are born. Evil spirits are assigned to human candidates within a territory and they naturally go where their efforts are proving fruitful. The demoniac from the Gerasenes, for instance, had hundreds or thousands of demons in him. Also keep in mind that only a third of the angels fell with Satan, so there's a limit to their numbers.

of the spirit because demons are going to fight tooth & nail to keep an individual in bondage to the sin in question. **Life's a fight, fight it.**

Of course, in cases where a person is partially or fully possessed, s/he would have to *first* be exorcized of the demon(s), followed by the applicable 2-step process above.

Earlier we saw that the word 'spirit' does not always mean a spiritual entity; it can simply refer to a person's character, as in Joshua had "a different spirit" than the other Hebrews (Numbers 14:24). So whereas I think it's unbiblical to say that a person has a spirit of a particular sin in reference to demonic spirits, you could say that s/he has a spirit of such-and-such sin in regards to *their developed character*. For instance: "Mark has a spirit of lust," "Carrie has a spirit of lying," "Alex has a spirit of rage" or "Zach has a spirit of legalism." This simply means that they've developed the *character* of the sin in question due to habitually giving-in to the flesh in that particular area. This is true in regards to noémas (mindsets/ideologies) as well. For instance, someone can have a spirit of **LIE**beralism.

It *is* biblical, however, to rebuke a "spirit of infirmity" if you genuinely discern that a person's disability is induced by a demon or demons. Examples from Scripture include a crippling problem (Luke 13:11,16), deafness and muteness (Mark 9:25) or mental illness (Mark 5:1-8). I suppose not all infirmities are directly caused by evil spirits, so you have to have spiritual discernment to effectively minister in these cases. And the only way you can do this is to have genuine spiritual sensitivity, which comes by drawing closer to the LORD, as well as eagerly *desiring* gifts of the Spirit rather than eagerly *denying* them (1 Corinthians 12:1,31 & 14:1,39). If you're not sure if a spirit is behind the infirmity in question, simply rebuke the ailment itself, as Jesus did (Luke 4:39). As a believer and co-heir in Christ you have the authority to do the works the Messiah did (John 14:12). So get in the habit of boldly declaring your authority in Christ, take charge over any sickness and command it to leave.

We'll address spirits of infirmities in more detail in chapter **21**.

We've explored how to deflect evil spirits in this chapter, closing with the three simple yet effective ways to repel demons—**1.** resist their attacks, **2.** draw near to God and **3.** purify your heart. Actually, God has provided an easy, surefire means to achieve this. I'm talking about the armor & arms of God, which we'll address in chapter **19**. But, first, Let's look at…

18

THE DIFFERENT TYPES OF PRAYER

Last chapter we talked about drawing near to God, as instructed in James 4:8, which brought up the topic of prayer, aka communication with your Creator. The best place to learn about prayer is what Christ taught on the subject when the disciples asked him about it:

> **"This, then, is how you should pray:**
>
> **'Our Father in heaven,**
> **hallowed be your name,**
> **¹⁰ your kingdom come, your will be done,**
> **on earth as it is in heaven.**
> **¹¹ Give us today our daily bread.**
> **¹² And forgive us our debts,**
> **as we also have forgiven our debtors.**
> **¹³ And lead us not into temptation,**
> **but deliver us from the evil one.' "**
>
> **Matthew 6:9-13**

This is typically referred to as "the Lord's prayer" and people sometimes pray it word-for-word, particularly when the occasion calls for a brief scriptural prayer, like ceremonies. This is fine, but it's really not a prayer to be spoken by rote. It's actually an *outline* of different **types** of prayer. In other words, it's a prayer *skeleton* that needs to be filled in with the "flesh" of our spontaneous prayers according to our unique expressions, communion, needs or desires and the specific people or situations touching us.

The outline can be broken down into seven parts as such:

- **Our Father in heaven** = Communion or fellowship with God.
- **Hallowed be your name** = Praise & worship.
- **Your kingdom come, your will be done on earth as it is in heaven** = Binding & loosing or intercession, that is, releasing God's will and kingdom into people's lives and situations on Earth, including your own.
- **Give us today our daily bread** = Petition, that is, praying for your needs and righteous desires.
- **Forgive us our debts as we also have forgiven our debtors** = Repentance, venting, and forgiveness where applicable.
- **And lead us not into temptation, but deliver us from the evil one** = Armoring up, praying for protection, watchfulness, speaking in faith, and deliverance.
- **For yours is the kingdom and the power and the glory forever. Amen** = Return to praise and close.

As you can see, each part of "the Lord's Prayer" refers to a specific type of prayer. Let's look at each (omitting the redundant 7th one)…

"Our Father in Heaven"

This refers to communion with God since the believer is addressing God as his or her "Father." 'Father' indicates *familial* relation and relationship requires communication, hence fellowship. Christianity at its core is a *relationship* with the Creator of the Universe, which is why the gospel is referred to as the *message of reconciliation* in 2 Corinthians 5:18-20. I encourage you to cultivate an intimate relationship with your heavenly Father where you're in constant communion throughout the day, even when you're in bed (Psalm 63:6). Paul referred to this as "praying without ceasing" (1 Thessalonians 5:17 KJV) and the "fellowship of the Holy Spirit" (2 Corinthians 13:14).

While people in the world mock of the idea of walking with God—such as making references to "your invisible friend"—relationship with the Creator is the first order of life and perfectly normal. This can be observed by several examples in the Bible:

- Adam communed with God in the Garden of Eden, even after his fall (Genesis 3:8-13).
- Enoch "walked with God" and they were so close that the LORD simply "took him away," presumably so they could be together in Heaven (Genesis 5:22-24), but also as a type of the future Rapture.
- Moses communed with God in the Tent of Meeting wherein the LORD dwelt on the mercy seat of the Ark of the Covenant between the two gold-sculptured cherubim (Exodus 33:11).
- Asaph walked with his Creator so closely that they figuratively held hands (Psalm 73:23-25).
- David, of course, was "a man after God's own heart" (1 Samuel 13:14 & Acts 13:22).

All of these people from the Old Testament had a **relationship with the LORD** despite the fact that they had an inferior covenant with God. Today a vastly *superior* covenant is available to all people through Jesus Christ (Hebrews 8:6-7). This is the awesome message of the gospel—we can reconcile with our Creator, be forgiven of sin, have a relationship, and receive eternal life & immortality (2 Timothy 1:10).

As far as prayer protocol goes, Christ instructed us to pray *to the* Father (Matthew 6:9) in the name of Jesus by the leading of the Holy Spirit (John 16:23).

"Hallowed Be Your Name"

This refers to praise & worship. To 'hallow' means to honor as holy and venerate, that is, treat with respect and reverence. God's name—YaHWeH—represents the Creator Himself so we are to hallow the Great "I Am" (Exodus 3:13-14). The only way you can accomplish this in prayer is by *telling* him. Praise is celebration and includes thanksgiving, raving and boasting, whereas worship is adoration. Praise naturally attracts God's presence and is in accordance with the law of respect: What you respect moves toward you while what you don't respect moves away from you. Worship, on the other hand, is adoration or awe, and is the response to being *in* God's presence. See Psalm 95:1-7 and Psalm 100 for verification.

We could further differentiate praise & worship as such: Praise celebrates the LORD whereas worship humbly reveres him; praise lifts God up while worship bows when he is lifted; praise dances before the Most High whereas worship pulls off his shoes; praise extols the Creator for what he's done while worship adores him for who he is; praise says "Praise the Lord" whereas worship demonstrates that he is LORD; praise is thanksgiving for being a co-heir in Christ while worship lays the crown at his feet.

Every believer is called to deeper praise & worship. It will literally *revolutionize* your life, as it has mine and continues to do so.

It's no accident that **communion with God** and **praise & worship** are the first two kinds of prayer Jesus mentions in his outline (Matthew 6:9-13). They're simply the most important. After all, what does the average father or mother want to hear from their children, particularly as the children grow and develop? Not, "Gimme, gimme," but rather simple communion: "Hi Dad! How are you doing today? You're awesome!" "Do you have time? I'd like to just hang out with you." "Mother, I have something I've been thinking a lot about and I'd like to share it with you to see what you think." "Mom, you're so beautiful!" "Dad, tell me more about that project you're working on; it's lookin' great so far." Etcetera. If this is the kind of communion our earthly parents prefer, why would we think it's any different with our heavenly Father?

You can have these types of conversations with God throughout the day, every day—when you wake up in bed, when you're in the shower, when you're driving, when you're walking down the hall, in the evening, etc. As noted earlier, Paul referred to this as "praying without ceasing" and the "fellowship of the Holy Spirit."

The Spiritual Warrior moves beyond the idea that we only encounter God when we go to church gatherings once or twice a week. This is an Old Testament mentality in the sense that the Israelites had to go to the Temple in order to meet with the LORD, as far as his presence on Earth goes. And, even then, he was hidden in the Holy of Holies where the Ark of the Covenant was located.

"Your Kingdom Come, Your Will Be Done on Earth"

This does not refer to praying for the Millennium to come. It refers to releasing God's will into people's lives on Earth, including your own, through prayer. It's binding & loosing or intercession.

If the idea that prayer "looses" God and his kingdom to function in people's lives sounds strange to you, it's in line with the principle of binding & loosing, as taught by the Mighty Christ:

> **"I will give you the keys of the kingdom of heaven; whatever you <u>bind</u> on earth will be bound in heaven, and whatever you <u>loose</u> on earth will be loosed in heaven."**
>
> **Matthew 16:19**

> **"I tell you the truth, whatever you <u>bind</u> on earth will be bound in heaven, and whatever you <u>loose</u> on earth will be loosed in heaven."**
> **[19]"Again, I tell you that if two of you on earth agree about anything you ask for, it will be done for you by my Father in heaven."**
>
> **Matthew 18:18-19**

In the first passage Jesus said he was going to give believers the "keys of the kingdom of heaven." "Keys" refer to authority or power. If you have the keys to a vehicle, you wield the power to take advantage of it. The "kingdom of heaven" of course refers to God's kingdom, the kingdom of light. The Lord was saying that he was giving his disciples the power to take advantage of God's kingdom. This is driven home with the second part of the verse: "whatever you bind on earth will be bound in heaven, and whatever you loose on earth will be loosed in heaven." You could put it like this: Heaven will back you up in any legitimate effort to manifest God's kingdom on Earth via faith and love, which are the terms of the New Testament. "Faith works in love" (Galatians 5:6).

What exactly does it mean to "bind" or to "loose"? The Greek word for "bind" is *deo (DAY-oh)*, which means to literally bind up or figuratively in the sense of prohibiting or hindering; "loose" is *luo (LOO-oh)*, which means to unbind or release. So *deo* means to lock up whereas *luo* means to unlock. As such, believers have the authority to **hinder** or **prohibit** the kingdom of darkness on Earth and to **release** God's kingdom. The kingdom of darkness is prohibited in Heaven so we can prohibit it on Earth; the kingdom of light reigns in Heaven so we can loose it on Earth.

In the second passage Christ links the principle of binding & loosing to prayer. We bind the kingdom of darkness and loose the kingdom of light through our prayers.

Do you want God's kingdom to reign in your life and the lives of others? Of course you do, but it has to be released through prayer. Do you want God's will to be done in your life and the lives of others? You have to loose it via prayer. In other words, God's kingdom will not come and reign on this Earth unless a believer releases it through prayer and action; and God's will is not done on Earth unless the Church looses it via prayer and action. Simply put, believers have the power to bind the kingdom of darkness in this fallen world and loose the kingdom of light.

When you grasp this, you understand why the apostle stressed: "The prayer of a righteous person **is powerful and effective**" (James 5:16).

Someone might understandably respond: "Well if God's so Almighty why doesn't he just automatically do everything? Why does he need believers to 'release' his will through prayer and service?"

It is true that the LORD is Sovereign, which means he "reigns supreme." The Bible describes God as "the king of all the earth" (Psalm 47:7) who owns the Earth and everything in it (Psalm 24:1, 50:12 & 1 Corinthians 10:26). Christ himself called Father God "Lord of heaven and earth" (Matthew 11:25). So there's no disputing that the Almighty reigns supreme and "does whatever pleases him" (Psalm 103:19 & 135:5-6).

However, it's also clear in Scripture that the devil is the "god of this age" and the "prince of this world" who rules the kingdom of darkness or Underworld, which is the dark spiritual dimension that underpins the world (John 12:31 & 14:30). Anyone who's not part of God's kingdom is subject to this dark kingdom because they're "by nature objects of wrath" (Ephesians 2:3); this includes everyone who doesn't have a covenant with the Almighty, meaning all unbelievers. The following verses verify this: 1 John 5:19, Revelation 12:9, 2 Corinthians 4:4 and Ephesians 2:1-2.

These passages show that the "whole world" is presently under the control of the kingdom of darkness, which is why the Bible refers to this current era as "the present **evil** age" (Galatians 1:4).

This doesn't, of course, mean that all unbelievers are frothing at the mouth with evil, but rather that they're subject to the kingdom of darkness, whether they realize it or not. The depth of their subjugation is dependent upon how far they choose to embrace the flesh, which is the satanic nature. It's also dependent on how far their belief system (noéma) deviates from biblical truth.

We see evidence of Satan's rule and influence all around us constantly: wars, crime, corruption, broken families, immorality, injustice, poverty, false religion, legalism, harmful ideologies, disunity, disease, addiction, death, etc. Don't be alarmed, however, because the above passages show that the devil's control is limited to those designated as "the world," which doesn't include blood-bought, spiritually regenerated believers, *Hallelujah!* Christians are the "church" of Jesus Christ, which literally means "the called-out ones" in the Greek. This signifies that believers have been rescued from satan's kingdom:

> **For he has rescued us from the dominion of darkness**
> **and brought us into the kingdom of the Son he loves,**
> **Colossians 1:13**

Not only have we been rescued from bondage to the kingdom of darkness, we've been transplanted into God's kingdom as his beloved sons and daughters!

When you pray for yourself and those linked to you—family, neighbors and people at school or work—you're binding up the kingdom of darkness and loosing the kingdom of light, which includes loosing the angels assigned to them (Matthew 18:10). Some of the people you intercede for are lost and some are Christians who are ignorant of these things; as such, the angels assigned to them are limited in helping them, to say the least. But your prayers can release them to work in their lives, one way or another.

This doesn't negate freewill, of course. No matter how much you pray for someone and no matter how much they're exposed to the Word of God, the moving of the Holy Spirit and the service of angels, he or she can still stubbornly resist. And that's *their* choice. You did your part; they have to do theirs. If they refuse, that's their problem and they'll be held accountable for it when they stand before the LORD.

Praying for those whom you regularly come in contact with is to your social relations what oil is to a bike chain. Without your prayers, the kingdom of light is hindered in these people's lives, which includes the service of angels. When this occurs the kingdom of darkness takes advantage of the situation: Unclean spirits will naturally have more freedom of movement and therefore more negative influence, which isn't good for the individual in question or for your relationship with him/her. Since godly believers are guaranteed to be persecuted, why open the door to unnecessary problems due to skipping out on your duty to intercede? See 1 Timothy 2:1-4.

My Example in Praying for People

Christian servant-leaders are called to set **an example** for believers (1 Peter 5:1-3), so allow me to share my example. What I usually do when interceding for several people is voice **a general prayer**, such as the apostle Paul's prayer for the Colossian believers:

> **...we have not stopped praying for you. We continually ask God to fill you with the knowledge of his will through all the wisdom and understanding that the Spirit gives, [10] so that you may live a life worthy of the Lord and please him in every way: bearing fruit in every good work, growing in the knowledge of God, [11] being strengthened with all power according to his glorious might so that you may have great endurance and patience, [12] and giving joyful thanks to the Father, who has qualified you to share in the inheritance of his holy people in the kingdom of light.**
>
> **Colossians 1:9-12**

Notice how Paul prays this excellent general prayer for all the Colossian believers rather than say a similar prayer for each person by name. This makes sense and saves time because it keeps you from saying the same general prayer over and over for each individual.

After praying a general prayer like this, I then lift up various names from my intercession list, praying in the spirit as led of the Spirit (Ephesians 6:18). When I get to a certain individual, a specific need might come up and so I pray about it—both with my understanding and by the spirit (1 Corinthians 14:15)—and then move on to the next person.

I mentioned an "intercession list," which is simply a list of names in my mind; in other words, a *mental* list (I'm good with names and have an excellent memory). But I sometimes pray from an actual list as well, at least a couple times a week, usually with Carol.

Praying for Governing Authorities

We talked about praying for people linked to you, whether family, friends, neighbors and people at school or work. With this in mind, be sure to also regularly pray for **governing authorities**, whether spiritual or political (1 Timothy 2:1-4). By *spiritual* authorities, I mean key ministerial leaders in your area, nation and otherwise.

If you need some inspiration on this topic, I encourage seeing the excellent 2015 movie *War Room*.

"Give Us Today Our Daily Bread"

This kind of prayer is petition, which means asking for what you need, as well as righteous desires. Notice what the Lord said about needs:

> **"So do not worry, saying, 'What shall we eat?' or 'What shall we drink?' or 'What shall we wear?' [32]For the pagans run after all these things, and your heavenly Father knows that you need them. [33] But <u>seek first his kingdom and his righteousness, and all these things will be given to you as well</u>."**
>
> **Matthew 6:33**

This shows that you don't need to blow a lot of time in prayer on your needs since these things will automatically be provided for the Spiritual Warrior who seeks God's kingdom and righteousness first and foremost. Please notice that the Lord said to seek these first and not *only*.

Right before Christ was apprehended, abused and crucified for the sins of humanity, he prayed this prayer:

> **"Father, <u>if you are willing</u>, take this cup from me; yet not my will, but <u>yours be done</u>."**
>
> **Luke 22:42**

The Messiah was not petitioning God for a financial need or healing here, but rather he was seeking the Father about **direction**, which involves **consecrating one's life** to fulfill the LORD's will. Christ on Earth was *both* God and man (Philippians 2:6-8). Being God, the Son, he knew that he was called to die for humanity (John 3:16) and that the next twelve hours of his earthly life were going to be an excruciating challenge, to say the least. Thus, being part man, he understandably sought the Father in regards to the possibility of another way—an easier way—yet he ended his prayer with "yet not my will, but yours be done."

Whenever you are seeking the LORD for direction, your flesh is naturally going to want to take the less grueling direction, yet God's plan for your life may involve challenges and difficulties that your human side is understandably going to be resistant toward. Thus, when praying for direction and consecration of your life, you can request what you desire, which is usually the comfortable route, but your ultimate attitude must be "Yet not my will, but yours be done." Why? Because you're a servant while God is your LORD (Luke 17:7-10 & Philippians 1:1), you are a son/daughter while God is the spiritual Parent (Romans 8:15 & Matthew 23:9).

The prayer of petition, however, is a different matter. Petition refers to requesting something and must be based on the promise of God's Word. What you ask for is received through faith:

> **This is the confidence we have in approaching God: that if we ask anything <u>according to his will</u>, he hears us. ¹⁵ And if we know that he hears us—whatever we ask—<u>we know that we have</u> what we asked of him.**
>
> **1 John 5:14-15**

For instance, we know in the Scriptures that God promises to supply our needs and even righteous desires (Matthew 21:22, John 14:14 & 16:23-24), as well as heal us when needed (1 Peter 2:24, Mark 1:40-41 & Matthew 8:1-3), thus we can pray for such things and **receive them by faith**. Notice how the Lord emphasized the importance of faith for answered petition:

> **"Have faith in God," Jesus answered. ²³ "Truly I tell you, if anyone says to this mountain, 'Go, throw yourself into the sea,' and does not doubt in their heart but <u>believes</u> that what they say will happen, it will be done for them. ²⁴ Therefore I tell you, whatever you ask for in prayer, <u>believe that you have received it</u>, and <u>it will be yours.</u>**
>
> **Mark 11:22-24**

With the prayer of petition, you don't include the phrase "if it be thy will" because you're praying based on the promise of Holy Scripture and you receive what you seek by faith. You must be *sure* it's the LORD's will based on the promise of God's Word because, otherwise, you'll likely doubt that God wants you to have what you're seeking and this will hinder faith and sabotage your spiritual warfare. For instance, you'll be apt to reason: "Maybe it's not God's will for *me* to be healed." When you think like this, you inhibit faith and thus won't get what you're seeking.

I should add that I specified *righteous* desires above to distinguish them from fleshly, worldly desires (James 4:3-4).

If you're struggling with faith to believe for answers in prayer petition, the answer is to:

1. **Increase your faith**, which comes by drawing nearer to the Living Word in relationship (John 1:1 & 6:51).
2. **Increase your knowledge** of the written word and the covenant promises thereof (Romans 10:17 & 2 Corinthians 1:20).

"Forgive Us Our Debts as We Also Have Forgiven"

This type of prayer refers to "keeping in repentance" (Matthew & Luke 3:8), which ensures the continuing release of God's forgiveness and grace into your life (1 John 1:8-9). Without it, unconfessed sin will block up your spiritual arteries and your faith covenant won't work.

It also means to forgive people where applicable. For instance, the Lord said "If your brother or sister sins against you, rebuke them; and **if they repent**, forgive them" (Luke 17:3). Notice that there's a condition for the offender to be forgiven, which holds the person accountable to his/her bad behavior. Christ also emphasized this in Matthew 18:15-17 wherein he plainly instructed that an impenitent offender is to be removed from fellowship and treated as an unbeliever (!). Speaking of confrontation, why even confront an offender if you're supposed to automatically forgive? In other words, you're *not* obligated to forgive, everyone for everything all the time, the faster the better. This is a religious myth that's thoroughly unbiblical. We're instructed to forgive offenders **as the LORD forgives** (Colossians 3:13 & Ephesians 4:32), and God only forgives the penitent.

Unforgiveness itself is not a sin since the LORD refuses to forgive untold millions and justly so, as observed in Revelation 20:11-15. Some people argue that Christ forgave his murderers when he was crucified, but this isn't true. He prayed to the Father that *he* would forgive them (Luke 23:34) and the only way God offers forgiveness to sinners is through humble penitence (Psalm 32:5). What Jesus did was *pray* for his offenders, which is in line with what he instructed us to do (Matthew 5:44 & Luke 6:28).

It's also important to cast your cares on to the LORD when someone sins against you, which is venting (Psalm 55:22 & 1 Peter 5:7). Just as you must remove physical waste from your body, so you must remove emotional waste. Venting is as vital to your spiritual-mental health as the large intestine is to your physical health—the waste *must* be removed. This is why venting is strongly encouraged in the Bible (Psalm 62:8).

Casting an offense on to the LORD and praying for the offender are mandatory in the life of the Spiritual Warrior, but neither of these are the same as offering forgiveness. To 'forgive' means to "dismiss the offense" or "cancel the debt" and this isn't mandatory *unless* the offender apologizes in some manner. If he or she is penitent then, by all means, forgive. After all, this is how God deals with you. We are to do the same to others.

For a good example of forgiving heinous offenders, read the story of Joseph and his carnal brothers, as detailed in Genesis 37,39-45,50. He was a type of Christ and he didn't automatically forgive his siblings, but rather used tough love tactics to bring them to a point of broken penitence. Only *then* did he forgive them. The Lord instructs us to be "shrewd as snakes and as innocent as doves" (Matthew 10:16), not gullible as ignoramuses.

For elaboration on this important topic see my books *QUESTIONS & ANSWERS From the Bible* and, especially, *How to Handle OFFENSES: Personal & Criminal*.

The sixth part of the prayer outline—"And lead us not into temptation, but deliver us from the evil one"—we'll address in detail in the next two chapters. But, first, let's look at something applicable to petition and spiritual warfare that every Spiritual Warrior needs to know:

When to ASK and When to SPEAK IN FAITH / DEMAND

Christ spoke of both **speaking in faith** and **asking for things** in prayer in the same breath:

> **So Jesus answered and said to them, "Have faith in God. [23] For assuredly, I <u>say</u> to you, <u>whoever says to this mountain, 'Be removed and be cast into the sea,'</u> and does not doubt in his heart, but <u>believes</u> that those things he <u>says</u> will be done, he will have whatever he <u>says</u>. [24] Therefore I say to you, <u>whatever things you ask when you pray</u>, believe that you receive** *them*, **and you will have** *them.*
>
> **Mark 11:22-24** (NKJV)

There was a mountain nearby and the Messiah spoke of it in a figurative sense, as if it were an obstacle in one's life. Jesus said that you can speak to such an hindrance by faith and what you speak will come to pass, assuming you believe.

NOTE that Christ mentions **speaking** three times and **faith** (belief) once. In other words, if you're having trouble *believing* for something then keep *speaking* in faith and it will have positive impact on your belief since words have the power of life and death (Proverbs 18:21 & Matthew 12:37).

After talking about speaking in faith, the Lord goes right into the topic of asking for things in prayer, which is petition. While the two are different they're obviously somewhat linked. They're both forms of spiritual warfare or prayer, but one involves speaking in belief in the sense of demanding something by faith and the other involves requesting. So when should you speak in faith (demand) for something and when should you ask for it? The answer lies in comparing a couple of statements by Jesus in the Gospel of John:

> **"Believe me when I say that I am in the Father and the Father is in me; or at least believe on the evidence of the works [miracles] themselves. [12] Very truly I tell you, whoever believes in me will do the works I have been doing, and they will do even greater things than these, because I am going to the Father. [13] And I will do whatever you <u>ask</u> in my name, so that the Father may**

be glorified in the Son. ¹⁴ You may <u>ask</u> me for anything in my name, and I will do it.”

John 14:11-14

“In that day you will no longer ask me anything. Very truly I tell you, my Father will give you whatever you <u>ask</u> in my name. ²⁴ Until now you have not asked for anything in my name. <u>Ask</u> and you will receive, and your joy will be complete.”

John 16:23-24

In both of these passages Christ is talking about *asking* for things. The same Greek word is used in both verses, as well as Mark 11:24 above, which is *aiteó (eye-TAY-oh)* or a variation of it. This can mean *ask* in the sense of making a request, yet it can also mean *demand* in the sense of speaking in faith. The context will determine the proper meaning.

For instance, in the first passage, John 14:11-14, the Lord was talking about performing "works," aka miracles, and says that believers will do these same works—and even greater works—because he was going to be resurrected and sit at the right hand of the Father in Heaven (Acts 2:33). As such, he was talking about speaking in faith—demanding—in order to receive a miracle. A few examples in the New Testament include when Christ commanded the paralyzed man to get up and walk home (Matthew 9:6-8) and another occasion with an invalid at the Pool of Bethesda (John 5:8), as well as Peter's similar miracle concerning a lame man at the Temple gate (Acts 3:6).

A miraculous healing in my own life required speaking in faith. I needed knee surgery in 2013, but didn't want to go that radical route for understandable reasons. So Carol & I prayed over my knee every day, speaking in faith for a healing. It took about three months, but the healing manifested and I was out skiing slopes in New York the following winter. This shows that sometimes **perseverance** is necessary in order to receive the miracle for which you're speaking in faith; and not just to **receive** your healing, but to **maintain it** as well (Hebrews 6:12).

I was simply speaking in faith as Jesus instructed in Mark 11:23—and adding perseverance—whereas Jesus and Peter in the above three examples were presumably operating in the gifts of the Spirit; nevertheless, both methods require speaking in faith, aka *demanding* the miracle in question.

When there's a need for a healing miracle you don't ask since healing is an important part of the gospel of Christ (1 Peter 2:24); and it is God's will that the person be healed. How can I say that with certainty? Because Christ was Immanuel—"God is with us (in the flesh)" (Matthew 1:23)—and so what the Messiah did during his ministry on Earth **reveals God's will** to us. For instance, people needing serious healings would approach Jesus and ask *"if* you are willing." The Lord *never* responded "No, it is not my will"; rather he plainly said it *was* his will (Mark 1:40-41 & Matthew 8:1-3).

I repeat, healing is part of the gospel of Christ (1 Peter 2:24), which is one of several reasons why it's "good news." The Bible promises a minimum of 70-80 years of life (Psalm 90:10) so, if you're under that age, you can claim this promise by faith (2 Corinthians 1:20). Even if you're over 80 you can believe and receive in faith in your awesome covenant with God simply based on your righteous desire (Mark 11:24, John 14:14, John 16:24).

Speaking of which, if there's a situation where the individual is done with life on this Earth for one legitimate reason or another and *wants* to pass on—like the situation my Dad was in, noted at the end of chapter **8**—I'm assuming the LORD will respond accordingly. The Creator doesn't force healing on anyone just like he doesn't force eternal life on everyone.

Chew on these Scriptures (Matthew 4:4) and you'll have increasing insight on when to ask for something in prayer petition and when to speak in faith for a miracle; always be led of the Spirit (John 14:26 & Romans 8:14).

<u>19</u>

THE ARMOR & ARMS of God

The Spiritual Warrior regularly takes advantage of the armor of God, which enables you to **1.** draw closer to the LORD, **2.** activate angels on your behalf and **3.** deter evils spirits. Those who don't **won't**. Thus it's important to have a basic understanding of God's armor & weaponry.

We'll first look at what each piece of the armor & arms is and then observe how to use each of these spiritual tools throughout your day. I encourage you to utilize either of the two 7-item breakdowns as a checklist until you can "put on" the armor & weaponry without even referencing a list.

Speaking of which, the armor & arms of God are not things you "put on" and that's it. They're obviously not literal pieces of armor & weaponry, but rather figurative of **spiritual things YOU DO, and continue to DO, throughout any given day**. Because of this, it's possible for a believer to be using the armor & arms of God without even knowing you're doing so. If this doesn't make sense, it will once you understand what each piece is.

You've perhaps heard sermons or read books or articles on this topic and that's great. But I encourage you not to limit your view of the armor & arms of God to the way you first heard it. I'm not saying that what you were taught was wrong, but simply encouraging you to be open to new insights. The armor & weaponry of God are instrumental to successful spiritual warfare and so a proper understanding of them is vital to a victorious walk with the Lord.

220

Let's start by reading the relevant text:

> **Finally, be strong in the Lord and in his mighty power.**
> **[11] Put on <u>the full armor of God</u>, so that you can take your stand against the devil's schemes. [12] For our struggle is not against flesh and blood, but against the rulers, against the authorities, against the powers of this dark world and against <u>the spiritual forces of evil in the heavenly realms</u>. [13] Therefore put on <u>the full armor of God</u>, so that when <u>the day of evil</u> comes, you may be able to stand your ground, and after you have done everything, to stand.**
> **[14] Stand firm then, with <u>the belt of truth</u> buckled around your waist, with <u>the breastplate of righteousness</u> in place, [15] and <u>with your feet fitted with the readiness that comes from the gospel of peace</u>. [16] In addition to all this, take up <u>the shield of faith</u>, with which you can extinguish all the flaming arrows of the evil one. [17] Take <u>the helmet of salvation</u> and <u>the sword of the Spirit</u>, which is the word of God.**
> **[18] And <u>pray in the Spirit</u> on all occasions with all kinds of prayers and requests. With this in mind, be alert and always keep on praying for all the Lord's people.**
> **Ephesians 6:10-18**

The first paragraph is simply an introduction to God's armor & weaponry wherein several important points are stressed:

- **God *wants* you to be strong in him and walk in his mighty power.** The way you do this is by putting on the armor of God and using the weapons provided. Speaking of which…
- **Use the FULL armor.** Twice we're encouraged to put on the *full* armor, not part of it, which shows that every piece is necessary to effectively withstand the enemy's attacks.
- **The identity and nature of the adversary.** Your enemy is not flesh & blood—that is, people—but rather "the spiritual forces of evil in the heavenly realms." This refers to the evil spirits commissioned to assault you & yours.
- **Your *need* for God's armor & weaponry.** Since evil spirits are spiritual in nature, and therefore invisible, it requires intangible protection & arms to overcome them.

- **The "day of evil."** This refers to *when* you are attacked by the kingdom of darkness. You are not attacked every second of every day (although, of course, you have to constantly contend with the evil desires of the flesh, but that's a different issue). There are *specific times* when the enemy will assault you. This is the "day of evil." The Bible is warning every believer that the enemy will attack. It's not a question of *if* you will be attacked, but rather a matter of *when*.
- **The *purpose* of God's armor & weaponry: Your victory.** The LORD *wants* you to be victorious when the enemy attacks; he *wants* you to withstand the assault. This is the very reason he provides these defenses & arms. You must get it through your head that God is on *your* side: He is *for* you and *not* against you (Romans 8:31).

When Paul wrote the epistle to the Ephesians he was under house arrest in Rome and so there were Roman soldiers constantly in his vicinity. As such, he was able to get a good look at their armor & weaponry and drew parallels to the intangible armor & arms that God provides for every believer, which includes YOU.

Here are the seven pieces and an explanation of each:

1. The Belt of Truth

This is the first piece of armor because truth is essential for victory in a world governed by the father of lies (John 8:44). Truth is *alétheia (ah-LAY-thee-ah)* in the Greek, meaning "reality" or "the way it really is." The belt of truth is simply **devotion to seeking and finding the truth and living according to it, utilizing the sources of truth that God has provided**. The other pieces of the armor & weaponry are *dependent on* this piece, which is why it's the first one.

There are two main sources of truth: **1. The Living Word**, who is truth (John 14:6), and **2. The written Word**, which is truth, assuming it's interpreted soundly, balancing out truth with truth (John 17:17). *Both* sources are essential: The first refers to seeking the Living Word so that you are led by the Spirit of truth (John 16:13) while the second refers to feeding from the written Word and acquiring truth through "rightly dividing" it (2 Timothy 2:15). The way you do the second is twofold—receiving from sound ministers of God (Ephesians 4:11-13) and receiving through personal study (1 John 2:27).

Be careful to pursue the truth above loyalty to a particular sect. Otherwise you'll fall into the pitfall of foolish sectarianism, which is a work of the flesh: The list of works of the flesh in Galatians 5:20 includes "factions," which is *hairesis* in the Greek *(HAH-ee-res-is)*. This refers to a religious or philosophical **sect** and the problems inherent with factionalism.

2. The Breastplate of Righteousness

Do you feel you're too sinful to serve God? Do you struggle with a sense of unworthiness that hinders your communion with the Lord (that is, your prayer life)? Do you think you're too unrighteous to fulfill God's call on your life? The LORD has provided this particular piece of spiritual armor to set you FREE and empower you to serve effectively.

This armor refers to accepting **the gift of righteousness** the LORD has provided you in Christ (Romans 5:17) and living out of your new nature— your spirit—because it was *born* righteous when you accepted the gospel and underwent spiritual regeneration (Titus 3:5). This is your "new self, which was **created to be like God** in true righteousness" (Ephesians 4:22-24). As you learn to walk according to this new nature with the help and guidance of the Holy Spirit you'll naturally walk in *practical* righteousness. So putting on your breastplate of righteousness is one-and-the-same as walking in the spirit (Galatians 5:16).

Of course, as a human being with a flesh, you'll inevitably sin; this includes the more common sins like envy, jealousy, rivalry, hatred, gossip, lying, greed or lust. Those who have their "breastplate" on will humbly 'fess up and receive God's forgiveness, which "purifies you from all unrighteousness" (1 John 1:8-9). Doing this is "keeping with repentance" (Matthew & Luke 3:8). The repentance/forgiveness dynamic is essential to spiritual growth because it ensures God's grace continually flowing in your life and your ongoing progress. It keeps your spiritual arteries clear of the clog-up of unconfessed sin.[16]

A Roman soldier's breastplate guarded his heart and other vital organs. Just so, the breastplate of righteousness guards your figurative heart—your

---

[16] Incredibly, there's this widespread false teaching amongst Evangelicals today which suggests that believers never have to repent of anything, ever. Jesus must have been walking in gross error when He instructed the Ephesian Christians to repent in Revelation 2:5 (sarcasm).

mind—and prevents it from being corrupted by things that would eventually destroy you (Proverbs 4:23).

3. The Gospel of Peace Shoes

The "gospel of peace" refers to the message of Christ, which is the "message of reconciliation" (2 Corinthians 5:18-21). 'Reconciliation' means "to turn from enmity to friendship." It's through the gospel that you have *peace* with your Creator and are reborn his beloved son & daughter (Romans 5:1 & 1 John 3:2,9). It's through this gospel that you become Christ's friend (John 15:14-15).

The Roman soldier's footwear was designed for firm-footing, which was a life-or-death matter in combat. When you face spiritual attack, your peace with God is likewise a matter of life and death—victory or defeat. The text says that the gospel of peace shoes grant the believer "readiness." This is the Greek word *hetoimasia (het-oy-mas-EE-ah)*, which means "foundation" or "firm-footing" without which you won't be ready or prepared for battle.

Putting this all together, your *relationship* with the Lord is foundational to withstanding spiritual attack. **Having your gospel of peace shoes on means developing a close relationship with God and maintaining it.** Someone might say that this sounds similar to the belt of truth, but the belt refers specifically to *acquiring truth* from both The Living Word and the written Word. The gospel of peace shoes, by contrast, are focused on your *relationship* with God period. In other words, the belt of truth concerns procuring the truth from the Living Word and the written Word whereas the gospel of peace shoes concerns your *rapport* with the Person of God. The belt has to do with learning **the principles of God's kingdom** whereas the shoes have to do with knowing **the Person of God**.

Make no mistake, without this vital relationship the enemy will chew you up and spit you out, one way or another. One of the enemy's favorite strategies is to mislead believers into the pit of sterile religiosity where they know *about* God, but don't *know* him. A good example from the Scriptures can be observed in Galatians 4:9. Some people might even be described as having "a form of godliness but deny its power" (2 Timothy 3:5), which is reminiscent of the lifeless Pharisees.

If the gospel of peace shoes—that is, your relationship with God—is foundational to your spiritual walk, why isn't it the *first* piece of armor to put on? Why do truth (the belt of truth) and walking in the spirit (the breastplate of righteousness) take precedence? Because the gospel of peace shoes relate to communion with God and therefore worship. And Jesus said "God is spirit, and his worshipers must worship in the spirit and in truth" (John 4:24). Think about it: Without the belt of truth, we can't worship God properly and our communion would be prone to error. Similarly, without the breastplate of righteousness we would fall into worshipping God out of our flesh rather than out of our spirit. So both the belt of truth and breastplate of righteousness come first.

4. The Shield of Faith

The Roman soldier's shield was huge and would cover his whole body when he knelt behind it, protecting him from arrows, spears and the like. Just the same, the shield of faith protects the believer by "extinguishing all the flaming arrows of the evil one." *But* you have to put this shield up or you'll get hit. Think about it in terms of the spacecrafts on *Star Trek:* If the Enterprise doesn't have its invisible shields up, the opponent could destroy them with phaser fire, photon torpedoes, etc. So it's imperative that you have your faith shield up to protect yourself from enemy attacks.

How do you do this? Simple: Regularly release your faith by speaking according to the promises of God in the five general areas of satanic attack. Remember, your tongue has the power of life and death (Proverbs 18:21). As you give voice to God's Word your angels will be employed to serve you accordingly. They'll erect a "hedge of protection" around you. What are these five areas of attack? They are **1.** physical ailments, **2.** mental maladies, **3.** defeat to human enemies, **4.** premature death and **5.** financial attack.

Consider the first one as an example: If you use the power of your tongue to speak death by confessing something like "There's a flu bug going around so I'll probably get sick" you just threw your shield out the window and opened yourself up to attack. This foolishly prevents your angels from doing their job of protecting you. Instead, erect your shield and activate your guardian angels by saying "That virus that's going around is under my feet and has no authority on my body; by the torture of Christ, who redeemed me from all curses (Isaiah 53:5), I'm free of all sicknesses &

diseases." If you do this and *believe*,[17] whatever virus that's going around will hit your invisible shield and not harm you whatsoever. *Never ever* talk sickness & disease. Speak health and blessing.

You must understand that every blessing in the New Covenant is *attained* and *maintained* by faith, including your salvation (Romans 10:9-10). What is faith? Faith is not belief in fantasies or fantastical things, like Leprechauns, but rather belief based on the knowledge of truth (reality) that you acquire; which is released through the power of your tongue.

How is this invisible "shield" erected and maintained around you as you walk in faith? By the angels assigned to you, who obey the voice of God's Word (Psalm 103:20). This is their occupation—obeying the voice of God's Word. The Hebrew word for 'voice' is *qol (kohl)*, which means "sound, voice." That's what angels obey—the sound or voice of the Word of God. But does your Bible make any sounds of itself? Does any passage make a sound when you read it or study it? No, it only makes sound if you speak it! That's why it's so important that you get the power of your tongue into play and start speaking the Word of God in faith. This is covered in detail in my book *ANGELS*.

The text says that the shield of faith "can extinguish *all* the flaming arrows of the evil one." In other words, if you have your faith defenses up, no curse will be able to hit you. For instance, Carol & I always have our shields up concerning sickness & disease and so we're hardly ever hit. I say "hardly ever" because there are three kinds of exceptions, which we'll look at below when we cover the sword of the spirit.

5. The Helmet of Salvation

The helmet protected the Roman soldier's head. Likewise, the helmet of salvation protects the believer's mind from distress when undergoing satanic attack. As you apply the wisdom principles of God's Word and "fight the good fight of faith" as led of the Holy Spirit (1 Timothy 6:12), it's guaranteed that the LORD will deliver you (2 Peter 2:9). This assurance grants you peace of mind that transcends understanding in the

---

[17] There are three ways that faith grows, as detailed in *FREEDOM From Doubt and Unbelief* of chapter **2** and *Rise Up and Walk in Your Authority!* of chapter **21**.

midst of attack. In short, the helmet of salvation prevents your mind from going squirrelly when experiencing demonic assault.

As an example, I underwent a serious attack last fall, but I had peace of mind about it and therefore had the grace to endure the ramifications of the assault, which lasted exactly 40 days, the biblical number of perfection in testing or judgment.

The helmet of salvation is the absolute assurance that God will deliver you when you suffer attack as you walk in faith & perseverance and don't give up.

This certainty of salvation includes the most important salvation—eternal salvation. Your eternal salvation is guaranteed as you continue in faith and endure (John 10:29 & Colossians 1:22-23).

The last two pieces of the armor of God are notable in that they're not solely defensive in nature, but offensive as well. That's because they're not actually armor, but rather **weaponry**…

6. The Sword of the Spirit

This weapon is defined as "the word of God." How does this piece differ from the belt of truth, which refers to the truth of the rightly-divided Word of God? Simple: The sword of the spirit does not refer to the pursuit of truth, as does the belt, but rather to the Word of God spoken in bold faith as a weapon. To do this, of course, you have to first *acquire* the word of truth by "putting on" the belt. This shows that the belt of truth is a foundational piece of the armor & arms of God, which is why it's the first one you don.

How does this differ from the shield of faith which is erected by speaking the Word of God in faith? Simple: The shield is strictly designed for defense whereas the sword is intended for both defense and offense. Since believers are ambassadors of the kingdom of God and function on Earth as enemies in enemy territory it's necessary to have your shield of faith up at all times to protect yourself from unforeseen attacks. (Think of it in terms of potential sniper fire when soldiers are in war zones). The sword of the spirit, by contrast, isn't pulled from its figurative "scabbard" *until* there's evidence of enemy attack in one of the five general ways noted above, whether concerning you or someone for whom you're interceding. Similarly, Roman soldiers wouldn't pull out their swords until the opponent actually assaulted them or if they went to the enemy to attack them. Either way, the adversary must be in sight to use the sword.

Speaking of which, devils obviously won't manifest in your life in the form of red cartoony figures with pitchforks. When evil spirits attack, it will manifest via one of the five general curses noted earlier—physical maladies, mental illnesses, unjust human attack, premature death and financial lack. We observe this in the enemy's attacks on Job (Job 1-2). When one or more of these curses show up in your life you are under enemy assault and it's time to get your sword out and start swinging! If you don't, you'll be defeated. There are also five other kinds of enemy attack, which apply to spiritual things and are addressed next chapter.

We'll further differentiate the sword of the spirit from the shield of faith below and elaborate on when and how to use both.

7. Praying in the Spirit

Most ministers omit this last article when teaching on the armor of God, but it's a vital piece of spiritual weaponry. Paul instructed us to "pray in the Spirit on all occasions with all kinds of prayers and requests." What does it mean to "pray in the spirit"? Notice how the Bible defines it:

> **For if I <u>pray in a tongue</u>, <u>my spirit prays</u>, but my mind is unfruitful. [15] So what shall I do? I will <u>pray with my spirit</u>, but I will also <u>pray with my understanding</u>; I will sing with my spirit, but I will also sing with my understanding.**
>
> **1 Corinthians 14:14-15**

As you can see, God's Word defines praying in the spirit as praying in another tongue via your spirit by the Spirit. This is different than typical prayer, of course, which is to "pray with your understanding," meaning to pray with your mind using the language with which you're most familiar. In my case it would be English. Paul said he did both: He prayed (and sang) with his spirit and he also prayed (and sang) with his understanding. We need to do both as well; Paul was our example. And please notice that he lists praying in the spirit *before* praying with your understanding, which implies that it's at least *as* important.

Also observe that he instructs us to "pray in the Spirit on **all occasions** with *all kinds of prayers and requests*" (Ephesians 6:18). In other words, we should include praying in the spirit every time we pray; and with every *type* of prayer! We looked at the different types of prayer last chapter; they are: communion; praise & worship; binding & loosing or intercession; petition; and confession of sin, venting & forgiving. Get in the practice of praying in the spirit with all these different kinds of prayers on "all occasions."

Speaking of which, I encourage you to go on the offensive with this spiritual weapon. In other words, don't simply use it when you discern you're being attacked. Use this awesome gift on "all occasions" day and night. Evils spirits will run away screaming in all directions!

If you don't yet have the baptism of the Holy Spirit, then make it a priority to receive it. This awesome gift is available to *all* believers and is received subsequent to experiencing spiritual rebirth. All true believers have the indwelling Holy Spirit, of course (1 Corinthians 3:16), but the baptism of the Spirit is a gift received *after* experiencing spiritual regeneration, even if it's immediately afterward (Acts 10:44-48 & 19:4-7). Unfortunately, much of Christendom is either ignorant of this gift or deceived about it, erroneously insisting that it "passed away" when the biblical canon was completed. Don't buy the lie. God's Word encourages us to eagerly *desire* spiritual gifts, not eagerly *deny* them (1 Corinthians 12:1,31 & 14:1,39). These gifts include the gift of personal tongues, otherwise known as glossolalia *(gloss-ah-LAY-lee-ah)*.[18]

Paul didn't provide a metaphor for praying in the spirit as he did with the other pieces of God's armor, like "belt," "shield" and "sword." I suspect this was because there was no Roman armament that could compare to the weapon of praying in the spirit. I like to refer to it as *the missiles* of praying in the spirit because you can pray for people and situations on the other side of the planet; in fact, you can pray for situations you're not even cognizant of because when you pray in the spirit you bypass the limitations of your mind—your understanding—through your spirit with the help of the Holy Spirit.

---

[18] For details, see the article *Baptism of the Holy Spirit ("Tongues") and It's Benefits* at the FOL site. This information is also available in my books *The SIX BASIC DOCTRINES of Christianity* and *The Four Stages of Spiritual Growth*.

For instance, you might lose your job in a few months, but you don't know about it so can't pray **with your understanding** on the matter. However, the Holy Spirit knows about it and so the issue can be addressed by praying in the spirit. When the time comes, a new means of earning money is in the works because you covered it through praying in the spirit guided by the Holy Spirit. See Romans 8:26-27 and related passages for insights.

Separating the Shield of Faith and Sword of the Spirit

Now that you understand what each piece of the armor & weaponry of God is, let's go into a little more detail on *distinguishing* the shield of faith from the sword of the spirit.

A question might have occurred to you: If the shield of faith "extinguishes *all* the flaming arrows of the evil one" why is the sword of the spirit necessary? In other words, how does a curse that's assaulting you get past your shield and require you to get out your sword? There are four possible reasons:

- If you don't have your belt of truth on, your faith won't be effective as a shield because faith comes through first being exposed to the truth (Romans 10:17). In short, if you don't have the truth, you won't have the faith. This, again, reveals why the belt of truth is the first piece of armor you don.
- For one reason or another, your shield wasn't up. For instance, you canceled your shield by speaking doubt and unbelief. This, of course, deactivates your protective angels because angels are commissioned to obey the voice of God's Word (Psalm 103:20).
- You opened the door to the enemy through unrepentant disobedience, whether a sin of commission or sin of omission. (A **sin of commission** is something you *do*, like slander someone through malicious gossip, whereas a **sin of omission** is something you *didn't* do that you should've done, like give a poor person some money as the Spirit led you).
- You're undergoing a **Maturing-Intended Trial**, which means that you're suffering attack for righteousness' sake. In this type of trial, the LORD is permitting the assault for the purpose of testing your motivations and spurring growth through actively confronting challenges and working your faith muscles. Consider Job's trials detailed in Job 1-2: It is clearly established from the get-go that Job was blameless and upright so we know he didn't open the door to

the enemy through disobedience. Nowhere does it state that Job opened the door to the devil through fear or waywardness; in fact, God praised Job to the devil as *blameless!* However, the LORD was compelled to allow satan to attack Job to test his motivations: Was Job's piety a charade for the sake of acquiring God's blessings? Would Job curse the Almighty or deny God's existence if his many blessings were removed? Although the rest of the book of Job shows him struggling greatly and seriously venting to the LORD during his long trial (e.g. Job 10:1-3), Job didn't turn away from his Creator, but rather went directly *to* him, which takes faith; not to mention he persevered. Job therefore passed the test and God restored him and doubly blessed him (Job 42:10).

When one or more of the five general curses manifests in your life, honestly search your spirit and discern how it got past your shield (assuming your shield was up) and respond accordingly:

- If your words had no power when you spoke in faith because you failed to don your belt of truth, then put on your belt by going to God's Word and feeding on the truths relevant to your trial (Matthew 4:4). Then start speaking in bold faith accordingly.

- If you either failed to put up your faith shield in the first place or canceled out your shield by using your tongue to speak unbelief, it's necessary to repent and do as above: Feed on God's Word in the relevant area and then speak it in authoritative faith. Remember: Your enemy is spiritual in nature, so defeating demonic assaults requires spiritual warfare, not physical. This and the previous point could be filed under **Self-Inflicted Trials** because you're only being attacked due to your spiritual negligence or unbelief.

- If you are convicted of a sin immediately 'fess up and God will forgive you; then start swinging your sword as necessary. This is a **Discipline-Intended Trial** where you opened the door to the enemy through unrepentant sin (Ephesians 4:27). Hence the attack is a disciplinary measure on God's part. Just a few days ago Carol said she felt sickness trying to come on her at work and, upon searching her heart, she was convicted of walking out of love with a contentious baby Christian (remember, "faith works in love," so if you walk out of love, you walk out of faith). She swiftly repented, started swinging her sword, and the sickness withdrew. By the time she arrived home there was zero evidence of sickness.

- If you *know* your shield was up and you're walking in obedience according to the terms of your covenant—"faith working in love"

(Galatians 5:6)—then you can be sure that you're undergoing a **Maturing-Intended Trial**. Simply resist in faith and the enemy will flee in due time like a pathetic cur with his tail between his legs (James 4:7); in the meantime, stand and endure. As was the case with Job, God will "restore you and make you strong, firm and steadfast" "**after** you have suffered a little while" (1 Peter 5:8-10). You will experience greater maturity and favor with God as a result, just as Job did. Now, someone might complain that spiritual warfare is complicated by the fact that it requires you to determine if the malady is a disciplinary measure on God's part due to unrepentant disobedience or an attack from the kingdom of darkness for righteousness' sake, permitted by the Sovereign LORD. It's this very factor that calls for an actual *relationship* with God through "the fellowship of the Holy Spirit" (2 Corinthians 13:14). Relationship is what true Christianity is about and this separates it from mere human religion. What do I mean? If a believer has a genuine relationship with God s/he will be able to discern fairly easily if the curse that's assaulting him/her is due to a **Self-Inflicted Trial** (SIT), a **Discipline-Intended Trial** (DIT) or a **Maturing-Intended Trial** (MIT). On the other hand, believers who fail to cultivate communion with God will have a harder time distinguishing SITs, DITs and MITs, particularly DITs and MITs (as SITs are always obvious). So this is a spur to go deeper in your walk with God. We'll look at these different types of trials further next chapter.

"Putting On" the Armor of God on Any Given Day

As noted earlier, the armor & arms of God are figurative of the spiritual tools the LORD has provided us in order to overcome spiritual attack. "Putting on" the armor is not something you do at the beginning of the day and that's the end of it. The armor & weaponry of God are spiritual principles to be practiced throughout your day and week. They empower you, shield you from satanic attack, activate your angels and guarantee victory.

Let's succinctly rundown all seven pieces as you would practice them on any given day (since each is explained above, I'm going to limit scriptural references to additional insights):

1. **The Belt of Truth:** Make a genuine effort to seek the truth—reality—through the two main sources of spiritual truth: **A.** The Living Word via the Spirit of truth. **B.** The written Word via the balanced teachings of sound ministers and your own readings.

2. **The Breastplate of Righteousness:** Endeavor to live out of your new nature, which was "created to be like God in true righteousness." The Bible calls this "participating in the divine nature" (2 Peter 1:4). Cultivate a pliable, humble heart that's quick & willing to 'fess up if you succumb to the corrupt desires of the old nature. God is faithful to dismiss the sin and "purify you from all unrighteousness." Guard your heart as the wellspring of life by regularly rooting-out negative, destructive thoughts & desires (Proverbs 4:23).

3. **The Gospel of Peace Shoes:** Put on your gospel shoes by cultivating a prayer life, regularly communing with the LORD, as detailed last chapter. Your relationship with God is foundational and offers you sure-footing when facing spiritual attack.

4. **The Shield of Faith:** Use the power of your tongue to erect a shield around you by speaking in faith concerning the blessings that are yours in Christ. Do not speak doubt & unbelief or you will cancel out your shield and deactivate your angels. Every blessing provided in your covenant comes through faith *and* perseverance; so never ever give up.

5. **The Helmet of Salvation:** Guard you mind by being conscious of God's promises of deliverance as you walk in faith & endurance. This assurance of salvation—including eternal salvation—will keep your mind from going batty during an attack.

6. **The Sword of the Spirit:** Use the Word of God as a defensive and offensive weapon by speaking it in bold faith when discerning an attack by the enemy on you or yours. Also use it in intercession.

7. **Praying in the Spirit:** Pray in the spirit on all occasions with each type of prayer noted in the Lord's prayer outline (Matthew 6:9-13). This weapon is especially useful in situations where you don't know what to pray with your understanding or have limited knowledge concerning it. Pray and sing in the spirit! Get in the habit of praying in the spirit full blast for five-ten minutes or so when you get up in the morning. It will get your day off to an awesome start.

The reason it's necessary to understand and utilize the armor & arms of God is because donning this armor and taking up your weapons empowers you by protecting you from evil spirits and their schemes; it activates angels on your behalf and guarantees your victory.

Someone might say, "But it's so simple." Yes, it is. Victory in Christ is easy as pie. That's the beauty and genius of it. There *is* a yoke and burden to serving the LORD, but the yoke is easy and the burden is light (Matthew 11:28-30). But religious people evidently want a hard yoke and heavy burden, speaking of which…

An Erroneous Reaction to the Armor & Arms of God

It boggles my mind when I come across sincere believers who respond negatively to the purpose of the armor & weaponry of God. Such people embrace the sickness, defeat, death & poverty gospel. They basically fight for their right to be downtrodden by curses, like physical maladies, mental illness, defeat to enemies, premature death and poverty/lack. They have a sick masochistic martyr complex.

I want to make it clear that **every believer will be attacked in these areas**. That's how the kingdom of darkness manifests, not as quaint red devils with horns! Even if you have your shield up, which "extinguishes all the flaming arrows of the evil one," you'll have to get your sword out and fight the good fight of faith with perseverance, as explained above. When this occurs, you're going to "suffer for a little while," as Peter put it, but the LORD *will* restore you and make you strong, firm and steadfast (1 Peter 5:8-10).

Consider the example of Paul, the great apostle, who undertook several missionary journeys to reach the world for Christ. Notice what he said:

> **I am not saying this because I am in need, for I have learned to be content whatever the circumstances. [12] I know what it is to be in need, and I know what it is to have plenty. I have learned the secret of being content in any and every situation, whether well fed or hungry, whether living in plenty or in want. [13] I can do all this through him who gives me strength.**
>
> **Philippians 4:11-13**

Paul starts off by insisting that he *wasn't* in need—which is a "positive confession" for sure—but admits that he experienced times of need in his ministry travels, as well as times of plenty. He then unveils his secret of contentment in every situation "whether well fed or hungry, whether living in plenty or in want": He can do all things through Christ who gives him strength. In short, Paul's resources—his finances, in essence—were assuredly attacked at times, but he endured in faith knowing that he was rich in Christ (2 Corinthians 8:9). As such, he knew the resources would come as he persevered in faith. **And they always did.** He could "do all things through Christ who strengthens him" (KJV). That's the secret to contentment during satanic attack and the suffering thereof.

You see Paul had his helmet of salvation on. He had his shield of faith up. He *didn't* cancel out his shield by giving-in to doubt and speaking unbelief, like "I don't think God's going to come through this time; I'm not going to make it." No, he held on in faith and endured; and the resources always came. Praise God!

A Personal Example

I shared this example last chapter, but let me do so again with pertinent details. In the winter of 2013, my left knee swelled up and I could hardly bend it. Simply walking across the room or climbing stairs was painful. This was a malady that obviously got past my shield of faith. It was a Maturing-Intended Trial, an attack by the enemy for righteousness' sake. I needed surgery, but decided instead to claim healing and stand in faith. It took over three long months but my healing finally manifested and by Christmas time I was snow skiing.

Needless to say, it wasn't fun during those 3½ months that I was suffering. Sometimes panicky thoughts would cross my mind, like *"Why are you allowing this to happen, God?! I'm seeking you and serving you more than ever!"* But I rejected the victim mentality and the corresponding verbiage. I refused to blow money on doctors, meds and surgery. I stood in faith, swinging my sword. Carol & I kept laying hands on my knee, praying and believing. And the healing eventually manifested! Before the year was over, I was skiing down huge hills in New York! God is Good!

By the way, I'm not saying that you shouldn't go to the doctor. As emphasized in chapter **8**, do what you have the faith to do as led of the Holy Spirit. Luke was a physician by occupation and I encourage regular check-ups. During my trial I was simply directed to receive healing from the Great Physician rather than blow time & money on earthly doctors. In order to do this, you have to develop stubborn faith regarding the benefits that Christ bought for you.

<u>20</u>

THE BASICS OF SPIRITUAL WARFARE

What good is it to know about the armor & arms of God if you don't know *when* the enemy is attacking you or someone else? You must understand that the devil & his loser minions aren't going to manifest as cartoonish characters with cloven hooves and pitchforks. They're *spiritual* beings and therefore invisible to the human eye. The way they attack is by trying to put one or more curses on you and those linked to you.

I don't mean "curse" like in those old horror flicks, e.g. *The Curse of the Mummy's Tomb*, but rather in a biblical sense. In this chapter we're going to define the five general curses of the Law that the enemy uses to attack believers. We're also going to look at five other curses which threaten believers' *spiritual* blessings, ten curses in all.

Let's first establish that…

Jesus Christ Was *Your* Substitutionary Curse

Most believers know that Christ suffered substitutionary death for them. In other words, the Messiah died in our place—the innocent for the guilty—that we might have the benefit of eternal life. However, the majority of Christians don't know that Jesus was their **substitutionary curse** period. Notice what the Bible says on this point:

> **Christ redeemed us from the curse of the law <u>by</u> <u>becoming a curse for us</u>, for it is written: "Cursed is everyone who is hung on a pole."**
>
> **Galatians 3:13**

Christ *redeemed* us from the curse of the Law. 'Redeem' means to release from the power of something through purchasing. What was the price for our redemption? The blood of Christ; that is, the very life of the Mighty Lord. In short, **Jesus suffered & died for you to be redeemed**.

How did Christ redeem us from the curses of the Law? The text says "by becoming a curse for us"! In other words, he suffered being cursed so that we don't have to be cursed. How exactly was he cursed? Paul cites Deuteronomy 21:23 in reference to Christ's crucifixion: "Cursed is everyone who is hung on a pole." So when the Messiah suffered and died during his last 12 hours he became *our* substitutionary curse—an innocent human being cursed so that the guilty might be blessed. That's you & me and all people.

The Five General Curses of the Law

The text specifies that "Christ redeemed us from *the curse of the law*." What precisely is the curse of the Law? This phrase refers to the five general curses detailed in Deuteronomy 28:15-68: **1.** physical ailments, **2.** mental maladies, **3.** defeat to human enemies, **4.** premature death and **5.** financial lack. **Yeshua suffered all of these curses in his last hours so that you can be released from the power of them.** This is different than saying you won't be attacked by them, because the enemy *will* certainly try to oppress you with them.

Observe how the Anointed One suffered each of these curses:

1. **Christ suffered severe physical wounds to purchase health & healing for the believer:** "by his wounds you have been healed" (1 Peter 2:24 & Isaiah 53:5). Precisely what kind of wounds did the Messiah suffer? Read on…
2. **Christ suffered extreme mental anguish to redeem us from mental illness.** His suffering includes the psychological distress of the various tortures experienced during his final hours on Earth: Severe scourging that ripped his flesh, unjust mocking & physical blows, a crown of thorns rammed on his head, his hands & feet

literally nailed to a huge stake and the corresponding agony of crucifixion, which is one of the most painful executions conceived and is where we get the term "excruciating." This form of execution, by the way, was reserved for the worst of criminals, as well as foreign enemies. On top of all this, there was the mental anguish of being utterly separated from God wherein the Son cried out to the Father: "My God, my God, why have you *forsaken* me?" (Matthew 27:45-54). Lastly, the phrase "by his wounds you have been healed" refers to *both* physical and mental healing.

3. **Christ suffered defeat to his human enemies, which heretofore never happened.** While Jesus was attacked by people throughout his 3½ years of ministry on Earth, they were never victorious over him. He always eluded them or stumped them, one way or another; in other words, he was always ultimately triumphant. For instance, he refused to allow his opponents to unjustly apprehend and kill him on multiple occasions, as documented in Luke 4:28-30, John 7:30,44, 8:59 and 10:31,39. The only time he submitted his life to the hands of his enemies was when he was arrested in Gethsemane because it was God's will that he suffer and die for the redemption of humanity. We have to get away from this ludicrous religious idea that the Messiah was some kind of timid doormat when he was anything but that (Mark 11:15-18).

4. **Christ suffered premature death by obediently dying at 33 years of age.** The Bible promises 70-80 years minimum (Psalm 90:10 & 2 Corinthians 1:20). The only God-approved exception to this promise is if a believer is called to martyrdom for the advancement of the kingdom of God, like Stephen (Acts 7:54-8:4). In such cases, the Spirit will reveal this to the believer and give him/her the grace to handle it, as was the case with Stephen. It should be stressed that the believer has the victory even with this exception, as shown in Philippians 1:21-23.

5. **Christ "*became* poor, so that you through his poverty might become rich"** (2 Corinthians 8:9). Christ wasn't poor during his lifetime on Earth; he was a carpenter who attracted business due to his honesty, diligence and superb craftsmanship (Proverbs 22:29). Nor was he poor during his 3½ years of ministry because his team had a treasury, which Judas regularly stole from without the disciples even detecting it (John 12:6). The Messiah only "became poor" during his last 12 hours when he was arrested, tortured, stripped of his very clothing and literally nailed to a huge stake, i.e. "cross," not to mention literally forsaken by the heavenly Father. This was the depth of poverty—physically, mentally and spiritually.

As you can see, "**Christ redeemed us from the curse of the law by becoming a curse for us**" (Galatians 3:13). He released us from the power of the five general curses by willfully suffering these curses in one form or another in our place. **He was our substitutionary curse.**

The "Hour When Darkness Reigns"

Those last horrible hours of Christ's life on Earth were when satan & his devils were released to assault him. Notice what they hit him with—**all five of the general curses of the Law.** Is it any wonder that Jesus referred to this time period as the "hour when darkness reigns" (Luke 22:53)?

What did he mean by that? Simply that it was the window of opportunity for the devil & his evil spirits to freely assault him, as permitted by the Sovereign LORD. And how did they attack him? **Through the five general curses of the Law.**

When satan Attacks, He Uses One of the Five Curses

Let's now observe further scriptural evidence that the kingdom of darkness uses one or more of the five general curses of the Law when they attack a person. We just witnessed the example of Christ, so let's consider the examples of two righteous men from the Old and the New Testaments respectively, Job and Paul.

God was compelled to allow satan to attack Job in order to test him and observe if he would forsake the LORD once the devil stripped him of his many blessings (Job 1-2). Observe how Job suffered the five general curses of the Law when satan was released to assault him:

- **Physical ailments:** Job was stricken with painful boils from head to toe (Job 2:7).
- **Mental illness:** Job was thrust into dire mental anguish after the satanic assaults to the point of craving death and hurling audacious accusations at the Almighty (Job 3, 10:1-3 & 30:31).
- **Human attack *and* defeat:** The neighboring Sabeans and Chaldeans, who up to that point lived peacefully by Job, unjustly attacked and killed almost all his employees and stole his wealth (Job 1:14-15 & 17). Keep in mind that this curse does not refer to simply

human attack, but rather human attack *and* defeat, which is why I also describe it as 'defeat to human enemies.'

- **Premature death:** Job's ten children and nearly all his employees were killed (Job 1:14-19). Job's life was not at stake because the LORD wouldn't permit it (although in the second round God allowed his body to be attacked). So satan struck down the next "best" thing—Job's offspring and the bulk of his loyal workers.
- **Financial attack:** Job's great wealth consisted of numerous employees and thousands of sheep, camels, oxen and donkeys; all but four of his workers were killed and all his animals were either stolen or destroyed (Job 1:14-17).

Job passed his great test because he turned *to* God rather than away from him. Yes, he severely vented *to* God and accused him of crimes against humanity based on his limited understanding of reality, but he never cursed his Creator or forsook him.

As noted in chapter **18**, venting is a healthy practice which the Bible describes as "casting your cares on the Lord" (Psalm 55:22). We're instructed to do this because the LORD cares about us and doesn't want immaterial burdens to weigh us down or limit us, which will inevitably happen if we don't vent in some manner. To "cast all your anxiety on him" (1 Peter 5:7) means to literally **go to the LORD in prayer and hurl your burdens on him**. This is what Job did. The burdens you are to hurl on God include unjust offenses and the sense of violation & anger they produce, which can tempt you to become bitter.

Why cast your cares on the LORD? Because we can't handle them. **Just as we must remove physical waste from our bodies so we must remove emotional waste.** No wonder venting is strongly encouraged in the Bible (Psalm 62:8) and there are repeated examples of it (Psalm 142:1-3 & Jeremiah 20:7-18).

So Job passed his test and the LORD restored him and blessed him doubly (Job 42:10). Keep in mind that Job was presumably under the covenant of the Patriarchal Age,[19] which refers to the covenants the LORD made with Abraham, Isaac and Jacob (Acts 3:25 & Exodus 6:4-5). The terms of this covenant were obedience to God's revealed law at the time, which included circumcision (Genesis 17:1-14,23) and, of course, keeping with repentance, which Job devoutly followed. This explains why God boasted

---

[19] See Job 1:5, for instance.

of him as "blameless" (Job 1:8 and 2:3), which is not the same as sinless. The only sinless human being who ever lived was Jesus Christ.

Now let's consider Paul, who was under the New Covenant in which the terms are **faith working in love** (Galatians 5:6):

- **Physical maladies:** Paul was stricken with some type of physical ailment according to Galatians 4:13, which provided the opportunity for him to preach the gospel to the Galatians. The word for "illness" in this text could also be translated as "weakness" as it does in Matthew 26:41, which reads: "The spirit is willing but the body is *weak*." If it does refer to physical weakness, some theorize that it could apply to Paul after he was stoned and left for dead in the Galatian city of Lystra (Acts 14:8-20). They speculate that Paul would surely need time for his body to fully heal from the abuse, which may be why he referred to the situation as a trial for the Galatian believers (Galatians 4:14). But this seems unlikely since Paul received an immediate healing and walked right back into the city (!), not to mention he left to preach in another city the very next day (!!). Other possibilities include malaria, which was common in the area, or an eye disease in light of Paul's statement, "If you could have done so, you would have torn out your eyes and given them to me" (verse 15), although this could simply be a figure of speech. Regardless of what Paul's physical problem was, he resisted the attack in faith & perseverance, received healing, and lived over another decade to fulfill God's apostolic assignment from Jerusalem to Rome and all points between, not to mention write many other important epistles by the Spirit, like Romans and Ephesians.
- **Mental ailments:** The apostles went through many hardships as they determined to advance the kingdom of God. Second Corinthians 11 details Paul's numerous sufferings, including being thrown into prison multiple times, severely flogged five times (typically 39 lashes!), beaten with rods three times, stoned and left for dead, shipwrecked three times, and more. Not to mention all of his labor, sleepless nights and the pressure of all the churches he oversaw (verses 23-29). Facing such horrendous attacks, trials and pressures, Paul and the other ministers were understandably assaulted by negative emotions at times, like fear, doubt, frustration, anxiety and wanting to quit. This is why Paul said they were "sorrowful, yet always rejoicing" (2 Corinthians 6:10); he also mentioned "fears within" and being "downcast" (2 Corinthians 7:5-6). But they never allowed such dark emotions to take root in their hearts and derail

their faith and mission for God. There's no evidence of this in Scripture. They withstood in faith & patience and overcame. Take, for example, when Paul was about to be shipwrecked due to a great storm in Acts 27:21-26; instead of caving-in to the fear and despair—e.g. *"We're all gonna die!!"*—he received instruction from the LORD and boldly spoke in faith.

- **Human attack *and* defeat:** Paul was attacked by a man named Alexander the metalworker who caused him "a great deal of harm" (2 Timothy 4:14-15), but Paul overcame and wasn't defeated or dead. He was able to warn Timothy and believed that the Lord would pay Alexander back for what he had done. Another good example is from Acts 16:22-34 where we observe Paul and Silas being unjustly attacked in Philippi after exorcizing a demon from a slave girl. They were beaten, flogged and thrown in prison. This was a serious attack indeed, but Paul and Silas withstood in faith and perseverance. At midnight they were praying and singing hymns in their gloomy, smelly jail cell (!). They refused to be defeated. They refused to give-in to doubt, frustration and despair. They knew that victory was theirs no matter how bad the situation appeared. The next thing you know there was an earthquake and the cell doors flew open! God clearly responds to such stubborn, fervent faith. Not only did they escape, the jailer and his family were saved and baptized! Paul and Silas even stayed at their house that night and dined.

- **Premature death:** Paul healed a crippled man in Lystra, which was a powerful testimony to the people there, but some Jews came and stirred the crowd against him. As noted above, they stoned Paul and dragged him outside the city, supposing him to be dead. But Paul received an incredible healing after the disciples gathered around him and he went right back into the city! The next day he was well enough to leave for another town to preach, which indicates a total healing (Acts 14:8-20). Another example would be when Paul sailed to Rome as a captive in Acts 27. A great storm came and seriously threatened all their lives. Keep in mind that, according to Job 1:16,19, satan has the ability to utilize nature for his diabolic purposes. The devil didn't want Paul to fulfill his divine commission of carrying the gospel to Gentile kings; hence, he tried to kill him on the open sea via the storm, but it didn't work because Paul received divine instruction and stood in faith (verses 21-26). Yet the devil didn't stop there. No sooner was Paul shipwrecked on the island of Malta then a deadly viper bit him (Acts 28:1-10). The islanders expected the apostle to drop dead at any moment but he withstood in faith—meaning he utilized his "sword of the spirit," which is the

Word of God spoken in bold faith—and ended up having a powerful healing revival!

- **Financial lack:** Paul pointed out in Philippians 4:12-13 that he knew what it was like to be in need and also to have plenty; he knew what it was like to be hungry and to be well fed. He also testified to his brushes with financial attack in 2 Corinthians 6:10. So we know Paul went through experiences where physical resources were seriously limited. Yet, he shared in the Philippians passage his secret of being content in any situation, whether living in plenty or in want: He said he could do all things through the Lord Jesus Christ who strengthened him. In other words, he stood in faith. He didn't give-in to worry or despair in times of need and cry, *"God has forsaken us—we're not gonna make it!"* Likewise, in the Corinthians passage he admitted to having nothing, but countered it with an expression of faith, "yet possessing everything." Consequently, he always made it through times of lack with a peaceful contentment (Hebrews 13:5). He fully understood that blessings come via faith & patience in our covenant, and faith works in love. Jehovah Jireh always eventually provided and the apostle fulfilled his many missionary assignments. Late in his life, when Paul was in custody in Caesarea, Governor Felix frequently went to him hoping Paul would offer him a bribe (Acts 24:26). This indicates that even under house arrest Paul was financially blessed since wealthy politicians don't try to milk people who are impoverished and have no money.

  A good example from the life of Christ would be when, out of nowhere, tax collectors required Peter and Yeshua to pay the annual Temple tax, which amounted to about $500 each (Matthew 17:24-27). Jesus wasn't taken off guard and, interestingly, didn't even ask treasurer Judas to get the money from their ministry earnings. He had faith that God provides the power to get wealth (Deuteronomy 8:18) and knew precisely where to get the amount they needed by the Spirit. Hence, the LORD provided.

Jesus Christ, Job and Paul are *our* **examples**. When any of the five general curses of the Law show up in your life it means you are under satanic attack.

When this happens, the first thing you need to do is determine if the assault is a **Self-Inflicted Trial** (SIT), a **Discipline-Intended Trial** (DIT) or a **Maturing-Intended Trial** (MIT). Here's an explanation of each:

- SITs are obvious; the result of one's own folly, like being injured due to reckless driving and the subsequent wreck or suffering physically due to a junk food diet. In both cases the person's travails are *not* due to some satanic plot, but simply his/her foolish choices. The answer to SITs is learning wisdom.
- A DIT means the curse is hitting you due to disobedience, whether a sin of commission or a sin of omission. If this is the case, immediately 'fess up and God will dismiss the charge (1 John 1:8-9); then take up your weapons and fight the good fight of faith until the curse departs.
- An MIT means that the curse is striking you for righteousness' sake and the LORD is allowing the enemy to assault you in order to test your character and, once your character is proven, turn the negative situation around to your good (Romans 8:28). That's the genius of MITs: God takes something in which the enemy intends to destroy you with—or, at least, hinder you—and ultimately turns it around to your good, making you "strong, firm and steadfast" "after you have suffered for a little while" (1 Peter 5:8-10). Of course, this is providing you fulfill *your* role by fighting the good fight of faith and enduring. (Remember: the LORD is your *"helper,"* not your do-everything-for-you-so-you-don't-have-to-do-anything-at-all-er). This is precisely what happened with Joseph (Genesis 50:20).

The reason this data is essential is so that you know with certainty *when* you're under satanic attack. After all, what good is the armor & arms of God if you can't even recognize when you're being assaulted?

This material is also essential so you don't mistake a satanic attack for "God's will." For instance, a genuine Christian woman was diagnosed with life-threatening cancer and concluded that, whether she lived or died from the cancer, it was God's will. No, **it's satan's will to take out fruit-bearing believers prematurely**.

The obvious problem with this woman's type of fatalistic reasoning is that, if you *think* something's God's will, you won't fight it. You'll accept it and suffer the consequences. But if you recognize something as a satanic attack, you'll fight it tenaciously.

Needless to say, ***don't* accept any curse of the Law on the mistaken grounds that it's "God's will"**! If a curse shows up in your life due to your own folly or rebellion, you're evidently undergoing an SIT or DIT;

simply repent and proceed to fight the good fight of faith. The curse *will* flee from you as you persevere in faith.

If, however, you're walking blamelessly before the LORD, keeping with penitence, you're obviously undergoing an MIT. *Don't* embrace the curse as "God's will." Tenaciously fight the good fight of faith and don't give up. The curse will eventually depart and the LORD will turn around the negative situation for your good "after you have suffered for a little while".

Handing an Unrepentant Believer Over to satan

Speaking of Discipline-Intended Trials (DITs), this type of trial explains something curious Paul said to the Corinthian believers. It concerned an unrepentant man in their assembly who was having sexual relations with his father's wife. Paul instructed the church to "hand this man over to Satan" (1 Corinthians 5:5). What did he mean by this? Simply that the man must be excommunicated from the fellowship since he was unwilling to repent of his sin. The hope was that he'd be spurred to penitence whereupon he'd be forgiven and warmly welcomed back. Thankfully, this is precisely what panned out, as revealed in Paul's subsequent letter (2 Corinthians 2:6-11).

To explain, a dis-fellowshipped believer is removed from the protective community of the church and placed outside where the "god of this world" is at liberty to have his way with him/her, so to speak. The enemy will thus assault the individual with one or more of the curses of the Law because this is *how* satan & evil spirits attack people. They don't manifest as spooky boogeymen; they attack through one or more of the curses of the Law.

Let me emphasize: the purpose for "handing a person over to Satan" is to win him/her back. Paul's goal was in line with God's love; in this case *tough* love. The hope was that banishment from the church community and suffering one or more of the curses of the Law would humble the man, provoke desperation, and ultimately shock him back to his spiritual senses, at which point he would be warmly welcomed back into the fellowship just like the prodigal son humbly returned to his father (Luke 15:11-32). So handing a person over to Satan is one-and-the-same as handing him/her over to a Discipline-Intended Trial.

God Motivates Us *Through* the Attraction of Blessings

The blessings of the Mosaic law are naturally the opposite of the curses of the Law; they are:

- Physical health.
- Mental health (e.g. peace of mind, faith, hope, love, etc.).
- Victory over human enemies and their unjust attacks.
- Long life.
- Financial provision.

Every sane person on Earth *wants* these five general blessings operating in his or her life. They're intrinsic to our spiritual/mental DNA. After all, no one wants sickness & disease, mental illness, defeat to enemies, premature death or poverty—*no one!* If someone says otherwise, they're either a liar, a fool or cracked.

Is it any wonder, therefore, that the LORD used these blessings to motivate Israel to obey his laws? Read Deuteronomy 28. It's a long chapter, but it establishes "the terms of the covenant" that God had with the Israelites (Deuteronomy 29:1,9). In modern lingo 'covenant' means *agreement* or *contract*. Every contract has terms. If you hire a company to provide a new roof for your abode the terms are *x* amount of money for a new leak-proof roof. The LORD's terms for the covenant (contract, agreement) that he had with the Israelites were: Blessings for obedience to the Law and curses for disobedience. In short, God used humanity's natural attraction to the five general blessings and our aversion to the five general curses to inspire compliance and discourage transgression.

Yet the entire Old Testament is testimony to the fact that the Israelites *couldn't* comply with these terms. Why? Because something was seriously wrong with their "spiritual DNA." The condition of spiritual death—which is the state of being dead to God—and their sinful natures rendered them incapable of fulfilling the simple terms of their covenant.

For Israel—and people in general—to fulfill such terms they would have to have a spiritual regeneration whereby they acquire a new spiritual nature that's united with God and, even more, indwelt, empowered and guided by the Holy Spirit. The attainment of eternal life is an awesome "fringe benefit." This is what the New Covenant is all about and explains why…

The New Covenant Is *Superior* to the Old Covenant

The New Covenant that believers have with God is superior to the Old Testament that the Israelites had. Notice what the Bible blatantly says on this point:

> **But in fact the ministry Jesus has received is as superior to theirs as the covenant of which he is mediator is superior to the old one, since the new covenant is established on better promises.**
> **[7] For if there had been nothing wrong with that first covenant, no place would have been sought for another.**
>
> **Hebrews 8:6-7**

For the New Covenant to be superior to the Old Covenant it would have to contain all the benefits of the Old Covenant plus *more*. For instance, if I buy a new car that's superior to my old one, it would have to have everything the old one had *plus* be new and likely have additional benefits, otherwise it wouldn't be superior. If the Old Testament promised the five blessings of the Law under the condition of obedience how could the New Testament be superior if it doesn't, *at least*, provide these blessings?

The New Covenant does provide them because the New Testament expressly assures us that "For no matter how many promises God has made, they are 'Yes' in Christ" (2 Corinthians 1:20). "In Christ" is a covenant phrase, meaning *in covenant* (in contract) with God through spiritual regeneration via the gospel of Christ. No matter how many promises God made in the Old Testament they are 'Yes' to those in covenant with God through Yeshua. In other words, a believer can claim any of the general blessings provided in the Old Covenant by faith.

For further proof, notice how the New Testament promises the five general blessings to believers:

1. **Physical health/healing:** 1 Peter 2:24 and 3 John 1:2.
2. **Mental wellness:** John 14:27, Philippians 4:6-9 and 3 John 1:2.
3. **Victory over unjust human attack:** 2 Timothy 4:17-18 & Luke 18:1-8.

4. **Long life** (with the exception of cases where God calls the believer to martyrdom for the advancement of his kingdom): 1 Peter 3:9-12.[20]
5. **Financial provision:** Mark 10:30, 2 Corinthians 8:9 & 9:11 and Philippians 4:19.

While these blessings are promised to New Testament believers, the terms of our Covenant are different than the Old Covenant. The terms are not obedience to the Old Testament Law because **1.** the dietary and ceremonial laws were fulfilled in Christ and are not applicable to New Testament believers (Colossians 2:16-17); and **2.** the moral laws—also fulfilled by Christ—are fulfilled in our lives by simply living according to our new nature, "created to be *like God* in true righteousness," with the help of the Holy Spirit (Ephesians 4:22-24). The terms of the New Covenant are **faith working in love** (Galatians 5:6), which the Amplified Bible reads as **faith being *activated* by love**. As such, anyone who fulfills the first and second greatest commands of the Mosaic law automatically fulfills *all* of the moral law (Matthew 22:36-40 & Romans 13:8-10). These two simple commands have three applications: LOVE GOD and LOVE PEOPLE as you LOVE YOURSELF.

Do you want these five general blessings supernaturally operating in your life on a regular basis? Of course you do. **They manifest through faith working in love—love for God and love for people as you love yourself.**

Yet you must understand that the kingdom of darkness is going to attack you through the five general curses of the Law, just as the enemy did with Job, Jesus and Paul, which is why it's necessary to learn how to "fight the good fight of faith" (1 Timothy 6:12). If there's a fight to faith that means there are enemies to faith. You must know your adversary and how assaults from your enemy will manifest in order to be victorious in your fight. That's one of the purposes of this manual.

So you operate in the five blessings of the Law simply by walking in faith, which includes "fighting the good fight of faith." And faith is activated by

---

[20] The Old Testament was more concerned with long life on this Earth (Deuteronomy 5:33, Psalm 91:16 & Proverbs 10:27) whereas the New Testament is more concerned with acquiring eternal life period (John 3:36, 11:26 & 1 John 5:11-12). Nevertheless, with the exception of Holy Spirit-directed martyrdom for the advancement of God's kingdom (such as Stephen in Acts 7:54-60), the New Testament promises long life with conditions.

love—**loving God** and **loving people** as you **love yourself**—which includes *tough* love when appropriate.

There are, however, some things you need to keep in mind; let's start with…

Spiritual Laws Work *With* Natural Laws

Spiritual laws work in union *with* natural laws not in exemption from them. For instance, faith being activated by love is a spiritual law that works in conjunction with common sense principles. Consider these examples:

- The Bible promises physical health/healing, but if you consume unhealthy food on a regular basis, allow yourself to become obese or develop the habit of smoking, you'll naturally imperil your health.
- The Bible promises peace of mind, but this blessing will elude you if you choose to use your mind to dwell on negative, sinful things.
- The Bible promises deliverance from unjust attacks by enemies, but if you're an arrogant, contentious person who never prays for your enemies I wouldn't bank on it.
- The Bible promises long life but if you choose to be a reckless daredevil or obstinate chain-smoker your life could be cut short.
- The Bible promises financial provision within the framework of your calling, season and environmental context, but if you're lazy (2 Thessalonians 3:10), stingy (2 Corinthians 9:6) or stubbornly impenitent (Proverbs 28:13) don't count on it.

You see? Spiritual laws and parallel natural laws work in tandem. It's a matter of simple wisdom.

You probably know unbelievers who operate in some of the five general blessings of the Law simply by observing the corresponding natural laws. For instance, someone could be a staunch atheist and yet prosper financially because s/he is diligent and rises to levels of authority in his/her occupation (Proverbs 12:24). Yet, without the Lord's guiding hand, there can be a price to such "success," like the loss of one's marriage or mental/physical breakdown. For instance, how many rich & famous celebrities have committed suicide? For those in covenant with God, however, "The blessing of the Lord makes one rich, And **He adds no sorrow with it**" (Proverbs 10:22 NKJV).

Financial Blessing Is Determined by Season, Calling & Environmental Context

Financial provision is the blessing that tends to upset some Christians, as if they want to fight for their right to be impoverished. While there have been problems with dubious ministers who essentially make Christianity out to be a get-rich-quick scheme and have used it accordingly (1 Timothy 6:9), we shouldn't throw out God's conditional promises of financial blessing with the proverbial bathwater. Disregarding the false teachings of greed-loving "ministers," the problem some believers have with the concept of financial blessing begins with an erroneous image of what it means to be financially blessed of God in a fallen world. Moreover, their criticisms do not take into account issues like the season the believer's in, divine purpose or environmental context. Let's look at these:

An Erroneous Image of Financial Blessing in a Fallen World: Someone wrote to rebuke me in response to one of our videos where he mistook my references to "the good life." He evidently envisioned it to mean living like Hugh Hefner, as if true prosperity is *all about* owning a huge mansion and sipping cocktails while lounging at an in-ground pool with myriad half-naked women prancing around, etc. (I'm not saying, by the way, that a believer *can't* own a mansion or have an in-ground pool). For one thing, this is a worldly and shallow image of "prosperity." Secondly, the video itself defined the "good life" as being hooked up with God's will and fulfilling the objectives he gives you, whatever they may be, which includes having the resources to carry out these objectives. As noted in chapter **5**, an objective or purpose like this could be any number of things, including moving to a developing country and being a missionary. God's objectives—*courses*—for each believer are exciting and good because they're in line with your Creator's will who knows you inside out and therefore how you're "wired." Living in accordance with the LORD's purposes *is* "the good life," regardless of what that purpose is. There will be hardships and persecutions, of course, but God knows what you can handle and what you can't handle. He will provide the grace to make it through as you wisely fight the good fight of faith.

The Season You're In: You might be in God's perfect will and yet the season you're in will determine your prosperity to an extent. For instance, prosperity at 18 years-of-age is different than prosperity at 50. Consider the example of Joseph, who was a type of Christ: He was unjustly sold into slavery by his jealous brothers when he was 17 and became a slave, and then a prisoner, before eventually living in the palaces of Egypt many years later as second-in-command of the nation. This journey entailed about 13 years. When he was a slave in Potiphar's house, the LORD blessed Joseph and he prospered in that context, but he was still a slave (Genesis 39:2-6). Obviously, there are limitations to how much you can prosper as a slave. Likewise, Joseph prospered while an inmate in prison, but he was still a prisoner (39:21-23). So, the season you are in determines the extent of your prosperity.

Your Divine Purpose: Your God-given calling will also determine the scope of your prosperity. This is similar to the previous one: Joseph was called to be a slave for a season, and then a prisoner, before becoming the governor of Egypt. He prospered as a slave and prisoner, but it certainly limited his prosperity. Why would God possibly call Joseph to be a slave and prisoner for so many years? Because Joseph was being groomed to be second-in-command of one of the most powerful nations on Earth at the time. The way up is down. People are more apt to be quality leaders if they have personally experienced humiliating circumstances, unjust suffering and corrupt non-leadership. Another example is Paul who wrote at least four "prison epistles" when he was under house arrest in Rome around the age of 60, only a few years before his passing. He could only prosper so much in such a situation.

Your Environmental Context: A brother-in-the-Lord I know came from the more modest sections of Youngstown and, as he became increasingly successful, his fiancé wanted him to move to a better area before marrying. Yet he insisted that he was called to stay in that community to reach the people there. The LORD put them on his heart. Whether he knew it or not, this corresponded to Paul's exhortation to the Corinthian Christians: Generally speaking, believers should remain in the situation they were in when they were called in order to reach the people thereof, as directed by the Holy Spirit (1 Corinthians 7:17-24). After all, who better to reach a group of people than those *from that* community and culture? This was a general instruction and not an ironclad law. Obviously if a person is led of the Spirit to move outside of such a context, then that's what he or she should do. Paul, for example, didn't remain in the region of Tarsus, he became a world-traveler. The brother who felt led to stay in a modest area of Youngstown would indeed prosper there, but it would be a different expression of prosperity than if he were called to, say, Mulholland Drive or the jungles of the Amazon. What if your environmental context is a communistic country where the ruling elite ensure that everyone stays at an equally modest level (except for them, of course)?

Obviously, there's some overlap between the season you're in, your divine calling and your geographical setting. In any case, when you grasp these things, it helps set you free of envy and facilitates contentment in your God-given assignment (Hebrews 13:5).

What *Is* "Prosperity" Anyway?

This all brings us to the definition of prosperity. What exactly is prosperity for the believer? It's having enough resources for your needs and righteous desires in order to fulfill your God-given calling, which depends on the aforementioned season you're in, your specific assignment and the environment to which you're called. Righteous desires are, of course, not the same as *un*righteous desires, like greed, hedonism and pomposity.

People who lust after material things for the purpose of being better than the proverbial Jones and look down on others are walking in eye-rolling carnality. Yet there's nothing wrong with having a spirit-of-excellence and wanting what you have to reflect the glory of God. I praise the LORD for neighbors who maintain a nice home & yard rather than let things get rundown.

Nor is merely being rich evil, as noted earlier in chapter **15**. Abraham, Job, Solomon and David became quite wealthy. When Paul instructed the pastor Timothy on rich people in the congregation, he didn't tell him to rebuke them for being wealthy, he simply exhorted the young minister to tell them **not to be arrogant**, but to put their hope in God rather than their riches and "to be rich in good deeds and to **be generous** and **willing to share**" (1 Timothy 6:17-18). Why did Timothy have to tell them *not* to be arrogant? Because the accumulation of physical wealth tends to feed the carnal ego and tempts people to be condescending toward those with less. This is a form of greed, which Christ blatantly condemned (Luke 12:15); so is putting on airs to impress others. It goes without saying, if you're financially well off, don't let it puff you up. Instead, develop the spirit of a giver as giving is the antidote to greed (Romans 12:8). Yet don't become arrogant of your giving and look down on those you *presume* don't give as much and condemn them as not being truly saved or what have you.

Lastly, it's not money that's the root of all evil, but rather the *love of* money (1 Timothy 6:10). It's fine to have money; it's just not fine for money to have you.

Objections to the Blessing of Health/Healing

It's astonishing, but there are genuine Christians who sincerely love the LORD, but will fight tooth & nail for the right to be sick & diseased and prematurely perish. Yet a third of Jesus' earthly ministry was focused on physical health/healing:

> **Jesus went throughout Galilee, <u>teaching</u> in their synagogues, <u>proclaiming the good news</u> of the kingdom, and <u>healing every disease and sickness among the people</u>.**
>
> **Matthew 4:23**

> **Jesus went through all the towns and villages, <u>teaching</u> in their synagogues, <u>proclaiming the good news of the kingdom</u> and <u>healing every disease and sickness</u>.**
>
> **Matthew 9:35**

Christ's ministry was threefold: **1.** He taught the Word of God, **2.** he evangelized by preaching the Good News and **3.** he healed people of every disease and sickness. So his ministry consisted of **teaching, preaching & healing**. (Memorize that: **teaching, preaching & healing; teaching, preaching & healing; teaching, preaching & healing**).

One of the things he taught was that health/healing is a God-given right in covenant with the LORD. This explains how people whom Yeshua healed had the faith to be healed in reaction to his teaching & preaching (whether they heard the Word directly or indirectly):

> **Jesus turned and saw her. "Take heart, daughter," he said, "<u>your faith has healed you</u>." And the woman was healed at that moment.**
>
> **Matthew 9:22**

> **"Go," said Jesus, "<u>your faith has healed you</u>." Immediately he received his sight and followed Jesus along the road.**
>
> **Mark10:52**

> **Then he said to him, "Rise and go; <u>your faith has made you well</u>."**
>
> **Luke 17:19**

These verses are from three different occasions taken from three different Gospel accounts. Christ regularly taught and preached the truth of health/healing and thus these people had the faith to receive healing, each from three different physical maladies—a bleeding problem, blindness, and a skin disease. Yeshua was the conduit of God's power, but it was *their faith* that made them well. Everything in our covenant is by faith & perseverance, including salvation (Hebrews 6:12).[21]

By "conduit" I mean the channel through which God's power flows to an individual; or an article that inspires faith, or both. This could be a person, like Jesus or Paul (Acts 20:7-12), or a thing, like Peter's shadow (Acts 5:15-16), a handkerchief (Acts 19:11–12) or anointing oil (James 5:14-15). The LORD uses conduits like these because people obviously need them to inspire faith and it's their faith that ushers in healing via God's power. So it's not the conduit that heals the individual, but the power of God, which is appropriated through the believer's faith. But you actually don't *need* a conduit to receive a healing or any miracle; you can receive directly from the LORD, as Jesus said: "Whatever you ask for in prayer, **believe** that you have received it, and it will be yours" (Mark 11:24). Of course, it takes spiritual growth to receive directly from God like this, which is one of the key purposes of Fountain of Life and this very manual you're reading (Ephesians 4:11-13).

"But Paul left a man sick in Miletus," someone might point out, based on 2 Timothy 4:20. Obviously this man didn't have the faith to receive healing at the time, despite Paul's teaching & preaching, which shows that the conduit itself doesn't heal. However, if the man kept drawing near to God and feeding on the message of faith & healing, he would eventually have the faith to receive. We don't know if this ever happened because the Bible doesn't say.

If you want health/healing you're going to have to fight the good fight of faith for this God-given right in Christ. This is regardless of whether or not the problem is the result of simple wear & tear on your body, including age, or if it's demonic in nature (Luke 13:11,16). **Only a fool would fight for the right to be sick & diseased and die prematurely.**

---

[21] Faith that gives up isn't true faith, only faith that perseveres (Colossians 1:22-23 & 1 Corinthians 15:2).

Don't Be Like Job's "Friends"!

It goes without saying that none of this means that we should negatively judge believers who are suffering some physical malady or any other curse, like Job's "friends" did with him (1 Corinthians 4:5). Rather, we should do our part to help hurting believers receive their healing or blessing, which *may* include walking in tough love by correcting a sin issue that, on some occasions, opened the door to the enemy (which would be a DIT—a Discipline-Intended Trial). For instance, Christ saved an adulterous woman from the curse of premature death, yet he *also* corrected her sinful behavior which opened the door to this curse in the first place (John 8:1-11). True love corrects when appropriate, but don't presumptuously judge & condemn, like Job's "friends."

Many physical and mental maladies are passed down in one's family from generation to generation. People suffering these ailments didn't do anything to incur it. But, if they want to walk free, they're going to have to learn to fight the good fight of faith; and fight it tooth & nail because the enemy is going to do everything in their power to keep a person bound up so as to not be a threat to their kingdom. This is *why* I'm sharing the material.

The Five Main Blessings of Your Covenant

Now that you understand the five general curses of the Law and the corresponding five blessings of the Law, let's examine **the five main spiritual blessings** that are yours through Christ being your substitutionary curse:

1. **The apprehension of eternal life** (John 3:16 & 2 Timothy 1:10). The Son of God suffered the wages of sin—death—so that you might have eternal life (Romans 6:23).
2. **Reconciliation with God wherein you can have a *relationship* with your Creator** (2 Corinthians 5:18-20). 'Reconciliation' means to turn from hostility to friendship. Christ suffered separation from God on the cross so that you can be united with your Creator and have intimate fellowship (Matthew 27:46).
3. **Spiritual regeneration where you're *born* righteous in your spirit** (Ephesians 4:24). Jesus Christ never sinned when he was on Earth, but he suffered the curse of being "made sin" on the cross so that you "might *become* the righteousness of God" (2 Corinthians

5:21). 'Become' is translated from a variation of the Greek word *ginomai (GHIN-oh-may)*, which means to "come into being, to be born." This means that your spirit was made in-right-standing with God when you came to Christ. And explains why God *sees* you as holy—because you *are* holy, spiritually speaking (Colossians 1:22).

4. **Freedom from bondage to sin.** This blessing is a natural outflow of the previous one: Since Christ suffered being made sin on your behalf so that you can be *born* righteous & holy in Christ, you can walk free of bondage to the flesh simply by learning to live out of your new nature. The Bible calls this walking in the spirit (Galatians 5:16-17) or "participating in the divine nature" (2 Peter 1:4). Humbly "keeping with repentance" is a strategic key to maintaining this blessing (Matthew/Luke 3:8 & 1 John 1:8-9).

5. **A meaningful life with God-given purpose.** When Christ was forsaken by the Father on the cross, he suffered the utter meaninglessness of life for the first time in his life so that you can have a meaningful life with divine purpose (Matthew 27:46). Allow me to elaborate on this…

A Meaningful Life With God-Given Purpose

The LORD provided for us an *entire book* in the Holy Scriptures to illustrate the curse of the meaninglessness of life. I'm talking about Ecclesiastes, which isn't a long book so I encourage you to check it out if you're not familiar with it. Ecclesiastes happened to be the favorite book of an unbeliever I met who regularly read the Bible. Actually, this wasn't surprising because Ecclesiastes is the one book in Scripture that focuses on the *human perspective* "under the sun," a phrase repeatedly used in its twelve chapters.

This "under the sun" perspective refers to the mundane viewpoint, which is limited to the outlook perceived through the five physical senses. It's a viewpoint of life without the benefit of the divine, eternal perspective, which explains why Solomon—the writer—constantly laments the meaningless of life in Ecclesiastes. I've experienced this curse even after becoming a believer, yet only when I allowed myself to become distant from God for one reason or another, whether falling into sin or spiritual apathy. The good news is that Christ suffered this curse of mundane futility so that you can have the blessing of a purposeful life with God-given drive![22]

This blessing, along with knowing the LORD—that is, having an actual relationship with your Creator—will become the **driving force in your life** as you mature in Christ. Why is this important? Because these two blessings will enable you to endure the discomfort of the enemy's increasing attacks as you mature and increasingly engage in spiritual warfare (remember: "Higher levels, bigger devils"). For instance, how was Paul possibly able to face the incredible satanic attacks on his life and endure? (See 2 Corinthians 11:23-29). Because **his main goal in life was not *mundane* peace, prosperity, pleasure and the avoidance of pain, but rather pleasing God through fulfilling the works he called him to fulfill**. Doing so produces far greater peace, riches and joy because they're spiritual in nature.

I should add that the LORD and his will should be our *first* priority, but not our *only* priority (Matthew 6:33).

Reflect on these things and the Spirit will give you insight.

The Enemy WILL Attack These God-Given Blessings

Just as the kingdom of darkness will try to stop the five blessings of the Law manifesting in your life by trying to put one or more of the five curses of the Law on you, evil spirits will attack these five spiritual blessings, whether in your life or in the lives of those for whom you're interceding:

1. The enemy will attack your eternal salvation (I'll show you *how* in a moment, don't freak out).
2. The enemy will attack your relationship with God.
3. The enemy will try to prevent you from living out of your new nature, which is righteous, and get you back into the flesh.
4. The enemy will try to get you stuck in life-dominating sin bondage.
5. The enemy will try to prevent you from fulfilling your God-given purpose(s).

Let me elaborate on each:

---

[22] See chapter **5** for a biblical 3-point plan on how to discern God's will for your life and fulfill his purposes.

The enemy will attack your eternal salvation. The Bible certainly teaches that your salvation is secure (John 10:28-29), yet it's obviously contingent on *continuing* in faith (Colossians 1:22-23 & 1 Corinthians 15:2). Numerous passages clearly show that Christians can abort their salvation *if* they choose to neglect their faith and lose it (Hebrews 6:4-9, 2 Peter 2:20-21, 2 Timothy 2:11-13 & Titus 1:16). This is just common sense; after all, if it takes faith to be saved it naturally follows that people cannot be saved if they come to a point where they no longer believe. So, the Bible supports the doctrine of eternal security, but not the doctrine of *unconditional* eternal security.

Since it takes faith to be saved (Ephesians 2:8) and **salvation is secure as one continues in faith**, the only way the enemy can successfully attack a believer's salvation is by deceiving him/her with doctrines of demons in an effort to get them to come to the point where they no longer believe. This is done through corrupt noémas—erroneous indoctrination, as covered in chapter <u>17</u>. Let me give you an example: A man I knew, who was an evangelizing Christian for 25 years, foolishly read a book which championed atheism and he eventually publicly confessed that he no longer believed (!) and even encouraged others to read the book (!!). How did the enemy rob this man of his eternal salvation? Through false teachings that corrupted his mindset and therefore ripped off his faith.

Of course, this man's relationship with God must have been pretty feeble and his theology shallow for a mere atheistic book to derail his faith, but this just goes to show the importance of two pieces of the Armor of God— the gospel of peace shoes and the belt of truth, as covered in the previous chapter. Without these vital pieces of armor, the devil can rob you wholesale!

The enemy will attack your relationship with God. Did you notice that when the devil attacked Job his stated goal was to get him to curse the Almighty to his face? Make no mistake, the enemy's primary objective is to break the believer's relationship with God, with the first order of business being to break the fellowship. In short, evil spirits are obsessed with destroying your communion with the LORD.

The enemy will try to prevent you from living out of your new nature, which is righteous, and get you back into the flesh. Since any believer who learns to walk according to their new righteous nature will produce the fruit of the spirit—the very character traits of God—s/he naturally becomes a threat to the kingdom of darkness. As such, evil spirits will seek to keep believers from living according to their new nature, i.e. walking in the spirit.

The enemy will try to get you into the bondage of life-dominating sin. Since sin breaks fellowship with God and hinders believers from participating in the divine nature, the kingdom of darkness will do everything in their power to get believers in bondage to a particular sin wherein it becomes life-dominating. Some obvious examples include alcoholism, *pharmakeia* (drug-oriented sins), porn bondage, greed, fornication, sexual perversion, arrogance and pathological lying (1 Corinthians 6:9-11). When a person is captive to a particular sin—living it as *a lifestyle*—he or she is no threat to the devil's kingdom; in fact, s/he inadvertently supports it.

The enemy will try to prevent you from fulfilling your God-given purpose(s). Since any fulfillment of a God-given assignment is a direct threat to the kingdom of darkness, evil spirits will do everything they can to prevent believers from fulfilling their divine calling in whatever season they're in, however big or small.

Master the Ten Curses and Contrasting Blessings

Altogether there are ten curses and ten contrasting blessings—five curses of the Law and five spiritual curses; five blessings of the Law and five spiritual blessings.

- The five curses of the Law and the five blessings of the Law have to do with mundane things corresponding to your life on Earth.
- The five spiritual curses and the five spiritual blessings have to do with God, eternity and the things of the spirit (which, of course, affect your life on Earth).

This chapter is devoted to detailing these ten curses and ten blessings so that you'll readily recognize *when* you are under demonic attack and hence fight the good fight of faith accordingly. After all, how can you conduct spiritual warfare if you're not even aware you're being attacked? This goes for people you're interceding for as well.

You Must Fight the Good Fight of Faith for Your Rights!

The five blessings of the Law and the five spiritual blessings are **yours in Christ**. In other words, these ten blessings are **yours** by **right** in covenant (contract) with God through Jesus. Remember, you are a co-heir in Christ through spiritual regeneration wherein you're *born* of the Messiah's seed, that is, the Anointed One's spiritual sperm (Romans 8:17 & 1 John 3:9).

Here, again, are the ten blessings:

The Five Blessings of the Law
1. Physical health/healing.
2. Mental health.
3. Victory over unjust human attack.
4. Long life till you're satisfied (minimum 70-80 years).
5. Financial provision/blessing (not a get-rich-quick scheme).

The Five Spiritual Blessings
1. Eternal life.
2. Reconciliation and relationship with the LORD.
3. Spiritual regeneration wherein you're spiritually *born* righteous and can live by this new nature.
4. Freedom from bondage to sin via walking in the spirit.
5. Meaningful life with God-given purpose.

These ten blessings are your rights ('10' is incidentally the number of completion in the Bible). *But* they are attained and maintained through faith & perseverance. This includes your eternal salvation, as explained above. Like I said earlier, faith that gives-up is not true faith. That's why faith *and* perseverance/patience/endurance are often spoken of in the same breath in the New Testament (e.g. Hebrews 6:12).

These ten blessings are *your* earthly "Promised Land." To explain, the Israelites were promised the land of Canaan and victory over the inhabitants thereof, which were their enemies; yet they still had to get their swords out and take the land. Similarly, these ten blessings are promised to you, the believer, but you must put your armor on, get your weapons out, and fight the fight of faith in order to walk in them. Unlike with the Israelites, however, your enemies aren't flesh and blood (Ephesians 6:12). Your enemies are spiritual in nature and their attacks manifest through one (or more) of the ten curses above, which explains why it requires *spiritual* armor and *spiritual* weapons to overcome them.

I've heard Christians speak of the Promised Land as if it were a type of eternal life in the new Heavens and new Earth (typically referred to as "Heaven"). This is true as far as our *eternal* Promised Land is concerned. Even the Old Testament saints looked forward to the *eternal* Promised Land (Hebrews 11:10,16). Yet, just as they had an earthly Promised Land, so New Covenant believers have an earthly Promised Land, although it's not a piece of real estate. It's walking in the ten promised blessings above. This includes fulfilling whatever mission or dream the Lord gives you. In other words, the Hebrews' Promised Land is a type of your inheritance during your temporal life on this Earth.

The Hebrew's earthly Promised Land was Canaan where there were enemy nations that they had to conquer in order to obtain their Promised Land. Just as they had to put their armor on and take up weapons in order to inhabit their Promised Land, we believers have to put on our armor and take up our weapons to inhabit ours.

Needless to say, get your armor on, get your weapons out, and fight the good fight of faith—conquer *your* Promised Land!

'What About Hebrews 11:39?'

Before closing this chapter, we need to clear up an objection based on this passage:

> **These were all commended for their faith, yet none of them received what had been promised,**
>
> **Hebrews 11:39**

To properly interpret this verse, both the hermeneutical laws **context is king** and **Scripture interprets Scripture** must be applied. First, who is the subject of the text? Second, what specific promise(s) *didn't* they receive while on Earth? As far as the first goes, the writer is contextually referring to various Old Testament saints who, albeit flawed individuals, were commended for their faith as they endured great challenges and persecutions.

As far as the promise(s) they didn't receive on Earth goes, the context shows that it's referring to their *eternal* Promised Land:

> **By faith he** [Abraham] **made his home in the promised land like a stranger in a foreign country; he lived in tents, as did Isaac and Jacob, who were heirs with him of the same promise.** [10] **For <u>he was looking forward to the city with foundations, whose architect and builder is God.</u>**
>
>

Hebrews 11:9-10

> **All these people were still living by faith when they died. <u>They did not receive the things promised; they only saw them and welcomed them from a distance,</u> admitting that they were foreigners and strangers on earth.** [14] **People who say such things show that they are looking for a country of their own.** [15] **If they had been thinking of the country they had left, they would have had opportunity to return.** [16] **Instead, <u>they were longing for a better country—a heavenly one.</u> Therefore God is not ashamed to be called their God, for <u>he has prepared a city for them.</u>**
>
>

Hebrews 11:13-16

So the promise they didn't receive while on Earth is the new Jerusalem and, by extension, the new Heavens (Universe) and new Earth (2 Peter 3:13). The new Jerusalem is currently in Heaven but will "come down out of heaven from God" to rest on the new Earth in the eternal age to come (Revelation 3:12 & 21:2,10).

New Covenant believers are also looking forward to this promise and, like the Hebrews, will not receive it as long as we're on *this* Earth:

> **For here <u>we</u> do not have an enduring city, but <u>we</u> are looking for <u>the city that is to come.</u>**
>
>

Hebrews 13:14

Someone might understandably point out that verse 13 (of the Hebrews 11 passage cited above) infers more than one promise, as it says: "They did not receive *the things* promised; they only saw *them* and welcomed *them* from a distance." Answer: While the "promise" the Old Testament saints didn't receive on Earth mainly concerns the new Jerusalem and, by extension, the new Heavens and new Earth, it also naturally includes the foundational promises on which these future blessings are based: **1.** the promised prophet, Jesus Christ (Deuteronomy 18:15), and **2.** the New

Covenant established through his death and resurrection (Jeremiah 31:31,33). Every Old Testament saint listed in the Hall of Faith Chapter of Hebrews 11 died before these promises came to pass.

New Covenant believers have received these two promises, of course, otherwise we wouldn't be New Covenant believers; and this ties into something noted in verse 40:

> **These were all commended for their faith, yet none of them received what had been promised, [40]since God had planned something better for us so that only <u>together with us</u> would <u>they</u> be <u>made perfect</u>.**
> **Hebrews 11:39-40**

This distinguishes the Old Testament saint from the New Testament saint. The spirits of New Covenant believers were "made perfect" through spiritual regeneration when they accepted the gospel of Christ (Hebrews 10:14, 12:23 & Ephesians 4:24). Yet deceased Old Testament saints won't receive this promise *until* their resurrection. At that time "together with us" they will "be made perfect."

Lastly, twice previously in the book of Hebrews believers are encouraged to walk in faith & patience to inherit their promised blessings (Hebrews 6:12 & 10:36), so Hebrews 11:39 *cannot* be interpreted to discourage this. Not to mention, we have the entire rest of the New Testament. Scripture interprets Scripture.

21

DEALING WITH DEMONIC POSSESSION

In the Bible it is observed that the Lord delivered people from demons who *induced* insanity, deafness, muteness and infirmity (Mark 5:1-20, 9:17-29 & Luke 13:10-16). It's clear from the scriptural evidence that being possessed (or oppressed) by an evil spirit can induce mental or physical ailments. Such demons are "spirits of infirmities," which we'll address momentarily.

How many people in our mental institutions are being drugged up and essentially imprisoned for the rest of their lives when what they really need is exorcized of dark spiritual entities that have possessed them to one degree or another? Don't get me wrong here, I'm not against these kinds of asylums and realize that we, as a society, are just doing what we have to for such ailing people; that is, what we can.

Yet, what if someone of Jesus Christ's stature were around, someone who had the authority, faith and courage to rebuke demons and send them fleeing with their tails between their legs, so to speak? The first chapter of the gospel of Mark shows the Messiah exorcizing demons from numerous people and this is merely one chapter of the New Testament! (See verses 25-26, 34 and 39).

A Real-Life Experience With Demonic Possession

I know of one person who was seriously mentally ill all her life but the best that professional medical science had to offer couldn't deliver her. The best they could do was sedate her, try this or that (including shock treatments) and help her cope. Some of this is good to an extent, but *they could not **set her free***. She lived and died with this severe illness. I'm convinced that these symptoms were the result of some type of demonic possession/oppression. Other believers who were close to the situation have drawn the same conclusion. The signs pointed to a *partial* possession, which we'll look at shortly. If only I knew then what I know now and was the person I am now, I would have exorcized her of this spiritual subjugation without a second thought, as long as she was willing (which is necessary since God never heals or delivers people against their will).

Am I suggesting that we should let loose a bunch of religious kooks into our mental institutions to supposedly exorcize the severely ill of their (very possible) literal demons? No, but *if* some people show evidence of the power and boldness Jesus Christ walked in, shouldn't we? Didn't Yeshua come to "set the captives free," "heal the sick and brokenhearted" and "release the prisoners from the darkness"? (Luke 4:16-21 & Isaiah 42:5-9).

The fact that so few believers are walking in this authority, power, faith and boldness is a shame to the modern Church in general. It's also testimony to the powerless nature of so many counterfeit sects and "believers" who "have a form of godliness but deny its power" (2 Timothy 3:1-5). Not that all the believers within these camps are counterfeits, not at all. But their leaders are unaware, disingenuous or spiritually blind. And didn't Jesus say, "If the blind lead the blind, both will fall into a pit?" (Matthew 15:14).

One of the purposes of this book is to reveal the reality of dark spiritual entities, how their attacks manifest, and how to effectively combat them by faith.

The Believer's Authority

Where is the Church of Jesus Christ, the "called-out ones" who are called out of the darkness of this world? Why is the Church so inert and seemingly powerless when it comes to dealing with victims of demonic possession or oppression? I'm asking with humble concern, not arrogant denunciation; plus I'm including *myself* when I say 'the Church.'

Let's not forget the incredible authority the Lord gave believers:

> **"I saw Satan fall like lightning from heaven. [19] <u>I have given you authority to trample on snakes and scorpions and to overcome all the power of the enemy</u>; nothing will harm you. [20] However do not rejoice that <u>the spirits submit to you</u>, but rejoice that your names are written in heaven."**
>
> **Luke 10:18-20**

"Snakes and scorpions" are figurative of the devil and demonic spirits. Yeshua gave the disciples authority to trample them under their feet, that is, overcome their power. Hence, filthy spirits *had* to submit to them and the disciples were understandably elated (see verse 17). They delivered people from demonic oppression and possession; they healed the sick and brokenhearted; they set the captives free *because they had the authority and power to do so*. Authority is the right to rule whereas power is the ability to rule.

If Jesus' disciples—who weren't even spiritually regenerated at the time— had authority to overcome the powers of darkness, how much more so Christians who have been spiritually *born* of the imperishable seed of Christ?

Get a hold of this fact: If you're a believer, **YOU have authority over the kingdom of darkness! All the spiritual forces of evil are under your feet! They don't have the authority to overcome you; *you* have the authority to overcome them!**

Words have the power of life and death (Proverbs 18:21), so make this powerful positive confession:

> *I* [state your name] *have the authority to trample on snakes and scorpions and to overcome all the power of the devil and his wicked angels. Nothing will harm me. I have the victory in Jesus Christ—Hallelujah!!*

Make Biblical statements like this your regular confession. Speak them with fervor! Never speak disempowering words of doubt, defeat, fear or grumbling. Cast such things off on the LORD in prayer, which is venting (Psalm 55:22 & 1 Peter 5:7). When you spend quality time praising, adoring and communing with the Most High the very light of God's presence will squelch emotional waste like doubt, fear and worry. Do this regularly. God is the Fountain of Life and, in his light, we see light (Psalm 36:9); darkness vanishes!

Christ Is the Genuine Lion While satan Is a Counterfeit

The devil may prowl around like a roaring lion trying to frighten people immobile with his intimidating roar but, for the believer who walks in faith, he's a toothless, clawless, sinew-less lion. More than that, the Bible describes Jesus Christ as the *genuine* Lion of Judah. In other words, Yeshua is the real deal, while the devil is just a counterfeit—a fake—who prowls around *like* a roaring lion. Oh, sure, he can attack since he's "the god of this world" and we're invading his turf, but the Bible says that all we have to do is "submit to God and resist the devil" "standing firm in the faith" and the enemy will literally "flee" from us (James 4:7 & 1 Peter 5:8-10).

This is what the apostle Paul called fighting "the good fight of faith" (1 Timothy 6:12). When we stand in faith with our spiritual armor on and swing our spiritual swords, the forces of evil have no recourse but to "flee." One minister I heard said the imagery in the original language paints the picture of a dog running away with his tail between his legs—*"Yipe, yipe, yipe, yipe!!"* Picture that the next time you take a stand in faith against the enemy—including exorcisms—and have yourself a knee-slapping victorious laugh.

Walking in the Amazing Authority of Jesus Christ

We live in a generation that idolizes reason and pseudoscience above all. These are the only criteria for determining reality to the unspiritual man, and understandably so. Thus anyone who looks to the Holy Scriptures for truth and has the audacity to act accordingly is viewed with disdain and ridicule. Which explains why the Church is so powerless and timid when it comes to dealing with demonic possession or oppression: **We fear the scorn of the world.**

This reminds me of a Pentecostal pastor who told me about a prophet he had at his assembly for a few services. The prophet ministered to the people and apparently dealt with a couple cases of demonic oppression or possession. The pastor said he was uncomfortable with the man's ministry because it was sometimes awkward and even shocking. But dealing with filthy spirits can get ugly! Yelling, vomiting, screaming, wiggling on the floor, etc. come with the territory. We'll look at examples from the Scriptures in a moment. The pastor said that the experience made him "gun shy" of demonic deliverance and everything that goes with it. Unfortunately, he threw the baby out with the proverbial bathwater because his church had the most sterile atmosphere of any I've experienced; and it was "Pentecostal"! I'm not being mean or disrespectful, just telling you what I experienced at this fellowship.

I realize we have to "become all things to all people that by all possible means we might save some" (1 Corinthians 9:22). Hence, we have to "locate" where individuals are and act accordingly, otherwise we'll scare 'em off with things they simply can't handle, at least not presently. We need to do this to reach people, but let's not do it to the extent that we become as spiritually powerless as the world. We are the "light of the world" (Matthew 5:14), meaning that the Church is the light that inspires those lost in the darkness of this world. Those in the darkness "who have ears to hear and eyes to see" will naturally be drawn to the light and ultimately delivered; and the closer they get to *The* Light the freer they'll be (John 8:12,31-32). This is the way it's supposed to be.

But something's wrong when the Church allows the darkness of the world to squelch our light to the point that we're impotent and ineffective, all because we fear the world's contempt and ridicule! Needless to say, this is an example of allowing the world to mold us into its form; something the Bible instructs us *not* to do (Romans 12:2).

One of the things that drew people to the Mighty Christ was the genuine authority he walked in, which shouldn't be confused with pompous authoritarianism. This made his ministry—his service—effective, including demonic deliverance. Observe:

> **They went to Capernaum, and when the Sabbath came, Jesus went into the synagogue and began to teach. [22] The people were amazed at his teaching because he taught them as one who had authority, not as the teachers of the law. [23] Just then a man in their**

synagogue who was possessed by an evil spirit cried out, [24] "What do you want with us, Jesus of Nazareth? Have you come to destroy us? I know who you are—the Holy One of God!"

[25]"**Be quiet!" said Jesus sternly. "Come out of him!"**
[26]**The evil spirit shook the man violently and came out of him with a shriek.**
[27]**The people were all so <u>amazed</u> that they asked each other, "What is this? A new teaching—and <u>with authority! He even gives orders to evil spirits and they obey him</u>.**" [28] News about him spread quickly over the whole region of Galilee.

Mark 1:21-28

Verse 22 shows that the people were *amazed* at the aura of authority Jesus displayed merely with his public teaching. This was something the religious leaders of that day didn't have, like the Pharisees and the Sadducees; all they had was religious bluster. The people were even more amazed when the Messiah proceeded to **command evil spirits to shut up and come out of people**, as shown in verse 27. Unsurprisingly, news spread about him throughout the region.

Speaking of commanding demons to shut up, Christ typically did this when encountering possessed people (Mark 1:24-25 & Luke 4:35,41). Why? Because evil spirits are liars who have ages of experience duping even the brightest of people. In light of this, never talk with demons; just tell 'em to shut up and exorcize the individual, presuming the person is willing.

A pastor in my area testified of his first encounter with a demon-possessed man. The wicked spirit started a conversation with him that went on for a couple of hours (!) whereupon the pastor's head was spinning, so to speak. Then a seasoned fellow-minister, who just so happened to be visiting from out of state, entered the room and immediately discerned what has happening. He didn't talk with the foul spirit at all, but simply said *"loose"* and that was the end of it.

Rise Up and Walk in Your Authority!

Unlike 1st century Israel where Christ ministered, I realize most people reading this live in irreligious cultures of the post-Christian Western world (or, at least, Western-influenced). As such, we have to be careful how we minister and make sure we're led of the Holy Spirit. Regardless, you can be sure that if we boldly rise up and walk in our authority and people start getting miraculously healed or freed from life-dominating sin and demonic oppression or possession nothing will keep the news from spreading. It will light a spiritual fire in this dark, dying world and those who long for healing and freedom will literally come running for deliverance! Make no mistake, Jesus plainly said that "anyone who has faith" will do the works he did. In fact, he said such people would do even *greater* works (John 14:12).[23] Please note that he said "***anyone*** who has faith"; this means "anyone" who simply ***believes***!

Do you sometimes struggle with faith? All believers are *believers* precisely because they have "a *measure* of faith" (Romans 12:3). The wonderful thing is that this is merely the starting point of the faith walk because *faith can grow*. While we addressed this in chapter **2**, let's brush up on the three ways faith increases:

1. Getting closer to God, who is the Fountain of Life and therefore gushes life, light, power and belief into whoever gets close to him (Psalm 36:9).
2. Through regular *feeding* on God's Word, as shown in Romans 10:17 and Matthew 4:4. Whatever element of the Word you feed on is where your faith will grow. For instance, if you want strong faith in regards to the believer's authority, spiritual warfare and exorcism, then I encourage you to master the material in this chapter, as well as the previous two.
3. By praying in the Holy Spirit, as shown in Jude 1:20 (see also Ephesians 6:18, 1 Corinthians 14:14-15 and 2 Timothy 1:6-7).[24]

A pastor I know, Rick testified to something he experienced when he was in Bible college: He attended a big service where the Charismatic leader was ministering and Rick happened to be standing in the front row. The minister was not far from him when fear suddenly seized Rick and he felt paralyzed. The minister looked at him, but seemed to be focusing on something unseen over Rick's shoulder. He simply pointed to this *thing* and waved his hand, as if to say "Go," and the fear immediately left the brother.

---

[23] See the last section of chapter **8** for details on what this means.

[24] For details, see the seventh piece of the armor & arms of God in chapter **19**.

This minister was obviously walking in the gift of discerning of spirits (1 Corinthians 12:1-11), which is the ability to perceive what's happening in the spiritual realm. (Contrary to what some think, discerning of spirits is *not* the gift of carnal judgment and gossip/slander). An Old Testament example of this spiritual gift can be observed when Elisha's assistant was suddenly able to see into the spirit realm (2 Kings 6:15-17).[25]

Don't you want to walk in the gifting and authority that this minister functioned in when he delivered this brother seized by a spirit of fear? Of course you do; I do too. The material in this book is a good starting point.

Dealing With "Spirits of Infirmities"

At the beginning of this chapter, it was pointed out that Christ delivered people from demons which *induced* infirmities of one sort or another, including mental illness. Here are two biblical examples:

- **Deafness and muteness:** Mark 9:17-29.
- **Crippling:** Luke 13:10-16.

Let's look at both cases:

> **A man in the crowd answered, "Teacher, I brought you my son, <u>who is possessed by a spirit that has robbed him of speech.</u> [18] <u>Whenever it seizes him, it throws him to the ground. He foams at the mouth, gnashes his teeth and becomes rigid.</u> I asked your disciples to drive out the spirit, but they could not."**
> **[19]"You unbelieving generation," Jesus replied, "how long shall I stay with you? How long shall I put up with you? Bring the boy to me."**
> **[20]So they brought him. When <u>the spirit</u> saw Jesus, <u>it immediately threw the boy into a convulsion. He fell to the ground and rolled around, foaming at the mouth.</u>**
> **[21]Jesus asked the boy's father, "How long has he been like this?"**

---

[25] Since Paul, by the Spirit, didn't elaborate on the gift of the discerning of spirits, there must be a biblical precedent to define it. While the gifts of the Spirit are a New Testament phenomenon, Old Testament prophets obviously functioned in these gifts, as the Spirit willed.

"**From childhood**," he answered. ²² "**It has often thrown him into fire or water to kill him.** But if you can do anything, take pity on us and help us."
²³ " 'If you can'?" said Jesus. "**Everything is possible for one who believes.**"
²⁴Immediately the boy's father exclaimed, "I do believe; help me overcome my unbelief!"
²⁵When Jesus saw that a crowd was running to the scene, **he rebuked the impure spirit**. "**You deaf and mute spirit**," he said, "**I command you, come out of him and never enter him again.**"
²⁶**The spirit shrieked, convulsed him violently and came out.** The boy looked so much like a corpse that many said, "He's dead." ²⁷ But Jesus took him by the hand and lifted him to his feet, and he stood up.
²⁸After Jesus had gone indoors, his disciples asked him privately, "Why couldn't we drive it out?"
²⁹He replied, "**This kind can come out only by prayer.**"

Mark 9:17-29

This passage reveals several insights:

- This evil spirit *induced* muteness and deafness (verses 17 & 25).
- While the muteness and deafness were presumably constant conditions, the demon only seized the child on occasions, not 100% of the time (verse 18). Luke's account verifies that the spirit would leave him on occasion (Luke 9:39), which indicates a **partial possession**. (This was the situation with the person in my life, shared earlier). In this particular case of *partial possession* there was only one demon involved whereas in the example of *total possession* concerning the man from the Gerasenes there were hundreds, perhaps thousands, of demons involved (Mark 5:1-20).
- Speaking of partial possession, it's clear that the infamous serial killer Ted Bundy was demonically influenced to commit his atrocious crimes; and the evidence points to partial possession: When he was his normal self, he was affable and charismatic, which explains the inexplicable loyalty of several naïve people close to him, not to mention his mounting fan club (!). Many remained loyal *during* his eleven years of imprisonment before his execution in early 1989. Even the judge who sentenced him noted how likable and gifted he was. Yet his myriad wicked murders and subsequent abuse of the corpses indicated a wholly sinister side. An investigator

who visited Bundy's cell in Florida witnessed firsthand his satanic mood swings: During an ordinary conversation the murderer abruptly metamorphosed before his very eyes wherein Bundy's body & countenance weirdly altered and the investigator perceived an odor. He described the situation as extremely intense during this dispositional change, which lasted about 20 minutes.

- Getting back to Mark 9:17-29, when the demon took control of the boy it threw him to the ground where he foamed at the mouth, gnashed his teeth and became rigid (verse 20). Needless to say, it helps to recognize these characteristics of demon-possession.

- The demon **drove the boy to self-harm** by often trying to kill him via throwing him into fire or water (verse 22). This demon-influenced tendency is covered in chapter **9** of my book *ANGELS*.

- Christ rebuked the demon, calling it a "deaf and mute spirit," which simply means it was an evil spirit that had the ability to cause deafness and muteness (verse 25).

- Jesus *commanded* the demon to **come out of the boy**, adding **"and never enter him again"** (verse 25). This is an important addition.

- The spirit shrieked and convulsed the lad violently during the exorcism (verse 26). These are further characteristics we need to recognize when exorcizing demons.

- Explaining why the disciples couldn't cast out this particular wicked spirit, Jesus said "This kind can come out only by prayer" (verse 29).[26] Since prayer is communion with God, this indicates that a close relationship with the LORD and the corresponding increased spiritual sensitivity & anointing are required to operate in the authority necessary to deliver people from demons of this magnitude. Obviously some evil spirits are more powerful or obstinate and, hence, are more resistant to exorcism.

Now let's look at the other passage and cull insights from it as well:

> **On a Sabbath Jesus was teaching in one of the synagogues, [11] and <u>a woman was there who had been crippled by a spirit for eighteen years. She was bent over and could not straighten up at all</u>. [12] When Jesus saw her, he called her forward and said to her, <u>"Woman, you are set free from your infirmity."</u>**

---

[26] While some translations say "prayer and fasting" (e.g. the KJV), the earliest (and therefore most reliable) manuscripts available omit "fasting." It was likely added by an overzealous scribe at some point.

¹³**Then he put his hands on her**, and **immediately she straightened up** and praised God.
¹⁴**Indignant because Jesus had healed on the Sabbath, the synagogue leader said to the people, "There are six days for work. So come and be healed on those days, not on the Sabbath."**
¹⁵**The Lord answered him, "You hypocrites! Doesn't each of you on the Sabbath untie your ox or donkey from the stall and lead it out to give it water? ¹⁶ Then should not this woman, a daughter of Abraham, whom Satan has kept bound for eighteen long years, be set free on the Sabbath day from what bound her?"**

Luke 13:10-16

- The woman's crippled condition was *caused by* a demon (verse 11). This shows that evil spirits have spiritual powers that can negatively affect those in the physical world. Medical science has, of course, discovered various other causes of ailments, whether physical or mental, but this does not discount the effect the spiritual has on the physical. Furthermore, could it not be possible—even likely—that these spirits induced these "causes," as pointed out earlier?

- Unlike with the spirit that brought muteness and deafness, Christ did not rebuke the demon or command it to leave (at least Luke didn't cite this in his account). Jesus simply said, "Woman, you are set free from your infirmity," followed by laying his hands on her, and she was both delivered from the spirit and healed (verses 12-13). This shows a correlation between the two—being delivered from demonic oppression and receiving healing. Comparing the two accounts also shows that **1.** exorcizing demons and healing people are not one dimensional in nature as there are various methods we can employ, which grant the same result, and **2.** we should rely on the Holy Spirit's distinctive leading in each case.

- On a side note, this passage shows that legalists like the Pharisees— i.e. lifeless religionists—are prone to *opposing* genuine ministerial works, such as exorcism and healing. Big surprise, huh?

It's possible that not every infirmity is directly caused by evil spirits, so you have to have spiritual discernment in order to effectively minister in these situations. And the only way you can do this, again, is to have genuine spiritual sensitivity, which comes by drawing closer to the LORD, as well as eagerly *desiring* gifts of the Spirit rather than eagerly *denying* them (1 Corinthians 12:1,31 & 14:1,39). If you're not sure if a malady was induced by a demon, you can simply rebuke the ailment itself, as Jesus did here:

> **Now Simon's mother-in-law was suffering from a high fever, and they asked Jesus to help her. [39] So he bent over her and <u>rebuked the fever, and it left her</u>. <u>She got up at once</u> and began to wait on them.**
>
> **Luke 4:38-39**

As a New Covenant believer and co-heir in Christ you have the authority to do the works the Messiah did (John 14:12).

Closing Blessing

Rise up O man of God, rise up O woman of God, and walk in the authority that is yours in Jesus Christ. May you walk in faith and do the works Yeshua did! May you heal the sick and set the captives free through the power of God that's in you and upon you. Let it be so.

22

DEALING WITH HUMAN ENEMIES

We've briefly considered strategies on handling human enemies here and there, but it's a good idea to include a succinct chapter on the topic. In the Old Covenant, the Hebrews didn't have spiritual authority over the devil & his filthy minions because they lacked spiritual rebirth and the indwelling Holy Spirit. As such, they were mandated to fight their human enemies, literally, and the LORD would take care of evil spirits. This has been switched in the New Covenant: Because believers have spiritual regeneration and are temples of the Holy Spirit, we have the authority to fight demonic spirits and are not to fight people, generally speaking, which can plainly be observed here:

> **For <u>our struggle is not against flesh and blood</u>, but against the rulers, against the authorities, against the powers of this dark world and against the spiritual forces of evil in the heavenly realms.**
>
> **Ephesians 6:12**

This is fine, but what do you do when a person is overtly attacking you? If someone is *criminally* persecuting you, you can of course utilize the help of the governing authorities, which is what they're there for, as observed in Romans 13:1-6. We're talking more about *personal* offenses here, such as insults, gossip/slander, snubbing and so forth. The answer is simple: Pray for them, which both the Lord and Paul instructed (Matthew 5:44, Luke 6:27-28 & Romans 12:14-21). This 'releases' God to be at work in their lives, as detailed in chapter **18** in the section *"Your Kingdom Come, Your Will Be Done on Earth."* While you're praying, be sure to vent to the LORD your anger and frustration over the offense in question, which will protect you from bitterness (Psalm 55:22 & 1 Peter 5:7).

What to Do Behind the Scenes

Here's what the Messiah said on the topic:

> **Then Jesus told his disciples a parable to show them that they should <u>always pray and not give up</u>. [2]He said: "In a certain town there was a judge who neither feared God nor cared what people thought. [3]And there was a widow in that town who kept coming to him with the plea, '<u>Grant me justice against my adversary</u>.'**
>
> **[4]"For some time he refused. But finally he said to himself, 'Even though I don't fear God or care what people think, [5]yet because this widow keeps bothering me, I will see that she gets justice, so that she won't eventually wear me out with her coming!' "**
>
> **[6]And the Lord said, "Listen to what the unjust judge says. [7]And <u>will not God bring about justice for his chosen ones, who cry out to him day and night</u>? <u>Will he keep putting them off</u>? [8]I tell you, <u>he will see that they get justice, and quickly</u>. However, when the Son of Man comes, will he find faith on the earth?"**
>
> **Luke 18:1-8**

Understand that God isn't being equated to an unjust judge in this parable, but rather *contrasted*. If even a corrupt judge will give justice to the persecuted person who diligently appeals for justice against an enemy, how much more so our good LORD in Heaven?

Remember, "The prayer of a righteous person **is powerful and effective**" (James 5:16).

That's what you do behind the scenes, but what about face-to-face dealings? There are several…

Options for Directly Dealing With Your Enemies

As far as face-to-face tactics go, one option is to do something good for your persecutor, which is the powerful **principle of overcoming evil with good** (Romans 12:21). Treat the person out to eat. "Bless those who persecute you" rather than cuss 'em out (Romans 12:14). The reason this principle is effective is obvious: It's difficult for your enemy to continue hating you when you're being so good to him/her, which is also taught in the Old Testament (Proverbs 25:21).

Another option is to confront the person who's sinning against you in private, as Christ instructed (Luke 17:3-4). He gave additional instructions in Matthew 18:15-17: If the person isn't penitent after the confrontation (assuming the offense is even legitimate), the Lord said to procure the help of 1-2 mature believers for a second confrontation (whatever you do, don't enlist the help of *carnal* believers). If the person is still impenitent, you can share the offense with the assembly in order to socially pressure the offender to repentance. If s/he remains stubbornly impenitent, treat them as an unbeliever; in other words, no longer regard them as a brother or sister in the Lord. That's what Yeshua himself said to do.

Such a scenario happened in real-life at the church in Corinth in which an unrepentant fornicator had to be disfellowshipped from the assembly (1 Corinthians 5:1-5,12-13). We looked at this in chapter **20**. Thankfully, the guy later repented and so Paul encouraged the Corinthians to forgive him and warmly welcome him back into the fellowship (2 Corinthians 2:6-11).

Should you use these same instructions in dealing with personal offenses from *un*believers? These scriptural directives on praying for offenders, venting, confrontation and potential repentance/forgiveness are applicable to any relationship, like marriage, friendships, co-workers and neighbors. They're universal. They keep relationships alive and functioning; without them, problematic associations inevitably fall apart and walls develop, separating the individuals.

Let's say you work with an unbeliever who starts offending you in certain ways, like snubbing you, calling you names or badmouths you to co-workers and higher-ups. The first thing you'll want to do is cast your cares on to the LORD and intercede for this person. This is "turning the cheek" wherein you graciously overlook the offense to avoid unnecessary strife and you give the transgressor time to change for the positive. This is also taught in the Old Testament, as observed in Proverbs 12:16. If the offender stubbornly refuses, you'll have to eventually confront him/her as led of the Spirit. If s/he still refuses then you can get the supervisor involved, which would be the secular equivalence of getting mature believers involved in cases where the transgressor is a believer.

If the offender remains stubborn, then you are free to cut all relational ties while keeping him/her in prayer and continuing to cast your cares on to God. Your "relationship" with the co-worker becomes strictly business since they've rejected your grace. You can be sure that the LORD will address the situation, one way or another, and deliver you (assuming you're actually walking with the Lord and the offenses are legitimate). With these kinds of situations, the "turn-away principle" is in order, as discussed in chapter **1** (in the section *Weak Christians Will Object to Your Bold Willingness*).

It helps to understand that unbelievers are in spiritual darkness and lack the moral foundation of the Word of God, the reborn spirit and the indwelling Holy Spirit. Of course, they have a human spirit and grasp universal morality deep down inside, whether they care to admit it or not (Romans 2:14-16). In light of this, relationships with unbelievers require greater patience and mercy than those with the average Christian. Each case is dependent on **1.** you, **2.** your level of spiritual maturity and **3.** the guidance of the Holy Spirit, which explains Paul's carefully-worded instructions:

> **<u>If</u> it is possible, <u>as far as it depends on you</u>, live at peace with everyone.**
>
> **Romans 12:18**

Paul is encouraging believers to live lives of peace, which means being peaceable—avoiding strife and striving for harmony with all people in every situation, which includes unbelievers. This is also encouraged in Hebrews 12:14. Yet Paul adds a condition: "*If* it is possible, **as far as it depends on you**." Why does he phrase it like this? Obviously because peace is not possible in some situations since it depends on the antagonist's attitude and response.

Every situation is unique and you have to be led of the Holy Spirit, but sometimes you may have to make a bold stand and radically correct or break all ties, which are examples of tough love. In cases of severe offenses—and I'm talking about criminal acts—you may even have to defend yourself and your loved ones or enlist the help of authorities.

What does "as far as it depends on you" mean? Every believer is on a lifelong journey of spiritual development. The apostle Paul was spiritually mature and therefore far more able to walk in patient peaceable-ness in trying circumstances than a new believer fresh out of the world. In other words, your peace walk is dependent upon your level of spiritual growth. Whether you're a half pint or a gallon, live up to that level, as far as it is possible.

The passage—Romans 12:18—could be viewed as somewhat of a "safety valve." When you face unjust offenses from an unbeliever and respond by implementing the principle of overcoming evil with good (Romans 12:21) any reasonable person will be diffused and react positively to your graciousness & the Spirit's moving.

However, when an antagonist stubbornly refuses to respond in a positive manner—particularly after generous longsuffering on your part—you can be sure that s/he is a calloused fool of the lowest order. Such a person disqualifies himself or herself from any further merciful patience and you are released to completely cut ties or move toward **righteous radicalness** with God's blessing. A good example of the former is when Paul cut ties with hardened Jews at the synagogue in Ephesus after three months of ministry (Acts 19:8-9); a good example of the latter would be his radical dealings with a hostile magician on Cyprus (Acts 13:8-12). Peter did something similar with another sorcerer (Acts 8:18-24).

What If You KNOW the Confrontation Will Turn Ugly?

If you know a confrontation will turn ugly and bring out the worst in you—devolving into a fleshly melee—then don't confront the person. Only a masochist or fool would willfully enter into such a draining, unpleasant confrontation.

Someone might understandably contend: 'But the Lord said we *must* confront the individual in Matthew 18:15-17.' Actually, Christ's instructions apply specifically to handling offending Christians from one's own assembly, which naturally means his guidelines must be revised in cases where the transgressor is hooked up with another fellowship or is unchurched. The Messiah's words are more general instructions than unbendable rules that must be observed to the letter in each potential case.

For support, consider Paul's instructions to the believers in Rome:

> **I appeal to you, brothers, to <u>watch out for those who cause divisions</u> and create obstacles contrary to the doctrine that you have been taught; <u>avoid them</u>.** [18] **For such persons do not serve our Lord Christ, but their own appetites, and by <u>smooth talk</u> and <u>flattery</u> they deceive the hearts of the naive.**
>
> **Romans 16:17-18** (ESV)

Paul instructs believers to look out for those who tend to cause conflict and concludes by simply saying "avoid them." He doesn't say anything about confronting & correcting these troublemakers; he merely says to **keep away from them**. Were these contentious individuals believers or heathen? Paul was obviously denoting people functioning within the fellowship of Roman Christians who were at least professing believers. Whether they were genuine followers of Christ or not, Paul stresses in verse 18 that they *weren't* actually serving the Lord but rather their own appetites. He then reveals what marks such divisive people: They have a reputation for being *smooth talkers* who *deceive* naïve folks, that is, people who are incapable of discerning their carnal character.

What exactly is deceitful "smooth talk"? To be frank, it's bullcrap or another word that shares the initials of **B**ernie **S**anders. These types have a knack for telling stories and exaggeration. Put another way, they have the ability to dazzle listeners with their smooth talk; not everyone, of course, just those who are gullible and lack the ability to identify their bull for what it is. These are fabricators, braggarts and flatterers who naturally create discord and division wherever they roam since it's their very *nature*.

Guard yourself from such "believers" and steer clear of them. Don't approach and reprimand them because they'll despise you for it and turn the situation against you (Proverbs 9:7-9); they'll try to tear you to pieces like the (hidden) vicious predators they are. They want to lure you into the realm of the flesh, which is the plane from which they operate. They want to bring out the worst in you. Don't take the bait. Keep away from them; intercede for them and shield the naïve sheep in your midst from their smooth-talking devices.

I had an in-law years ago who was so offensive and argumentative that I had to stop taking his calls. I'd delete his messages without even listening. Why? Because speaking to him, or even giving ear to a voicemail, was like consuming poison; it would throw my day off course—destroying my concentration and draining my energy. I found out a Christian relative refused to take his calls as well. Neither of us did this hastily; it took ten years of merciful forbearance and prayer. But life is too valuable to squander on arrogant, disrespectful troublemakers and liars, even if they profess to be Christians. Don't give ear to such a *proven* contentious person unless you learn from a respected source that s/he is willing to speak with a smidgen of meekness and respect. If so, give it a try.

Here's another relevant text on the topic:

> **But understand this, that in the last days there will come times of difficulty. ² For people will be <u>lovers of self</u>, <u>lovers of money</u>, <u>proud</u>, <u>arrogant</u>, <u>abusive</u>, disobedient to their parents, <u>ungrateful</u>, <u>unholy</u>, ³<u>heartless</u>, <u>unappeasable</u>, <u>slanderous</u>, without self-control, <u>brutal</u>, not loving good, ⁴treacherous, <u>reckless</u>, <u>swollen with conceit</u>, lovers of pleasure rather than lovers of God, ⁵<u>having the appearance of godliness</u>, but denying its power. <u>Avoid such people.</u>**
>
> **2 Timothy 3:1-5** (ESV)

Paul gave these instructions to his acolyte, Timothy. He exhorted him to "avoid" these fleshly types who had an "*appearance* of godliness" yet no actual spiritual effectiveness (verse 5). This revealed that these were people who claimed to know the Lord but plainly lacked the power of a new life. Instead of fruit of the spirit—love, joy, peace, patience, kindness, humility and self-control (Galatians 5:22-23)—they show steady signs of hatred, selfishness, greed, boasting, arrogance, manipulation, ungratefulness, depravity, gossip/slander, recklessness and smugness. As with the passage from Romans above, the apostle doesn't even tell his protégé to confront & correct such individuals; rather he directs him to simply **keep away from them**.

If the offenders you are dealing with share these carnal traits, rebuking them is pointless because they lack the spiritual character to receive correction, the primary fruit being love. It's just not possible to correct bigheaded, rude, impulsive individuals without being pulled into a big nasty fight. It will likely drag you into the realm of the flesh and draw out the worst in you. These hardened types loathe spirituality and correction, regardless of whether or not they're confessing Christians, attend a certain assembly and shmooze with leaders. "**Avoid such people.**"

As you can see, the Bible's not one-dimensional on this topic. There are several effective options for you to implement when a human enemy rears his/her head in your life. These are action-oriented things you can *do*—things that will keep you active, both spiritually and physically—rather than be an inert doormat to abuse. Be led of the Spirit and, remember: If God is for you, who can be against you? (Romans 8:31). "The one who is in you is greater than the one who is in the world" (1 John 4:4).

Let's end with a couple of relevant proverbs:

> **The wicked flee though no one pursues, but the righteous are as bold as a lion.**
>
> **Proverbs 28:1**

> **Fear of man will prove to be a snare, but whoever trusts in the LORD is kept safe.**
>
> **Proverbs 29:25**

<u>23</u>

THE NINE TRAITS OF A GIANT-KILLER

We started this manual with the story of David's victory over Goliath. Every Spiritual Warrior is called to be a giant-killer, like David, just in a spiritual sense. Let's now return to this section of Scripture for further gems.

Since the passage is too long to quote here, I encourage you to brush up on 1 Samuel 17 in your Bible. This historical account reveals **9 traits of a giant-killer** as follows:

1. Giant-Killers Walk by Faith, Not by Sight

The Israelite soldiers were "terrified" because **they were walking by sight** (verse 11). Their senses took in the data that Goliath was 9½ feet tall, weighed over a thousand pounds with his armor & weapons and was utterly intimidating in manner & word. Their brains received this information and it moved them to *flee*.

David, by contrast, didn't respond this way because he was walking by faith, which means he was living out of the *sixth* sense (2 Corinthians 4:18, 2 Corinthians 5:7 & Hebrews 11:1). Thus David boldly faced the intimidating Goliath, even though he wasn't a soldier and was barely more than a boy at about 17-18 years-old.

2. Giant-Killers Understand Their Covenant With God

'Covenant' means contract. It's an agreement between two parties with conditions (although the agreement could be unconditional in rare cases). The LORD works with humanity through covenants. David understood this. After hearing Goliath's arrogant challenge, he responded, "Who is this *uncircumcised* Philistine that he should defy the armies of the living God?" (verse 26).

The reason David referred to Goliath as "uncircumcised" is because circumcision was the sign of the Abrahamic covenant that the Israelites were under, along with the Mosaic covenant (Genesis 17:1-14 & Leviticus 12:3). David was pointing out that Goliath didn't have a covenant with the Almighty whereas the Israelites did. As such, they didn't need to fear this colossal warrior no matter how intimidating he was.

3. Giant-Killers Know When to Grow-UP

We observe this in David's reply to King Saul after the monarch argued "You are not able to go out against this Philistine and fight him; you are only a young man, and he has been a warrior from his youth" (verse 33). David's literal response began with this statement: "Your servant *used* to keep sheep for his father" (verse 34 NRSV). Notice that David spoke of being a shepherd boy in the *past tense* even though he was tending sheep earlier that very day!

In other words, David instinctively sensed that this occasion was going to be a turning point in his life and so he no longer saw himself—or spoke of himself—as a lowly shepherd boy. That was something he "used" to do. Sure enough, he graduated from being a shepherd boy to being Israel's top warrior that very day!

The lesson? When the Spirit moves upon you to let something go that links you to your past, particularly something that ties into your identity, *DO IT*. Everyone grows older, but not everyone grows up. This is true physically and spiritually. There are Christians out there who are 20, 30, 40 years-old in the Lord, but they refuse to grow up spiritually and therefore are still in the childhood stage of spiritual growth. Giant-killers are not like that.

4. Giant-Killers Celebrate & Boast of God's Power in Past Victories

David's reply to the king of Israel shows *how* he had the extraordinary faith to take on the hulking Goliath: He said when he tended his father's sheep, a lion and a bear attacked the lambs on a couple occasions, and so the teen struck the carnivores and killed 'em. He figured that, just as the LORD granted him success over the king of beasts and the bruin when he bravely acted, so he'll have the victory over this giant (1 Samuel 17:34-37).

We could relate this to us today: If you haven't been tested with a situation where you needed 200 bucks and exercised your faith to receive it (Mark 11:24 & John 16:24), you're not likely going to have the faith to receive $2,000 when it's needed, or $20,000. If you haven't exercised your faith to receive healing for a serious headache or a painful back, you're not likely going to have the faith to overcome the 'Goliath' of cancer. Those smaller items would be your 'lion' or 'bear' whereas the bigger challenges would be your 'Goliath.'

So praise the LORD when you face those smaller items because God is allowing them in your life so that you can work your faith muscles, which will train you for greater challenges in the future.

5. Giant-Killers Go by the Spirit, Not by What Everyone Else Is Doing

This can be observed in verses 38-40 when King Saul insisted that David wear full armor and use his personal sword in squaring off with the giant. But David wasn't feeling it and so rejected the armor & sword. He didn't care "what everyone else was doing" and went with what he had a peace about—using a sling and a stone.

We need to do the same if we want to conquer our 'giants.' Disregard "what everyone else is doing" and be led of the Spirit (Romans 8:14); "let the peace of Christ reign in your hearts" (Colossians 3:15). In other words, don't do or say anything you don't have a peace about doing, even if it happens to be the hip thang to do.

6. Giant-Killers Are Bold as a Lion, Willing to Risk All

What was at stake in David's situation taking on Goliath? His life! In short, *everything*. If you want victory over your giants, you must be bold and willing to take huge risks as well (Proverbs 28:1). Life's a fight, FIGHT IT. And be willing to risk everything when the Spirit guides you.

At the same time, don't be a rash fool (Proverbs 19:2). Get tight with the Lord so you appropriately discern the leading of the Spirit as opposed to the *misleading* of your flesh (unrighteous anger, impatience, rashness, folly, etc.).

7. Giant-Killers Are Eager to Obey With Violent Faith

Christ said that the kingdom of Heaven is taken hold of and advanced by those with "forceful" or "violent" faith and diligence (Matthew 11:12). Yes, the "poor in spirit" possess the kingdom of Heaven (Matthew 5:3) but genuine meekness obviously includes bold tenacity, particularly when it comes to spiritual warfare, which is the example set for us by Christ himself in the gospels.

So, rise up in bold faith and don't shrink back (Hebrews 10:39)! You'll never outgrow spiritual warfare; you must simply learn to fight. That's what this manual is for—learning to fight, God's way, so you can effectively slay your giants. The LORD'll teach you how to fight in your superior covenant (Hebrews 8:6), just as he taught David how to fight in his (Psalm 18:34 & 144:1).

8. Giant-Killers Speak the Word of Faith

The Bible teaches that words have the power of life and death (Proverbs 18:21) and Christ emphasized the power of *speaking* in *faith* in Mark 11:23. In the literal rendition of that passage the mighty Messiah stressed speaking **three times** as opposed to believing, which he noted **once**. So, if you're having trouble believing something biblical or something the Spirit wants you to get a hold of, start speaking it in faith, even if you're struggling with believing it. Paul stressed believing & speaking too (2 Corinthians 4:13).

Both Goliath and David grasped this potent principle since they each implemented it for victory, as observed in verses 41-47. Because the giant was the champ of the Philistines for numerous years, he had much success with believing & speaking in faith. Yet David had a covenant with the Almighty whereas Goliath did not, which tipped the scales in the former shepherd boy's favor. He thus beat the intimidating hulk even though the odds of victory were minuscule from a natural standpoint.

If you want success over the 'giants' that rise up in your life who threaten you & your loved ones, you'll have to learn to speak God's blessings & truths into the circumstances by faith. Then follow-up with the corresponding actions guided by your Helper and Counselor (Romans 8:14).

9. Giant-Killers View A "Goliath" as a Stepping Stone to a Better Season

David's encounter with Goliath was a life-threatening occasion, yet because David understood his covenant with his Creator and boldly walked in faith accordingly, this grave challenge ended positively by drastically changing David's life for the good: One day he was a lil' unknown shepherd boy and the next he was an acclaimed warrior of Israel (1 Samuel 18:5-7), not to mention he received the formidable reward promised by King Saul—a great financial prize, the king's daughter in marriage and tax exemption for himself & his family (1 Samuel 17:25).

24

ELI, SAMUEL and the Book of RUTH

In 1 Samuel 3 we observe young Samuel being called to his prophetic ministry while he was staying with the elderly high priest, Eli, at the Tabernacle in Shiloh where the Ark of the Covenant was located. Samuel and Eli slept under the same roof somewhere outside the Tent of Meeting (i.e. the Tabernacle). The golden lampstand in the Holy Place was filled with olive oil and lit at dusk (Exodus 30:8); it was kept burning from nightfall until first light (Exodus 27:20-21).

Just before dawn when the light was flickering the LORD called Samuel:

> **The boy Samuel ministered before the Lord under Eli. In those days the word of the LORD was rare; there were not many visions.**
> **²One night Eli, whose eyes were becoming so weak that he could barely see, was lying down in his usual place. ³The lamp of God had not yet gone out, and Samuel was lying down in the house of the LORD where the ark of God was. ⁴Then the LORD called Samuel.**
> **Samuel answered, "Here I am." ⁵And he ran to Eli and said, "Here I am; you called me."**
> **But Eli said, "I did not call; go back and lie down." So he went and lay down.**

> **⁶Again <u>the LORD called, "Samuel!"</u> And Samuel got up and went to Eli and said, "Here I am; you called me."**
> **"My son," Eli said, "I did not call; <u>go back and lie down.</u>"**
> **⁷Now Samuel did not yet know the LORD: The word of the LORD had not yet been revealed to him.**
>
> **1 Samuel 3:1-7**

The question we want to answer is how does this story relate to us today in the New Covenant era? After all, the very purpose of such Old Testament accounts is to **teach us**, as observed in Romans 15:4 and 1 Corinthians 10:11.

The lamp of God was flickering and about to go out, but this didn't seem to concern the high priest. Young Samuel, however, heard something; and heard it again and again. It was the voice of the LORD. So he ran to the immediate religious authority for counsel, but the youth was readily dismissed.

Like Eli, the eyesight of some in the Church has grown dim and the elders can't see so well, at least not spiritually. They've become content with the day-to-day goings-on of the ministry wherein they keep going through the motions, lighting the lamps and so forth. A personal word from the LORD and visions rarely happens, if ever.

- When the Holy Spirit really does speak to someone willing to listen, they are automatically written off as unsophisticated or dreaming.
- When the Creator really does appear, the elders' eyes are too dim to see it.
- When the Almighty actually does move, they are resistant to accepting it for fear of tripping over something unknown—something fresh—in their weak-eyed darkness, which would be awkward and humiliating. *("The horror, the horror")*.

Sometimes today we might need to "examine ourselves" (2 Corinthians 13:5) and admit that the lamp of God is flickering and perhaps even at risk of going out. Things are not as they should be. Why isn't the glory of God breaking out of our places of assembly and illuminating our communities and beyond?

This is just food for thought for any Spiritual Warrior, small and great. Let's give credit to Eli in that he finally recognized that the LORD was speaking to Samuel and thus gave the youth proper instructions, as observed in verses 8-9. But this didn't prevent God's judgment from falling on him & his wicked sons as detailed in the rest of the account.

Insights for Today From the Book of RUTH

The short book of Ruth details the account of Naomi's family moving from Bethlehem in famine-stricken Israel to Moab, which was a 7-10 day trip to the Southeast by foot. The two sons married Moabite women but, unfortunately, Naomi's husband and sons soon died and thus Naomi & her two daughters-in-law were left without husbands.

While disillusioned, Naomi heard that food was available in Israel again and set out to return, but encouraged her daughters-in-law to stay in Moab. Orpah chose to stay, but Ruth insisted on sticking with her desperate mother-in-law and accompanied her to Bethlehem.

What are some key insights we can get from this moving story? Again, the very purpose of these Old Testament accounts is to **teach us** (Romans 15:4 & 1 Corinthians 10:11). Here are ten insights to chew on:

- Bethlehem literally means "place of bread," but unfortunately there was no bread (food) there so Naomi & family felt compelled to leave Bethlehem and go to Moab for sustenance. Quoting the Old Testament, Christ said "Man shall not live on bread alone, but on every word that comes from the mouth of God" (Matthew 4:4 & Deuteronomy 8:3). As such, people will understandably leave Church assemblies if there's not enough spiritual food to live on there. They'll go elsewhere to find sustenance. In some cases, they'll unwisely turn to the world for succor, like bars, alcohol, drugs (illegal or legal), therapists, psychics, sexual immorality, perversion, government idolatry, etc. In short, if there's no bread in the Church fellowship they're naturally going to look elsewhere for sustenance, even turning to the world in some sad cases.
- "The wages of sin is death" (Romans 6:23) and so going to Moab (the world) for succor results in heartbreak and disillusionment. Cruel Moab can destroy your marriage and steal the lives of your children. The world will rob you of your life-passion and leave you

embittered. It will "steal, kill and destroy" but, thankfully, the LORD "gives life and life to the full" (John 10:10).

- When Naomi "heard" that the LORD had come to the aid of his people in Israel and that there was food there, she dropped everything to return home for sustenance. The prodigals—i.e. people who leave the Church to find possible sustenance in the world (Luke 15:11-32)—will come back when they are desperate enough and know there is spiritual bread available.

- These prodigals probably won't come back alone. Ruth accompanied Naomi to Bethlehem—the house of bread—a place she's never been to before. In other words, the prodigals will bring those from the world—the unsaved—who've never been to a genuine Church assembly and experienced the abundant spiritual bread thereof (John 6:35 & 6:63). These are *hungry* people, longing for true spiritual sustenance since the cruel world has left them empty and bereft.

- Unfortunately, some, like Orpah, won't come because the reputation of the Church has been so sullied by lifeless legalists and the impotence of human religion. They thus choose to live and die in "Moab," the world (Ruth 1:8-14).

- Thankfully, there are those who are utterly sick of the world and *hunger* for truth, like Ruth (Matthew 5:6). They're willing to leave everything they know and go to "the house of bread" merely because it's rumored there's spiritual succor there.

- However, Ruth didn't stick with Naomi merely due to a rumor, but also because of **1.** a noble sense of loyalty to her deceased husband and, therefore, his mother. And **2.** Ruth discerned from her time with this flawed family that they had something she didn't have, spiritually speaking, even despite losing her husband and witnessing Naomi's disillusionment. She discerned they were a "golden connection" to something better, perhaps even the abundant life she so desired (John 10:10).

- Loyalty is underrated. Note Ruth's moving declaration of loyalty to her embittered mother-in-law:

> **"Don't urge me to leave you or to turn back from you.**
> **Where you go I will go, and where you stay I will stay.**
> **Your people will be my people and your God my God.**
> **[17]Where you die I will die, and there I will be buried.**
> **May the LORD deal with me, be it ever so severely, if**
> **even death separates you and me."**
>
> **Ruth 1:16-17**

- Ruth's moving loyalty and her passion to obtain spiritual bread by leaving everything she knew behind pays off as she meets & marries Naomi's relative, Boaz, and they have a son, Obed, who was the father of Jesse, the father of the great King David, which placed a Gentile in the lineage of the King of Kings (Luke 3:23-38). In short, those who refuse to starve to death in a spiritual desert, but wisely take advantage of the "golden connections" the Creator provides will be placed in the line of royalty! See 2 Peter 2:9 and Revelation 1:6 & 5:10.

- By calling a Moabite to be in the lineage of the coming Messiah, the LORD illustrated that the New Covenant would apply to *all* people of *every* skin-color around the globe and not just to the Israelites/Jews. Speaking of which…

God's Plan of Redemption Includes All Peoples

This can be observed in comparing Matthew's genealogy of Yeshua with Luke's version. Matthew traces Christ's heritage back to Abraham (Matthew 1:1-17) whereas Luke traces it all the way back to Adam (Luke 3:23-38).

The reason for this difference is that Matthew wrote his account primarily for Hebraic readers while Luke, believed to be a Gentile (a non-Jew), wrote chiefly to Gentiles with the hope that they would learn that God's love & truth reach beyond the Hebrews to the entire world. With Luke's list going all the way back to Adam, the first man (Genesis 2:7 & 1 Corinthians 15:45), it illustrates that the Messiah came for all humanity since *every* skin-color sprang from Adam's loins (Romans 3:29-30).

This shows that there is, in essence, only one race, the *human* race. And since Earth used to be one continent, Pangaea, we're all native to the same continent, the same Earth, regardless of the fact that the land mass eventually split into several pieces, including thousands of islands (Isaiah 51:5 & 66:19).

Secondly, observe what God said when he called Abram, aka Abraham:

> **The LORD had said to Abram, "Go from your country, your people and your father's household to the land I will show you.**

> 2"I will make you into a great nation,
>   and I will bless you;
> I will make your name great,
>   and you will be a blessing.
> 3I will bless those who bless you,
>   and whoever curses you I will curse;
> and <u>all peoples on earth
>   will be blessed through you</u>."
>
> **Genesis 12:1-3**

The Almighty would use Abraham, the father of faith (Romans 4:11), to express his heart and purpose for *all* peoples of Earth (Galatians 3:8). God's desire was to redeem humanity from the depths they had fallen after Adam's sin. Through Abraham, the LORD would send the Messiah to fulfill his awesome plan of redemption for the whole world.[27]

---

[27] For fascinating details on God's plan of redemption, see my books *QUESTIONS & ANSWERS From the Bible* or *ANGELS: Their Purpose and Your Responsibility*. Or read the free article at the FOL site.

<u>25</u>

FREEDOM, LIFE, JOY, POWER!

Let's end this manual on an inspiring note. *"FREEDOM! LIFE! JOY! POWER!"* is the official slogan for this ministry, Fountain of Life. Why? Because it's catchy but, more importantly, it's thoroughly biblical and reflects what we're all about. To explain, we'll consider all four words from a scriptural standpoint.

But, first, it's important to understand a couple of things…

God's Primary Will for People

The Creator's primary will is revealed in 1 Timothy 2:4 where it says that God "wants all people to be saved and to come to a knowledge of the truth." So God's will can be broken down into to two main parts:

1. For people to **be saved** from separation from the LORD and eternal death.
2. For them to **come to a knowledge of the truth**.

The first one—obtaining salvation—is apprehended through turning to the LORD in **repentance & faith** in response to the gospel (Acts 20:21) and the corresponding **spiritual rebirth** (Titus 3:5), which makes us **spiritually alive to God** (Romans 8:10).

God *then* wants us to **grow in the "knowledge of the truth."** Why? Because it's only through truth—through *reality*—that we'll be **set free** in this world of lies. The more we increase in accurate knowledge—reality— and the corresponding understanding and wisdom, the more freedom we'll experience. This is why Christ said "***If*** you continue in my word, then you will know the truth, and the truth shall set you free" (John 8:31-32).

The Kingdom of Darkness *Opposes* God's Primary Will

Understanding the LORD's primary will is important because it reveals the devil's primary will, which is **to stop God's two-pronged will from occurring!** In other words, the enemy is intent on:

- Keeping people from being saved.
- Keeping those who are saved from knowing the truth more than they already do.

To carry out the first objective, satan does his best to deceive the masses into believing that Christianity is all about bondage, lifelessness, drudgery and weakness, which of course is **the express opposite of the truth**. (Freshen up on these mind-blowing passages that reveal the devil's ability to deceive people: 2 Corinthians 4:4, 1 John 5:19 and Revelation 12:9).

If a person *is* saved through the gospel and the corresponding spiritual rebirth, the enemy resorts to his secondary objective—to keep that individual from increasing in the knowledge of the truth. Why? Because if he can keep people from growing in truth, he can limit their freedom and therefore their effectiveness as a believer, not to mention their quality of life.

One of the enemy's greatest ploys is to seduce believers into the realm of **dead religiosity**. Whether that's through morphing them into impotent cultural "Christians," who "have a form of godliness, but deny the power thereof" (2 Timothy 3:5), or by seducing them into being pharisaical sourpuss religionists, it's all *bad*.

Either/or, this saps the freedom, life, joy and power that God offers believers through Christ. Those who are duped then falsely represent Christianity to those who are lost and dying in the world.

The good news is that every believer can fulfill God's primary will, and subsequently hinder the devil's will, simply by **1.** learning of and **2.** walking in the **freedom**, **life**, **joy** and **power** that the LORD has for him or her. Let's go over each of these as it's imperative to understand how biblical all four are…

FREEDOM!

You've probably noticed that this manual is focused on teaching from the Bible in an honest, balanced and unbiased (non-sectarian) manner. Why is this so important? Because Christ said God's Word is **truth**—that is, reality or the way it really is—and it's only through continuing in God's Word that we'll know the truth. The more we know the truth—reality—the more we'll be set **FREE**! See John 17:17 and 8:31-32. This explains why God's Word is referred to as "the perfect law that gives **freedom**" (James 1:25). While counterfeit "Christianity"—legalism—puts people into bondage, true Christianity sets people **FREE** because it's rooted in living by the perfect law that gives **freedom**, God's Word.

What does the rightly-divided Word set us **FREE** from?

- **The flesh**, which is the sinful nature, the beast inside us all that veers toward what is negative, destructive and evil (Galatians 5:19-21).
- **Legalism**, which is a spirit of dead religiosity and the false veneer thereof (Galatians 5:1).
- **False teachings** (doctrine), whether religious or secular in nature.
- **Curses of the Law**, which we overcome through spiritual warfare (Galatians 3:13).

All four of these freedoms are rooted in the balanced, unbiased teaching of the God-breathed Scriptures and the corresponding knowledge, understanding & wisdom that results, which is what Fountain of Life is all about.

The best way to handle an un-free world is to be so absolutely free that your very existence is an act of rebellion—*righteous* rebellion.

LIFE!

Christ declared why he came: To give **LIFE** and **LIFE to the full** (John 10:10). He was referring to eternal **LIFE**, which is *aionios zoe (ay-OH-nee-us ZOH-ay)* in the Greek and could be rendered "the **LIFE** of the age to come." Since the age-to-come is perpetual, translators render *aionios* as "eternal," as in eternal **LIFE**.

Receiving eternal **LIFE** is a 2-phase process, which begins with spiritual rebirth where the believer's spirit is regenerated and receives the life-of-the-age-to-come, i.e. eternal life (John 3:3,6 & 1 John 5:12). This process is completed at the bodily resurrection where believers acquire immortal glorified bodies (1 Corinthians 15:42-44), which takes place at the time of the Rapture when believers are "caught up" by the Lord, as detailed in 1 Thessalonians 4:13-17.

We first touched on this topic in *Knowing the Six Basic Doctrines of Christianity* in chapter **4**, specifically the sub-section on *The Resurrection of the Dead*. For anyone who claims that the Rapture is not biblical, 'caught up' is one word in the Greek, *harpazó (har-PAD-zoh)*, which means to "snatch up" or "obtain by robbery." It's translated in Latin as "rapio" in the Vulgate, which is where we get the English "Rapture."[28]

Here's the point: You can tap into this abundant **LIFE**, this eternal **LIFE**—this **LIFE**-of-the-age-to-come—anytime you want simply by learning to live out of your new nature, which possesses eternal **LIFE** and was "created to be *like* God in true righteousness and holiness" (Ephesians 4:22-24). When you do this, you'll "participate in the divine nature" and naturally produce the fruit of the spirit (2 Peter 1:4 & Galatians 5:22-23). **Experiencing the life-of-the-age-to-come is the ultimate high** and carnal temptations lose their allure the more you taste of it (Psalm 34:8 & Hebrews 6:5).

---

[28] Both the Rapture and Jesus' return to the Earth are described in terms of "coming" in the Bible, which is the Greek word *Parousia* (Matthew 24:27,37,39 & 2 Thessalonians 2:8). They both represent his Second Coming, albeit two phases. You see, to believers, the Rapture is Christ's Second Coming whereas, to the unsaved, his return to Earth is the Second Coming. So, both refer to the Lord's Second Coming depending upon the spiritual condition of the individual; they're just two different phases of his return.

JOY!

JOY means "to be cheerful, happy, well-off, in a good frame of mind, rejoice-ful." Unlike worldly happiness, it's not dependent on outward circumstances being hunky dory. **JOY** is a fruit of the spirit (Galatians 5:22-23) and is therefore a character trait of the LORD. This explains David's statement that **there is fullness of JOY in God's presence** (Psalm 16:11). In light of this, it's a mistake to view the Creator *only* in terms of solemnity, holiness and judgment; those who do so are *unbalanced*. God **is JOY**.

Since your new nature was "created to be *like* God" (Ephesians 4:24), the more you learn to live out of your new nature—that is, be spirit-controlled rather than flesh-ruled—the more you'll experience **JOY**. Peter described it as **"inexpressible and glorious JOY"** (1 Peter 1:8). Moreover, since God *is* **JOY**, the more you hang out with the LORD, the more **JOY** you'll experience because **you become like those you spend time with the most**. It's the law of association, which works to the good as well as the bad (1 Corinthians 15:33 & Proverbs 13:20). Godliness—i.e. like-God-ness (not religion)—is the result of spending time with the Most High, as detailed in chapter **4** (in the section *Utilizing the Seven Keys to Spiritual Maturity*).

Why is **JOY** important? Because it's linked to vigor (Nehemiah 8:10) and freedom (Proverbs 29:6) and therefore health and quality of life.

POWER!

The Mighty Christ imparted **authority** and **POWER** to his disciples over the dominion of darkness (Luke 9:1). This was *before* justification was available via Yeshua's death and resurrection. Spiritually regenerated believers (that's **you**, if you're a believer) intrinsically possess these blessings because you're born-again of the seed of Christ, which is *sperm* in the Greek (1 John 3:9 & 1 Peter 1:23). It's due to this rebirth that you're a "co-heir" in Messiah (Romans 8:17). This means that believers share in the inheritance of the heavenly Father *with* the chief heir, Jesus Christ. If this doesn't get you excited, read it again; or check your pulse.

My point is that YOU have authority and **POWER** over the powers of darkness and the curses thereof. **Authority is the right to rule whereas**

POWER is the ability to rule. You possess both, but you won't boldly walk in them if you don't know it, which is why I'm sharing this with you.

Additional **POWER** is available thru the baptism of the Holy Spirit. If you don't yet have this baptism, drop everything and get it. Go over the pertinent passages from chapter **4** (in the section *Knowing the Six Basic Doctrines of Christianity*, specifically the sub-section that covers *Instructions on Baptisms*). This will increase your faith and you'll surely get it. I didn't receive this awesome gift until 2.5 years *after* my salvation.

Now chew on this: Nothing is impossible with God (Luke 1:37; 18:27) therefore you can do *anything* as the LORD **empowers** you (Philippians 4:11-13). Fan that **POWER** into flame, as encouraged in 2 Timothy 1:6-7!

Let's close with this important question…

Does Christianity Weaken People or Empower?

I was talking to a man who argued that Christianity weakens people and instills fear. He likened God and the devil to forest monsters in fairy tales that Christian leaders use to control and limit people through fear. While such a view may reflect some religious groups who propose to be Christian, it's not supported by the Bible in the least.

If Christianity weakens people why did Christ give the Holy Spirit to *empower* us (Acts 1:8)? Why did Paul say we haven't been given a spirit of fear, but a spirit of **POWER** (2 Timothy 1:7)? Why did the Messiah say he came to give us *"LIFE to the full"* (John 10:10)?

If Christianity uses the devil to instill fear, why did Christ give *authority* to believers "to *trample on* snakes and scorpions", which are types of the devil and demons, and "to *overcome all the power of the enemy*" (Luke 10:19)? He even added, "nothing will harm you."

If Christianity teaches that believers are to have a negative fear of God why does the Bible say "God is love…There is no fear in love. But *perfect love drives out fear*" (1 John 4:16,18)? The only fear believers are encouraged to have is a healthy, reverent fear of God because it's the "beginning of wisdom" and protects us from foolish paths (Psalm 111:10).

It's stunning how deceived people are about Christianity, all because they confuse it with the counterfeit—religious, legalistic non-Christianity.

FREEDOM, **LIFE**, **JOY** and **POWER** are there for you—**take hold of 'em with "violent" force!** (See Matthew 11:12).

Amen and Amen.

Bibliography

Brown, Francis/Driver, S.R./Briggs, Charles A. *Brown-Driver-Briggs Lexicon*. Peabody: Hendrickson Publishers, 1994

Bullinger, Ethelbert W. *A Critical Lexicon and Concordance to the English and Greek New Testament*. Grand Rapids: Zondervan Publishing House, 1975

Houdmann, Michael S. *Got Questions? (miscellaneous)*. Retrieved from https://www. gotquestions.org/, 2002-2024

Jennifer, Aisjen. *10 Ways God Speaks to Us*. Retrieved from https://www.instagram.com/p/C6hB7OiMsJD/, 2024

Jeremiah, David. *Answers to Questions About Spiritual Warfare*. San Diego: Turning Point for God, 2014

Kirkwood, David. *Your Best Year Yet!* Pittsburgh: Ethnos Press, 1996

Lindberg, Sara. *Autophagy: What You Need to Know*. Retrieved from https://www.healthline.com/health/autophagy, 2023

LORD, The. *Berean Standard Bible (BSB). Holy Bible*. The Bible Hub, 2022

LORD, The. *English Standard Version (ESV). Holy Bible*. Chicago: Crossway, 2001

LORD, The. *King James Version. Holy Bible*. Iowa Falls: World Bible Publishers

LORD, The. *New American Standard Bible. Holy Bible*. Nashville: Holman, 1977

LORD, *The. New International Version (Revised). Holy Bible*. Nashville: Holman, 2011

LORD, The. *New King James Version Study Bible: Second Edition. Holy Bible*. Nashville: Thomas Nelson, 2012

LORD, The. *New Revised Standard Version. Holy Bible*. Nashville: Nelson, 1989

LORD, The. *The Amplified Bible*. Grand Rapids: Zondervan, 1987

LORD, The. *Quest Study Bible: New International Version*. Grand Rapids: Zondervan, 2003

MacArthur, John. *The MacArthur Study Bible: New King James Version.* Nashville: Word Bibles, 1997

Otnow Lewis, Dorothy. Cited in *Deseret News: Bundy Psychological Problems May have Started in his Infancy.* Retrieved from https://www.deseret.com/1989/1/25/18792693/bundy-psychological-problems-may-have-started-in-his-infancy/, 1989

Reagan, David. *God's Plan for the Ages.* McKinney: Lamb & Lion Ministries, 2005

Servant, David. *God's Tests: A Book for Anyone Who has Ever Asked, "Why Me, Lord?"* Pittsburgh: Ethnos Press, 1993

Servant, David. *Heaven Word Daily.* Pittsburgh: Ethnos Press, 2009

Strong, James. *Strong's Exhaustive Concordance.* Grand Rapids: Baker, 1991

Tenney, Tommy. *The GOD Chasers.* Shippensburg: Destiny Image Publishers, 1998

Vine, W.E. *Vine's Expository Dictionary of Biblical Words.* Cambridge: Nelson, 1985

Waren, Dirk. *ANGELS: Their Purpose, Your Responsibility.* Youngstown: Soaring Eagle Press, 2017

Waren, Dirk. *Fountain of Life Teaching Ministry.* Retrieved from http://www.fountainoflifetm.com/, 2011-2024

Waren, Dirk. *Legalism Unmasked.* Youngstown: Soaring Eagle Press, 2013/2018

Waren, Dirk. *The Four Stages of Spiritual Growth.* Youngstown: Soaring Eagle Press, 2015

Yambar, Chris. *Manna Underground Press (Misc.).* Youngstown: MUP, 1983-1986

Fountain of Life
Teaching Ministry
(Psalm 36:9)

The mission of Fountain of Life is to **set the captives FREE** by **reaching the world** with the **life-changing truths of God's Word**, the **power of the Holy Spirit** and the **Awesome News of the message of Jesus Christ.**

**We're calling Spiritual Warriors all over the Earth
to partner with us in this mission!**

Books by Dirk Waren:

The Believer's Guide to FORGIVENESS & WARFARE
Legalism Unmasked
HELL KNOW! (full and condensed versions)
SHEOL KNOW! (full and condensed versions)
The Four Stages of Spiritual Growth
ANGELS: Their Purpose and Your Responsibility
THE LAW and the Believer
The SIX BASIC DOCTRINES of Christianity
GRACE: What Is It? How Do You Grow in It?
How to Handle OFFENSES: Personal & Criminal
WOMEN in Ministry ...in God's Service
The FIVEFOLD MINISTRY Gifts: Apostle, Prophet, Evangelist, Pastor, Teacher
Solomon's SONG OF SONGS and Issues of Love & Sex
QUESTIONS & ANSWERS From the Bible
SPIRITUAL WARIOR: The Manual